MW01634103

Evangelical Millennialism in the Trans-Atlantic World,
1500–2000

Evangelical Millennialism in the Trans-Atlantic World, 1500–2000

Crawford Gribben
Long Room Hub Senior Lecturer in Early Modern Print Culture
Trinity College Dublin, Ireland

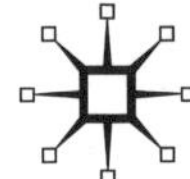

First published 2011 by
PALGRAVE MACMILLAN

Palgrave Macmillan in the UK is an imprint of Macmillan Publishers Limited, registered in England, company number 785998, of Houndmills, Basingstoke, Hampshire RG21 6XS.

Palgrave Macmillan in the US is a division of St Martin's Press LLC, 175 Fifth Avenue, New York, NY 10010.

Palgrave Macmillan is the global academic imprint of the above companies and has companies and representatives throughout the world.

Palgrave® and Macmillan® are registered trademarks in the United States, the United Kingdom, Europe and other countries.

ISBN 978–0–230–00825–0   hardback

This book is printed on paper suitable for recycling and made from fully managed and sustained forest sources. Logging, pulping and manufacturing processes are expected to conform to the environmental regulations of the country of origin.

A catalogue record for this book is available from the British Library.

A catalog record for this book is available from the Library of Congress.

10   9   8   7   6   5   4   3   2   1
20   19 18 17 16 15 14 13 12 11

Printed and bound in Great Britain by
CPI Antony Rowe, Chippenham and Eastbourne

For Martin Grubb

And I saw an angel come down from heaven, having the key of the bottomless pit and a great chain in his hand. And he laid hold on the dragon, that old serpent, which is the Devil, and Satan, and bound him a thousand years, and cast him into the bottomless pit, and shut him up, and set a seal upon him, that he should deceive the nations no more, till the thousand years should be fulfilled: and after that he must be loosed a little season. And I saw thrones, and they sat upon them, and judgement was given unto them: and I saw the souls of them that were beheaded for the witness of Jesus, and for the word of God, and which had not worshipped the beast, neither his image, neither had received his mark upon their foreheads, or in their hands; and they lived and reigned with Christ a thousand years. But the rest of the dead lived not again until the thousand years were finished. This is the first resurrection. Blessed and holy is he that hath part in the first resurrection: on such the second death hath no power, but they shall be priests of God and of Christ, and shall reign with him a thousand years. And when the thousand years are expired, Satan shall be loosed out of his prison, and shall go out to deceive the nations which are in the four quarters of the earth, Gog and Magog, to gather them together to battle: the number of whom is as the sand of the sea. And they went up on the breadth of the earth, and compassed the camp of the saints about, and the beloved city: and fire came down from God out of heaven, and devoured them. And the devil that deceived them was cast into the lake of fire and brimstone, where the beast and the false prophet are, and shall be tormented day and night for ever and ever.

Revelation 20:1–10

Contents

Preface

I have accumulated many debts in the years in which I have been researching and writing this book. Like its companion volume, *Writing the rapture: Prophecy fiction in evangelical America* (2009), and an earlier project, *God's Irishmen: Theological debates in Cromwellian Ireland* (2007), this book had its genesis during my postdoctoral fellowship in the Centre for Irish–Scottish Studies, Trinity College Dublin; it developed during my period of employment in English and American Studies at the University of Manchester; and it was completed after my return to Trinity and my subsequent and concurrent appointment as adjunct professor of church history at Westminster Theological Seminary. Throughout these years, my colleagues in each of these institutions have been a constant support and resource. In particular, I would like to thank Robert Armstrong, Terence Brown, Jeremy Gregory, Darryl Jones, Jeff Jue, Peter Knight, Graeme Murdock, Andrew Pierce, Amanda Piesse, Murray Pittock, Alan Rawes, Scott Spurlock, Mark Sweetnam, Carl Trueman and Brian Ward for many stimulating conversations on eschatological and related themes; Murray Pittock, David Alderson, Jane Ohlmeyer, Roger Stalley, Stephen Matterson and Darryl Jones for being ever supportive heads of school; Ian Campbell Ross and David Dickson, past and present directors of the Centre for Irish–Scottish Studies, for permitting and facilitating the development of the Trinity Millennialism Project; and the many colleagues and friends who have attended and participated in the Project's conferences. Among the latter, I have found the conversation of a series of graduate students of particular help: Jennie Chapman, Joe Purcell, Josh Searle, Katie Sturm, Jennifer Trieu and Sarah Wareham deserve special appreciation. My research has also been assisted by a wider circle of colleagues whose discussions have stimulated new ideas and new ways of approaching old ideas: their number includes Kenneth Newport and John Wallis of the Centre for Millennialism Studies at Liverpool Hope University, as well as Nigel Agnew, Michael Bath, David Bebbington, Ian Hugh Clary, John Coffey, James Davison, Amy Frykholm, Kenneth Gentry, Jerome de Groot, John Grier, Gary Harrison, Michael Haykin, Andrew Holmes, Barry Horner, Thomas Ice, Mark Jones, Richard Landes, David McKay, Patrick Mitchel, James Renihan, Mike Renihan, David Shedden, Nigel Smith, Kenneth Stewart and Arthur Williamson. I would also like to thank

John Gillespie, Doug Shantz, Michael Haykin, Nicholas Allen, Murray Pittock, Anthony Cross, John Briggs, Paul Muldoon and Nigel Smith for invitations to explore some of the themes of this book in lectures at the University of Ulster (2005), the University of Calgary (2006), Toronto Baptist Seminary (2006), NUI Galway (2008), the University of Glasgow (2009), Regent's Park College, Oxford (2009), and Princeton University (2010), and to thank Sheridan Gilley for the invitation to address the conference of the Ecclesiastical History Society (2010). My colleagues and friends in the Brethren Archivists and Historians Network, especially Neil Dickson, Timothy C.F. Stunt and Paul Wilkinson, have been of greater influence than they might realize. So too have the churches of which I have been a member during the writing of this project. The ministers and members of these and related congregations, particularly Matthew Brennan, Martin Grubb, Jason Isherwood, Shaun McFall, Stephen Rees, Stephen Roger and Mike Tardive, deserve special thanks.

This research has been made possible by the assistance provided by librarians at many North American institutions, including the Andover-Harvard Theological Library, Harvard Divinity School; the James P. Boyce Centennial Library, Southern Baptist Theological Seminary; the W.S. Hoole Special Collections Library, University of Alabama; the Mugar Library, Boston University; the Pre-Trib Research Center, Liberty University; the Speer Library, Princeton Theological Seminary; Toronto Baptist Seminary; and Westminster Theological Seminary. Enormous help has also been provided by librarians in many European institutions, including the Andersonian Library, University of Strathclyde; Bonn University Library; the British Library; Edinburgh University Library; the Gamble Library, Union Theological College, Belfast, especially Stephen Gregory; Glasgow University Library; Irish Baptist College; the John Rylands University Library, Manchester, especially Graham Johnson, archivist of the Christian Brethren Archive; Queen's University Belfast; the National Library of Ireland; New College, Edinburgh; Marsh's Library, Dublin; Reformed Theological College, Belfast; Trinity College Library, Dublin; the University Library, Cambridge; and Westminster College, Cambridge.

Some parts of this book have been developed from earlier publications, particularly the discussion of the Geneva Bible and James Ussher in *The Puritan millennium: Literature and theology, 1550–1682* (2000); my essay on 'John Gill and puritan eschatology', published in *Evangelical Quarterly* (2001); my chapter in *Prisoners of hope? Aspects of evangelical millennialism in Britain and Ireland, 1800–1880*, a collection of essays edited by Timothy C.F. Stunt and myself (2004); my chapter in *The emergence of evangelicalism: Exploring historical continuities* (2008), a collection of essays edited by Michael A.G. Haykin and Kenneth J. Stewart; my chapter in *Exploring Baptist origins* (2010), edited by Anthony R. Cross and Nicholas J. Wood; and my chapter in *The Edinburgh Companion to Scottish Romanticism*, edited by Murray G.H. Pittock. I am grateful to colleagues for their permission to return to these themes here.

Others of my debts are financial. The provision of a British Academy Small Grant facilitated Ian Hugh Clary's research in the libraries of a number of North American institutions in the summer of 2007, and I am hugely grateful for this vital assistance. I had hoped that the timely completion of this book would be made possible by a research sabbatical which was awarded by the University of Manchester and by further funding for an additional research sabbatical which was awarded by the Leverhulme Trust for the academic year of 2007–8, but this was made impossible by my departure from the United Kingdom. Further research assistance was, however, provided by Trinity's Start-Up Fund (2008) and by its Arts and Social Sciences Benefactions Fund (2008 and 2009), which supported the short-term research assistance of graduate students Mark Sweetnam and Kelly Pederson. Finally, I wish to thank Michael Strang and Ruth Ireland, my editors at Palgrave Macmillan, who have shown enthusiasm for the project since its inception – and enormous patience as 'the end' continually failed to materialize. And, of course, it should go without saying that I alone should be held responsible for the errors of fact or interpretation that remain within this book.

Reflecting on the 15 years I have spent investigating this tradition, it is tempting to remember the widely attributed maxim that the study of eschatology 'either finds a man mad or leaves him so'. There may be examples of both trends in the writing described in this book; but this book is written in the conviction that eschatological hope has been and should continue to be central to the common faith of Christians. It is in that context that the dedication records a formative debt. Greatest thanks, as always, are due to my family, especially mum and dad, Pauline, Daniel, Honor and Finn. *Tar chugainn, a Thiarna Íosa.*

Crawford Gribben
Trinity College Dublin

Glossary[1]

Amillennialism

The belief that the period of one thousand years described in Revelation 20:1–10 does not refer to an end-time period and is instead a metaphor for all or a substantial part of the period between Christ's incarnation and second coming. This appears to be the reading of Revelation 20: 1–10 assumed in the major reformation confessions of faith.

Antichrist

The church's theological enemies are described as 'antichrist' in several New Testament passages (1 John 2:18, 22; 1 John 4:3; 2 John 7). In popular discourse, however, 'the Antichrist' is a single figure who tends to combine elements of the various eschatological enemies described in Daniel and Revelation. The older protestant identification of the Antichrist as the Pope has given way to a range of other opinions under the influence of *futurist premillennialism* and *preterism*.

Apocalyptic

A Biblical genre, with disputed characteristics, that has given its name to a wider approach to the understanding of world affairs. Apocalyptic literature emphasizes the sudden (and often imminent) end of all things. In contrast to the *millennium*, the apocalyptic mode can seem dualistic (evil is in constant struggle with goodness), pessimistic (world conditions are not likely to improve), deterministic (the future has been planned by God), ethically passive (if conditions are not likely to improve, there is little that can be done to make the world a better place), and final.

Christian Reconstruction

The belief, developed in the later twentieth century, that the *postmillennial* coming of Christ will be preceded by the establishment of 'godly rule' on earth. This 'godly rule' will be marked by an unprecedented revival of Christianity and the international adoption of the Mosaic judicial and penal codes.

Dispensationalism

A variety of *premillennialism* which emerged in the 1830s to argue for a radical disjunction between Israel and the church and which teaches that the 'secret rapture' will precede the *tribulation*. Dispensationalists commonly mark seven distinct stages in the development of the history of redemption, which may or may not have different conditions of salvation. Dispensationalism has developed through three major stages: classical dispensationalism, which is best represented by the *Scofield reference Bible* (1909; second edition 1917) and the writings of L.S. Chafer and J. Dwight Pentecost; revised dispensationalism, which is best represented by the *New Scofield Bible* (1967); and progressive dispensationalism, which is best represented by the writings of Craig Blaising and Darrell Bock.

Eschatology

Classically, the study of the 'four last things' – death, judgement, heaven and hell – but the term has been expanded in use to refer to other aspects of end of the world belief. Evangelical eschatology can be either pessimistic, in its expectation of *apocalyptic* events, or optimistic, in its expectation of the *millennium*.

Futurism

A system of hermeneutics that understands New Testament prophecies to be chiefly concerned with the last few years before the second coming of Christ. Futurists tend to argue that the *Antichrist* will not be a pope. Futurism is common among *amillennialists* and *premillennialists*, and is a basic feature of *dispensationalism*.

Historicism

A system of hermeneutics that understands New Testament prophecies to detail all or part of the course of history in the period before the second coming. The identification of the Pope as the Antichrist is common in protestant historicist interpretation; but the identification of the establishment of Israel in 1948 as a fulfilment of prophecy also represents an historicist interpretive approach. 'Historicist' *premillennialism*, one variant of which is represented in the writings of Hal Lindsey, should be distinguished from 'historic' (i.e., non-dispensational) *premillennialism*, as advanced by G.E. Ladd, which may or may not be historicist, and which Lindsey would certainly oppose.

Millenarian / Millennialist

Conventionally, scholars working in millennial studies have followed Ernest L. Tuveson in distinguishing 'millennialists' (believers who adopt *postmillennial*, optimistic and gradualist theologies) from 'millenarians' (believers who adopt *premillennial*, pessimistic and radical theologies). Ernest R. Sandeen has noted, however, that the terms are interchangeable in the literature of the emerging fundamentalist movement and a strict distinction should probably not therefore be imposed.[2]

Millennium

A utopian period whose general characteristics are based on the description of the binding of Satan in Revelation 20:1–10 and the prophecies of the renewal of the natural world in the Hebrew prophets. Its specific characteristics vary according to the interpreter, and the millennium can be used as a trope for a wide and sometimes contradictory range of political, cultural and religious presuppositions. The three most common of evangelical millennial schemes, *amillennialism*, *premillennialism* and *postmillennialism*, should not be anachronistically read into older material. Not every exegete would share the basic assumption of these schemes, the idea that Revelation 20:1–10 refers to only one thousand-year period. The *Oxford English Dictionary* dates the development of the *premillennial* and *postmillennial* terms to the mid-nineteenth century, though the interpretive paradigms they represent can be traced to the reformation; it does not provide any information on the development of 'amillennial,' though it approximates to the eschatological position of the reformation creeds.

National election

The idea, popular in ancient Israel, reformation Britain and modern America, that God has chosen a nation, invested its progress with the earthly display of his glory, and will therefore make certain its dominance. This is not necessarily an uncritical nationalism, however; national election points to the responsibilities as much as the privileges of being God's chosen people, and can often lead to a jeremiad on the decay of truth among the chosen. It is based on a providential worldview that recognizes the hand of God in the drama of human history, and lies behind some forms of the American 'redeemer nation' myth.

Postmillennialism

The belief that Christ will return after the *millennium* has substantially reformed life on earth. Postmillennialists can be either *apocalyptic* or gradualist, and vary in the extent to which they believe the *millennium* can be expedited by their own effort. Postmillennialism has been revived among some conservative Presbyterians, particularly those with interests in *Christian Reconstruction*, but, among evangelicals more generally, remains much less popular than *premillennialism*.

Premillennialism

The belief that the second coming of Christ will take place before the *millennium*. Historic premillennialism teaches that Christ will return after the *tribulation* (and is consequently designated 'post-tribulational'); this was the view of, for example, C.H. Spurgeon and G.E. Ladd. *Dispensational* premillennialism, developed from the works of J.N. Darby, argues that Christ will return for the 'secret rapture' before the *tribulation* (and is consequently designated 'pre-tribulational'). This rapture will 'catch up' believers in order to take them into heaven while the *Antichrist* rages on earth. The second coming proper will take place at the end of the tribulation, and Christ will then usher in the *millennium* and reign over the world for one thousand years. Premillennialists debate whether believers will live on earth during the *millennium* and debate the specific roles of Israel and a range of other powers in this end-times scenario.

Preterism

A system of hermeneutics that understands New Testament prophecies to be chiefly concerned with the Roman assault on Jerusalem and the end of Temple worship in AD 70. Preterism has influenced a number of recent evangelical *premillennial* and *postmillennial* Bible commentaries.

Tribulation

The belief (shared by many *premillennialists*) that the Bible predicts a final seven-year period of terrible suffering during which the *Antichrist* persecutes believers and God pours judgement on the world.

Note on the text

Unless otherwise noted, all biblical quotations are taken from the King James (Authorized) Version.

Notes

1. This glossary is revised and expanded from earlier versions which I first published in Crawford Gribben and Andrew R. Holmes (eds), *Protestant millennialism, evangelicalism and Irish society, 1790–2005* (Basingstoke: Palgrave Macmillman, 2006), x–xii, and Crawford Gribben, *Writing the rapture: Prophecy fiction in evangelical America* (Oxford: Oxford University Press, 2009), 171–4.
2. Ernest L. Tuveson, *Redeemer nation: The idea of America's millennial role* (Chicago: University of Chicago Press, 1968), 33–4; Ernest R. Sandeen, *The roots of fundamentalism: British and American millenarianism 1800–1930* (Chicago: University of Chicago Press, 1970), 5 n. 3.

Introduction

This book provides an account of the eschatological commitments that
have evolved over five centuries to dominate large and influential sections of contemporary evangelicalism in the trans-Atlantic world. Its
companion volume, *Writing the rapture: Prophecy fiction in evangelical
America* (2009), attended to one manifestation of this distinctive habit
of mind – the 'rapture' novels and films that developed through the
twentieth century to attract unprecedented levels of celebration and
notoriety after the success of Left Behind (1995–2007), one of the
best-selling fiction series in American literary history.[1] This book, by
contrast, provides a canvas of description that is significantly broader
and less specific in its chronological and generic concerns. In a survey of
aspects of the print culture of one variety of popular Protestantism, this
book will describe the origin, development and divisions of competing
and contested formulations of the eschatological hopes and fears that
evangelicals, throughout their history and on both sides of the Atlantic,
have developed in their reading of the apocalyptic and millennial texts
of Scripture.

Evangelical millennialism in the trans-Atlantic world, 1500–2000 is of
broader significance than its title might suggest. Evangelicals constitute
one important element of the global rise of religious conservatism.[2]
Although they remain marginal to the political life of Canada and the
European nations, evangelicals represent a significant American subculture, and recent attempts by evangelicals to gain influence in American
political life, and even to seize control of the presidency, have been
widely documented.[3] Many of these politically active evangelicals have
assumed that they are living in apocalyptic times, just as many generations of believers had done before them. Citing Biblical prophecies
about the end of the age, drawing upon older ideas of national election

and a providential reading of American history, they have insisted on supporting Israel against the Arab and Islamic worlds in a robust and often isolationist geopolitical vision; and they have done so even as many of their number have outlined their expectations of an imminent 'clash of civilisations' and the subsequent and catastrophic decline of Western civilization into an apocalyptic tyranny that will identify Jews and evangelical Christians as being among its principal victims.[4]

But now, according to many of their critics, these American evangelicals are acting as the agents of a descent into apocalyptic terror.[5] Dominating a significant section of the base of the Republican Party, evangelicals have mounted an illiberal, a reactive and, some of its advocates and critics have argued, an evidently theocratic attempt to reverse the direction of American modernity.[6] These evangelicals have argued for the teaching of 'intelligent design' above the teaching of Darwinian evolution, have supported the promotion of premarital sexual abstinence above the provision of contraception for school children, have voted against 'pro-choice' politicians and in defence of traditional definitions of marriage, and have provided biblical sanction for an unpopular 'war on terror' and the uncompleted projects of 'regime change' it has so far involved. If evangelicals are not yet the victims of one expected variety of apocalyptic terror, their critics argue, they may be responsible for the construction of another. These evangelical prophecy believers and the critics they have alarmed cannot both be right – but both are agreed that they live in apocalyptic times.

Of course, many Christians have always believed themselves to be living in apocalyptic times – at least in principle. Those believers who have maintained the historic orthodoxy of their faith have confessed that, in the words of the Apostles' Creed, Jesus Christ will return to 'judge the quick and the dead,' and they have often insisted on the imminence of that event. But many of those who have expected this return have gone far beyond the basic formulation of eschatological hope provided by that most historic and ecumenical confession of faith. In the first and second centuries, a series of significant Christian leaders developed expectations of 'latter-day glory' which they associated with the idealised final age of spiritual and environmental utopia which they found described in such Old Testament passages as Isaiah 11:6–9 and Isaiah 65:25 and, uniquely in the New Testament, in Revelation 20:1–10.[7] These beliefs in an earthly millennium were deconstructed by Augustine, most remarkably in his *City of God* (written between 410 and 425), and were thereafter generally condemned.[8] But this eschatological optimism endured, flaring up at the end of the first millennia, and repeatedly returned to haunt the medieval catholic imagination.[9] Of course, this millennial imagination identified its enemies, and, at various stages in the medieval tradition, Jews, Muslims and even occupants of the papal throne were 'outed' as the Antichrist.[10] But, in the centuries after Augustine, the custodians of orthodoxy consistently defined themselves in opposition to an earthly millennial hope. This rejection of millennialism was shared by early protestants, whose eschatological conclusions otherwise marked a moment of profound discontinuity with those of the medieval church.[11] It was during the first century of reformation that the millennial and apocalyptic convictions that continue to shape significant elements of evangelical discourse took on many of their leading characteristics and were institutionalized in patterns of confessional identity. But it was only in the nineteenth century that they developed into the discrete prophetic paradigms that continue to dominate the thinking of evangelicals to the present day. In a social history of ideas that ranges from the early sixteenth to the late twentieth century and across the north Atlantic, this book will describe these changes, their consequences, and their ongoing significance within the changing theological, social, political and geographical contexts of evangelical belief.

I

Given this kind of chronological, geographical and thematic breadth, the terms of this book's discussion will need to be clarified. Its title begs many questions, for in recent years the definitions of 'evangelical,' 'evangelicalism,' and 'millennialism' have become the focus of significant scholarly debate. (Some readers, familiar with these scholarly debates about definitions, may wish to skip this section and move to the conclusion of the Introduction.) The title of this book signals that its interest is in aspects of the print culture developed by those evangelicals who have embraced varieties of millennial faith. This book does not describe its subjects as 'millennialists,' a term frequently encountered in the scholarly literature, for the complexities of evangelical belief, like those of most other varieties of religious faith, cannot be reduced to a single explanatory doctrine – even though 'millennialist' might be easier to define than 'evangelical.' The term is certainly slippery. Evangelicals had been debating the definition of this descriptor for many decades before that discussion was appropriated by professional historians in the 1980s. And they have not always been careful to distinguish 'evangelical' from 'evangelicalism.' It is the latter term – describing an evangelical movement – that has stimulated most interest. Since the 1980s the 'volume of literature on evangelicalism' has 'increased with remarkable speed,' according to one of the premier historians of the movement, Darryl G. Hart.[12] In 1978, he noted, a standard annotated bibliography, *American Religion and Philosophy*, did not even include 'evangelicalism' as a term in its subject index, and referenced fewer than 20 titles dealing with the movement. Fifteen years later, the 'flood of historical literature on evangelicalism had become so large that bibliographers could fill two volumes with books and articles' on the subject: *Twentieth-century Evangelicalism: A guide to the sources* (1990), by Joel A. Carpenter and Edith L. Blumhofer, and *American Evangelicalism: An annotated bibliography* (1990), by Norris Magnuson, were followed by another supplementary volume covering the period to 1996.[13] And it was not only that scholarly study of evangelicalism had increased – so too had the importance attached to the movement by students of wider social and cultural trends. By the mid-1990s, evangelicalism was increasingly being identified as 'one of the most important interpretive tools for historians studying the relationship between religion and United States society.'[14] Consequently, Hart has concluded, 'evangelicalism was a distinct expression of American Christianity lost on most church historians prior to 1980,' but, one decade later, it was 'hard to avoid in the study of American religion.'[15]

This remarkable scholarly revolution should not be understood to imply that the identity of evangelicalism had been resolved. In 1984, George Marsden provided the 'working definition' of the movement for religious historians in North America.[16] Conceptually, this definition was based upon a shared sense of heritage which referenced the reformation and seventeenth-century Puritanism, as well as pietistic, Methodist and revivalist traditions in and after the eighteenth century; a shared sense of identity in a 'religious fellowship or coalition'; and five doctrinal emphases which Marsden believed marked that coalition's boundaries, namely the 'final authority of Scripture,' the 'real, historical character of God's saving work recorded in Scripture,' 'eternal salvation only through personal trust in Christ,' the 'importance of evangelism and missions,' and the 'importance of a spiritually transformed life.'[17] Marsden's descriptive 'pentagon' had a great deal to commend it, but European historians have tended to work with another proposal. Outside North America, David Bebbington's monumental study of *Evangelicalism in modern Britain: A history from the 1730s to the 1980s* (1989) did most to identify and call attention to the emergence of this new field of historical enquiry and the movement upon which it centred. Bebbington's early work argued that 'evangelicalism,' as a religious movement, had its origins in the 1730s, as Enlightenment categories of self-reflexive knowledge undermined older, slower and more self-critical protestant theologies of salvation, and as the energizing preaching of Jonathan Edwards and the Wesley brothers pushed converts into a life of constant Christian activity. The definition of evangelicalism advanced in Bebbington's early work gathered around four distinctive themes: 'Biblicism,' an emphasis on the centrality, though not necessarily the inerrancy, of Scripture; 'crucicentrism,' an emphasis on the unique significance of the work of Jesus Christ on the Cross; 'conversionism,' an emphasis on every individual's need to be converted to Christian faith if they were to escape the punishment of sin and gain salvation; and 'activism,' an insistence that every Christian ought to be diligent in doing good works, and especially in sharing the gospel (that is, 'evangelizing').[18] Bebbington's later work has been more careful to nuance the apparent novelty of the movement he described, and has played down notions of a sharp distinction between modern evangelicals and their puritan forebears, but this careful re-statement of his argument has not precipitated any decline in the extraordinary influence of his most important book. This influence has continued as the boundaries of the movement manifestly blur. Even the assumption that evangelicalism is an inherently protestant movement has recently been shaken: in 1999 a Gallup survey indicated that 21 per cent of American Roman Catholics were also identifying themselves as 'evangelical.'[19] Hart, in his sceptical reading of this historiography, *Deconstructing Evangelicalism* (2004), has attempted to explain the difficulties of definition by arguing that it was these Gallup surveys that transformed 'a sectarian form of Protestantism' into 'the faith of ordinary Americans.'[20] This explains, he claims, why the size of the evangelical constituency is measured not by listing the combined membership of the churches affiliated to the National Association of Evangelicals (with a total of 4.5 million members in 1992), but rather by appealing to the results of opinion polls (in which, two years earlier, almost ten times as many respondents had identified themselves as 'evangelical').[21] At its broadest, Hart worried, evangelicalism had become no more than 'a coalition of decentralized discontent within America's denominations.'[22] But, he has insisted, it cannot be said to exist as a definable movement.

As Hart's comments suggest, it is clear that these early advances in scholarship, now two decades old, must be historicized and qualified.[23] The landmark studies by Marsden and Bebbington were published in the context of the political re-engagement of conservative evangelicals, and consolidated the paradigmatic boundaries of a surge of scholarly activity that accompanied their re-entry into the mainstream of American public life.[24] In North America, this new scholarly field became identified by increasingly frequent publications on evangelical history in such respected publications as *Church History*.[25] In both Britain and North America, the historians associated with this first generation of serious historical scholarship took care to fashion themselves as a delineated cohort, often through relationships with the Institute for the Study of American Evangelicals, a research centre based in Wheaton College, the 'evangelical Harvard,' while never attempting to disguise their significant differences of approach to their shared subject. Their efforts were consolidated in such publications as the jointly-edited collection of essays, *Evangelicalism: Comparative studies of popular Protestantism in North America, the British Isles and beyond, 1700–1990* (1994). More recently, some of the 'founding fathers' of the study of evangelicalism have participated in the production of a significant multi-volume series documenting the movement's history. Mark A. Noll's *The rise of Evangelicalism: The age of Edwards, Whitefield and the Wesleys* (2004) was followed (in order of chronological attention) by John Wolffe's *The expansion of Evangelicalism: The age of Wilberforce, More, Chalmers and Finney* (2007), David W. Bebbington's *The dominance of Evangelicalism: The age of Spurgeon and Moody* (2005), Geoff Treloar's *The disruption of Evangelicalism: The age of John R. Mott, J. Gresham Machen and Aimee Semple McPherson* (forthcoming) and Brian Stanley's *The global diffusion of Evangelicalism: The age of Billy Graham and John Stott* (forthcoming). This series has begun to institutionalize this field of scholarly enquiry even as it has largely confirmed the assumptions in sociology, theology and historiography of the first generation of practitioners.

Of course, this attempt at definition and control has not gone uncontested. In particular, Bebbington's proposal that 'evangelicalism' emerged in the 1730s and largely in discontinuity with earlier versions of popular Protestantism has been widely and, in recent years, frequently challenged. The assumptions of this school of historiography have been most thoroughly investigated in two recent publications, *Early Evangelicalism: A global intellectual history, 1670–1789* (2006), by W.R. Ward, an historian based at the University of Durham, and *The emergence of Evangelicalism: Exploring historical continuities* (2008), a collection of essays edited by two North American historians based in evangelical institutions, Michael A.G. Haykin and Kenneth J. Stewart. Ward's work reflected on his long investigation of early modern Protestantism to offer a challenging and ground-breaking analysis of what he described as the 'roots' of this new religious movement. His account of the origins of evangelicalism was developed on the basis of a three-fold critique of the existing scholarly narrative: he suggested that the existing secondary literature had inappropriately concentrated on British and American contexts, had given too late a date for the emergence of evangelicalism as a discrete religious movement, and had not provided a sufficiently broad description of evangelical identity. Ward advanced this critique by re-contextualising evangelicalism within a European intellectual environment that juxtaposed popular Protestantism with alchemy, the Cabbala, mysticism, anti-Aristotelianism, theosophy and apocalyptic enquiry – and consequently presented a movement the contours of which were quite different from those described by many of his peers. In some respects, Ward's treatment of evangelical identity is perhaps a little eccentric, ousting doctrine from the centrality of position it had enjoyed in the Marsden and Bebbington theses without clearly explaining why a much less defined notion of 'identity' could take its place. Ward's repeated claims that evangelicalism set itself up in opposition to or even, as he put it, in 'tremendous hostility' to systematic theology certainly needed a more careful exploration than that provided in his book; indeed, it is possible that his treatment of millennial eschatology, which he frequently made central to the development of this evangelical 'identity,' was less than precise, and, as a consequence, some elements of the argument should have been more carefully qualified. Similarly, the book's elaboration of an 'evangelical hexagon' – perhaps its clearest challenge to the Bebbington 'quadrilateral' or the Mardsen 'pentagon' – was never heuristically advanced to outline an alternative approach to the subject. But the iconoclastic spirit and intellectual breadth of *Early Evangelicalism: A global intellectual history, 1670–1789* should have been applauded: it was perhaps inevitable that the book's impressive scope should sometimes require a more careful articulation of key ideas.

The emergence of Evangelicalism (2008), on the other hand, represented a more wide-ranging interdisciplinary investigation of the Bebbington thesis. The contributors to the book, of which this author was one, were largely identified as evangelical believers, being drawn from across British and American denominational boundaries but generally representing the movement's conservative or Reformed constituencies. The book itself was published by two established evangelical firms, IVP, in the UK, and Broadman and Holman, in the USA.[26] One early reviewer noted with concern that the doctrinal preferences of the editors and of many of the contributors prevented any real kind of sympathetic engagement with the Methodist and other non-Reformed expressions of evangelical faith that Bebbington had identified as representing some of the earliest stages of the movement's emergence: it was as if the project had been flawed from its inception, its design making it incapable of reflecting or engaging, with appropriate scholarly sympathy and reserve, the broad notion of early evangelicalism.[27] Nevertheless, there is some evidence that the criticisms offered in this volume have encouraged some careful modification of the Bebbington thesis. Bebbington's response to the criticisms offered by the contributors to *The emergence of Evangelicalism* was included as the project's final chapter. While admitting that some of his earlier arguments about the novelty of evangelicalism would need to be qualified in future work on the subject, he continued to insist that the 'rise of the movement did represent much that was new.'[28] His response indicated that the arguments of *The emergence of Evangelicalism* necessitated a modification of existing historical approaches rather than the development of an entirely new explanatory paradigm.

The current book necessarily engages with a number of these debates. Some of its assumptions may concern some careful readers – particularly the use of 'evangelical' to describe multiple varieties of protestant faith in the trans-Atlantic world in the period before the eighteenth-century emergence of the movement that shared the name. The definition of this term is, of course, key, for it will limit the number of those individuals, institutions, movements and publications whose stories can usefully be juxtaposed. And, in this respect, due care will be required, for evangelicals have often found themselves sharing in a culture of millennial expectation that ranged far beyond their widest doctrinal boundaries, while other millennial believers travelled through evangelical experiences or institutions finally to find themselves outside the boundaries of the movement altogether. Some non-evangelical millennial movements shared evangelical habits and ideas. The followers of the eighteenth-century prophet Joanna Southcott, for example, were 'sincere, earnest Christians,' J.F.C. Harrison has reported, 'dependent for guidance on a literal interpretation of the Bible. They had pondered long over the scriptures, especially the prophecies and promises of the coming of Christ's kingdom, and were committed members of existing churches and sects.'[29] But if these Southcottians, many of whom embraced premillennialism while remaining within the Anglican establishment, had accepted the teachings of their prophet, they would have added a female and fourth person to the Godhead, and evangelicals, whatever minimalistic shortcomings there may be in the 'Bebbington quadrilateral,' the 'Marsden pentagon' or the 'Ward hexagon,' must surely be defined within the boundaries of the historic orthodoxy of the early ecumenical creeds.[30] Similarly, evangelicals must be committed to the sufficiency and finality of the (protestant) biblical canon: no one has challenged Bebbington's identification of the movement as being 'Biblicist.' Debates among evangelical millennial believers have been about the proper interpretation and application of biblical texts, not about whether new texts, whether the inspired utterances of a charismatic leader or the recently discovered contents of a new revelation, should be considered as divine: evangelical millennial movements are not in that sense 'prophetic.' There have been radically leader-centred evangelical millennial movements – the group of Brethren who at the end of the nineteenth century left Plymouth, England, to begin a community at Kyneton, Australia, far outside the boundaries of the Roman Empire they expected to be revived, were being driven by their shared appreciation for the prophetic exegesis of B.W. Newton, for example.[31] But these believers were being motivated by their convictions about the meaning of texts accepted as canonical throughout the Christian world. Prophetic movements, led by charismatic leaders who provide their people with new source texts, take people out of evangelicalism: the movement as a whole remains resolutely 'Biblicist.'[32]

It is, nevertheless, quite dangerous to make a decision that leaves one using a single term to describe competing or successive varieties of scholarly or popular Protestantism in complex and diverging ecclesiastical and geographical situations over five centuries of constantly changing social, cultural, political and intellectual contexts. But in making that decision, and in arguing for the utility of a single descriptive term, I want to avoid both a lazy reductionism in taxonomic usage and the implication that there existed a stable and uncontested evangelical movement throughout this chronological and geographical range. It is relatively easy to justify the use of the term in the contexts of the sixteenth century, for historians of the reformation are now using 'evangelical' as an alternative to 'protestant' or 'Lutheran' in their analyses of this period.[33] Diarmaid MacCulloch, in his survey of European reformation, makes that kind of decision. He explains that 'protestant' had a very specific and limited range of reference within the political cultures of the German states and the Holy Roman Empire throughout much of the sixteenth century, while the term 'evangelical' was being 'widely used and recognized at the time' and was much less of a denominational marker.[34] There were evangelicals before evangelicalism, therefore, and, like their successors, they can be identified across the confessional spectrum of early modern Europe. This book, following

Bebbington's arguments, will identify the evangelical movement as first emerging in the early decades of the eighteenth century, in a post-confessional age, when differences between protestant denominations were increasingly regarded as being less important than the doctrine and piety that Christians were believed and encouraged to share. Earlier evangelicals had held to a wide range of detailed but competing confessional positions, but members of the later evangelical movement were often involved in the deliberate reduction of creedal obligations in favour of a generic popular piety. This book will therefore identify as evangelicals believers ranging from sixteenth-century reformers to the fundamentalists and neo-evangelicals that emerged to dominate the religious marketplace on both sides of the Atlantic in the middle and later twentieth century, even as it describes an evangelical movement from the early eighteenth century, paying attention to the distinctive features of contemporaneous, successive, separatist and competing subcultures within the wider evangelical world. This discussion will proceed by addressing a number of the most important challenges to the Bebbington thesis. It will trace a greater degree of continuity between the theology and praxis of early modern and modern evangelicals than the Bebbington thesis generally allows, but it will also identify some important theological discontinuities within that shared tradition. And these discontinuities continue to be important, for the evidence provided by changing patterns of millennial belief suggests that patterns of disruption in theology and praxis can be traced in places other than those identified by many advocates and critics of the Bebbington thesis: I have attempted to reflect on this tension between continuity and change in this book's conclusion. This book will therefore argue that eschatological interests have been one of the key indicators of the shape of the ideological evolution of the trans-Atlantic evangelical movement throughout its history – albeit an indicator the general significance of which has hardly been recognized.

II

But it is not only that 'evangelical' and 'evangelicalism' need to be defined – so too does this book's usage of the vocabulary of eschatology. Full definitions of this range of terms are provided in the glossary, but at this stage in the introduction it is appropriate to signal that the title of this book indicates that its primary interest is specifically in one element of a wider protestant eschatological tradition, the millennial interests of evangelicals in the trans-Atlantic world. This book, therefore, does not provide a general description of protestant eschatology or apocalyptic thinking throughout this period.

Classically, in the Christian tradition, 'eschatology' has referred to discourse upon the 'four last things' – death, judgement, heaven and hell – but in popular usage the term has been expanded to refer to other aspects of end-of-the-world belief. Evangelical eschatology can be either broadly pessimistic, in its expectation of the apocalypse, or broadly optimistic, in its expectation of a golden age (sometimes known as the millennium) before the apocalypse. These expectations are generally derived from texts which represent, according to the conclusions of the Society for Biblical Literature, 'a genre of revelatory literature with a narrative framework, in which a revelation in mediated by an otherworldly being to a human recipient, disclosing a transcendent reality which is both temporal, insofar as it envisages eschatological salvation, and spatial, insofar as it involves another, supernatural world.'[35] This apocalyptic literature therefore emphasizes the sudden (and often imminent) end of all things. It can seem deterministic (the future has been planned by God), dualistic (good and evil exist in constant struggle), pessimistic (world conditions are not likely to improve), ethically passive (if conditions are not likely to improve, there is little that can be done to make the world a better place), and final. In contrast, millennial aspiration focuses on a utopian period the general characteristics of which are based on the description of the binding of Satan in Revelation 20:1–10 (which is read as a consequent limiting of evil) and the expectations of the renewal of the natural world recorded in Old Testament prophetic writing. The specific characteristics of this utopian age, which have been widely theorized, have varied according to the interpreter, and the millennium has been used as a trope for a wide and contradictory range of political, cultural and religious presuppositions.[36]

It is also important to note that the three most common contemporary evangelical millennial schemes (amillennialism, premillennialism and postmillennialism) should not be retrospectively projected onto older material, which often posited a much broader range of exegetical conclusions than those offered by recent writing on the subject. Not every exegete through the five centuries of tradition described in this book would share the basic assumption of contemporary schemes, the idea that Revelation 20:1–10 refers to only one period of one thousand years: in the seventeenth century, this view was denied by Thomas Brightman, James Ussher and Johannes Cocceius, and in the later twentieth century, it appears to have been denied by Norman Shepherd, sometime professor at Westminster Theological Seminary, a bastion of conservative Presbyterianism in North America.[37] And as one recent commentator has argued, the 'traditional criterion of classifying millennialism on the basis of when Christ would appear is ... virtually meaningless for the emerging systems prior to 1800.'[38] Confirming this observation, the *Oxford English Dictionary* dates 'millenarian' to 1626, 'millenarianism' to 1650 and 'millennial' to 1664, and its citation of usage demonstrates that the dominant modern terms emerged with 'premillennial' in 1846 and 'postmillennial' in 1851.[39] The *OED* fails to provide any information on the development of 'amillennial,' which is perhaps surprising given its frequent deployment in twentieth-century theological debate.

Of course, the evangelical eschatological tradition – and the discussion it has engendered – is much more complex than the history of its definitions might suggest. But these terms are still important. Amillennialism is the term used to describe the conviction that the one thousand years described in Revelation 20:1–10 is not a specifically eschatological reference and is instead a metaphor for all or a substantial part of the period between Christ's incarnation and his second coming. Amillennialism was the dominant millennial position in the early reformation period, and it has been growing in popularity with evangelicals throughout the course of the last century, especially in Europe and in the North American Reformed communities most responsive to European theological developments. But many evangelicals, especially in North America and throughout the twentieth century, have retained a firm conviction that the description of one thousand years in Revelation 20:1–10 does predict a specific future period, though they have differed as to whether the return of Jesus Christ will precede or succeed it. Postmillennialists argue that Christ will return after the millennium has substantially reformed life on earth. Postmillennialists, who were well represented among British and North American exegetes of the seventeenth and eighteenth centuries, can expect either the apocalyptic or the gradual transformation of human societies, and vary in the extent to which they believe the millennium can be expedited by human efforts. Postmillennialism has been recently revived among some conservative and Reformed evangelicals, particularly but certainly not exclusively among politically orientated North Americans with interests in Christian Reconstruction, but, more generally, this eschatological system remains much less popular than premillennialism among contemporary believers. Most contemporary evangelicals, especially in the USA, agree that the second coming of Christ will take place before the millennium. There are two important variants to this position.

'Historic' premillennialism is the belief that Christ will return after a several-year period of apocalyptic distress known as the 'tribulation' (and so it is sometimes described as being 'post-tribulational'); this was the view of a number of early Fathers, as well as the nineteenth-century London Baptist minister C.H. Spurgeon and the twentieth-century biblical scholar G.E. Ladd.[40] 'Dispensational' premillennialism, which coalesced into an innovative prophetic paradigm in the early nineteenth century, argues for a distinctive reading of the biblical history of redemption, the seven epochs of which may or may not have different conditions of salvation, and insists that Christ will return for the 'secret rapture' before the tribulation (and hence it is sometimes described as being 'pre-tribulational'). This rapture will 'catch up' believers in order to take them into heaven while the Antichrist rages on earth. The second coming proper will take place at the end of the tribulation, when Christ will usher in the millennium and reign over the world for one thousand years. Dispensationalists debate whether believers will live on earth during the millennium and debate the specific roles of Israel and a range of other powers in this end-times scenario. Dispensationalism is a hugely popular prophetic system, briefly expounded within a social and intellectual elite associated with the universities of Dublin and Oxford in the 1830s, then transplanted in North America to become the dominant eschatological paradigm available to modern evangelicals. And, of course, it has evolved. The schema has developed through three major stages: 'classical' dispensationalism, which developed from its first formal elaboration in the writing of J.N. Darby to be best represented by the *Scofield reference Bible* (1909; second edition 1917) and the writings of L.S. Chafer and J. Dwight Pentecost; 'revised' dispensationalism, which is best represented by the *New Scofield Bible* (1967); and 'progressive' dispensationalism, which is best represented by the writings of Craig Blaising and Darrell Bock, and which offers a significant and sometimes surprising reformulation of earlier dispensational belief.[41]

While these terms reflect specific exegetical and theological convictions, others have been developed to denote particular kinds of social and ethical responses these convictions can engender. Conventionally, scholars working in millennial studies have followed Ernest L. Tuveson in distinguishing 'millennialists' (believers who adopt postmillennial, optimistic and gradualist theologies) from 'millenarians' (believers who adopt premillennial, pessimistic and radical theologies).[42] But Ernest R. Sandeen has noted the fluidity of terminology in the literature of the protestant eschatological tradition, and, as he has argued, a strict distinction should probably not therefore be imposed.[43] His conclusion seems particularly important within evangelical millennial cultures, where, for example, the common assumption that premillennial convictions will encourage social passivity fail to account for the tireless activity of many representatives of the Christian Right, and where the common assumption that postmillennial convictions will generate ideas of evolutionary human development fail to account for the radically interventionist political theories advocated by many Christian Reconstructionists.[44] Scholars working in millennial studies ought therefore to adopt a wider range of descriptive labels than those provided by exegetically concerned theologians. Sociologists and political theorists have important contributions to make. Bryan R. Wilson has focused attention on millennial believers rather than millennial systems, and has distinguished these believers as being 'objectivists,' either in advocating the divine revolution of society, the human reformation of society, introversion from society, or the utopian reconstruction of society; 'subjectivists,' in advocating that God is more concerned with changing individuals than world systems; or 'relationists,' either in advocating that it is the believer's perception of the world, rather than the world itself, that should be changed, or in advocating that millennial belief should only encourage a hope for miracles.[45] Jürgen Moltmann, similarly, has drawn upon the work of political theorists to proffer another taxonomy, which distinguished 'political millenarianism' (the identification of an individual political system with the reign of God), 'ecclesiastical millenarianism' (the identification of the institutional church with the reign of God), and 'epochal millenarianism' (the identification of one historical period with the reign of God), all of which, he argues, exist in tension with the this-worldly hope outlined in biblical prophecy.[46]

But exegetical differences are still important. Systems of eschatology are generally driven by the hermeneutical decisions that inform their biblical base. Evangelicals have tended to choose between four methods of interpreting Revelation: 'idealism,' 'preterism,' 'historicism,' and 'futurism.' Those commentaries that adopt an idealist perspective tend to argue that Revelation was not written with specific historical application in mind, but was intended to teach a series of timeless truths applicable to a wide variety of social contexts which the text itself did not intend to predict. Throughout the last century, idealist approaches have been most commonly adopted by amillennial exegetes. Preterists, by contrast, understand New Testament prophecies to be chiefly concerned with the Roman destruction of Jerusalem and the end of Temple worship in AD 70, though some exegetes have pointed to fulfilments of prophecy as late as the fourth century AD. Preterism has influenced a number of recent evangelical pre- and postmillennial commentaries, and is regarded as being particularly important by contemporary Reformed scholars. Historicism refuses to identify an end-point for biblical prophetic fulfilment, and argues instead that these prophecies refer to specific events in the entire course of church history. The identification of the Pope as the Antichrist is common in protestant historicist interpretation (though Roman Catholic writers also adopted historicist readings to counter early Lutheran claims regarding the papacy). Within the terms of this book's discussion, it is important for readers to distinguish 'historicist' premillennialism, one date-suggesting variant of which is represented in the best-selling writings of Hal Lindsey, from 'historic' (i.e., non-dispensational) premillennialism, which may or may not be historicist, and which Lindsey would certainly oppose: in this discussion, 'historic' refers to an exegetical conclusion about the interpretation of Revelation 20:1–10 while 'historicist' refers to exegetical conclusions about the range of reference of the entire book of Revelation. Readers need not be alarmed by these kinds of nice distinction for the most common hermeneutical approach among contemporary evangelicals, especially in North America, is not historicism but futurism. This system of hermeneutics understands New Testament prophecies to be chiefly concerned with the last few years before the second coming of Christ, and its advocates tend to argue that the Antichrist will not be a pope. Futurism is common among amillennialists and premillennialists, and is a basic feature of dispensationalism. It is futurism's insistence that most biblical prophecies refer to an extraordinarily short period of time at the end of the age that drives the millennial expectation of the largest number of contemporary evangelicals on both sides of the Atlantic.

Nevertheless, as we have noted, evangelical believers have never held a monopoly on millennial convictions: as a great deal of recent scholarship has demonstrated, similar patterns of belief can be traced in cultures as far apart as underground UFO cults and mainstream theological traditions in Judaism and Islam, as well as in the Roman Catholic and Orthodox churches and in 'liberal' or mainstream protestant traditions. But while it is not unique to evangelicalism, millennial belief has certainly been central to its historical evolution, on both sides of the Atlantic. In Europe, W.R. Ward's discussion of the roots of the evangelical movement has highlighted that evangelical piety frequently emerged from and developed alongside radically millennial interests.[47] And in North America, Philip Jenkins has claimed that a 'fundamentalist evangelicalism with powerful millenarian strands' has been the 'largest component of the [American] religious spectrum ... since colonial times.'[48] But the history of evangelical millennialism has been a history of religious change, both within and across the trans-Atlantic world. While both traditions shared common roots in the popular piety of the early modern period, they evolved in distinct contexts of human geography, and negotiated their own relationships to social and political climates that, on either side of the Atlantic, appeared increasingly to diverge. Subsequent chapters in this book will document this process of divergence, and the manners in which contemporary differences between European and North American evangelicalism can to some extent be explained by their differing varieties of millennial belief, and by differing degrees of importance that have been attached to these varieties of millennial belief. The difference is particularly marked in the contemporary period, in which North American evangelicals are increasingly identified by a shared adherence to a variety of millennial belief that originated in Britain and Ireland in the first half of the nineteenth century but that no longer commands the allegiance of any more than a tiny minority of British and Irish believers. This book will argue that the differences have always been as significant as the similarities in eschatological thinking represented in trans-Atlantic evangelical print culture.[49]

III

As this argument suggests, the comparative and print cultural approach adopted in this book takes seriously the communication networks in which early modern and modern evangelicals have operated across the trans-Atlantic world.[50] The European component of the Atlantic community is of course much broader than merely Britain and Ireland, but, despite the presence of some important French, Dutch and German millennial theorists, especially in the earlier period, it has been British and Irish evangelicals who have been most closely associated with millennial aspiration. Their interests had an unlikely context of origin. The major confessions of faith produced by the emerging protestant traditions constructed a pan-European rejection of earthly eschatological hope. The Augsburg Confession (1530) of the Lutheran movement, the Forty-two Articles of the Church of England (1552) and the Second Helvetic Confession (1566) of the Reformed churches each condemned the 'Jewish dream' of an earthly golden age. But, by the beginning of the seventeenth century, a number of prominent voices began to suggest that the period or periods of one thousand years in Revelation

20:1–10 might have some actual historical or future reference to an age of idealized conditions for the church. These voices developed a conversation that stretched across the continent and which would have enormous implications in the intellectual cultures of the Stuart kingdoms. The focus of debate shifted: European scholars were increasingly taking part in a British, and even an English, millennial discussion. As the seventeenth century progressed, this conversation came to take on important trans-Atlantic dimensions, as puritans in the New World defended their emigration and delineated their new societies on the basis of distinctive patterns of millennial hope.[51] These early American evangelicals generated their own eschatological traditions, and, throughout the early and mid-eighteenth centuries, recycled older expectations of the revival of true religion in an overtly eschatological context. By mid-century, British evangelicals had become the receptors of this new American millennial thinking, as the celebrated revivals of religion known as the Great Awakenings drove high ambitions that the long-awaited glorious conclusion of history was finally at hand. But in the nineteenth century, the general direction of influence was again reversed, as the dispensationalism that had been developed in circles associated with aristocratic Anglicans in Ireland and the south of England gained a dominance of the American cultural mainstream unanticipated by previous varieties of millennial hope. The success of dispensationalism in American evangelical culture would be nuanced by the influence of another European import – the amillennialism associated with such influential Dutch Reformed theologians as Herman Bavinck, Louis Berkhof, William Hendricksen and G.C. Berkouwer, which, in sympathetic American editions, filtered back to believers in Britain and Ireland. Canadian and non-Anglophone European writers have often exercised enormous influence in trans-Atlantic evangelicalism, but this study will reflect the popular cultural dominance of Irish, British and American writers.

This focus on the trans-Atlantic generates important contexts for this book's discussion. The question of the significance of millennial belief is naturally bound up with the question of its human geography; and the uniqueness of particular systems of belief can only be tested in some kind of comparative context. As J.F.C. Harrison has noted, the history of millennial aspiration 'is incomplete if limited chronologically or geographically'; and, he noted, the trans-Atlantic comparison is the 'obvious, though by no means the only possibility for such an approach,' though strangely it has not been regularly adopted.[52] As the preceding survey of the circulation of ideas had demonstrated, the trans-Atlantic context is vital for the study of evangelical faith. Some millennial paradigms were developed on one side of the Atlantic but enjoyed distinctive patterns of success to the other: dispensationalism is a good example of this trend. Other prophetic paradigms were developed simultaneously on each side of the Atlantic: the millennial aspirations associated with American revivals appeared more or less simultaneously in the writings of Jonathan Edwards and Isaac Watts. Other paradigms evolved on one side of the Atlantic in relative isolation from the other: recent discussions among American evangelicals about 'progressive dispensationalism' and Christian Reconstruction have, for example, found no sustained counterpart in the print culture of European evangelicals. Throughout their history, therefore, evangelical millennial believers have embraced prophetic schemes which they endowed with a universal and even cosmic importance. But it is not the case, as this book will demonstrate, that those millennial believers who have embraced similar prophetic creeds in Europe and North America have always understood their implications in quite the same way.

IV

This book will describe the evolution of millennial ideas, avoiding the imposition of a misleading teleology, within the shared context of a trans-Atlantic evangelical movement. It will adopt an essentially chronological approach. This text focuses on print culture: its method of survey will make it difficult to access oral millennial traditions or personal reflections which exist in unpublished manuscript, or to ask questions about the reception, distribution, or sharing of individual texts, or the significance of their ownership. This book is not an ecclesial investigation: it can deal only in a limited way with the question of whether the content of ideas remained constant as they were received and transmitted by those who were not trained theologians. This book is not a psychological study: it cannot address the factors that encouraged individuals or groups to adopt millennial beliefs. Neither is this book a sociological study: it cannot ask wider questions of why certain societies are more likely than others to foster this kind of aspiration, nor can it describe in detail the social composition of millennial movements or the readers of millennial publications, nor delineate the processes by which millennial beliefs oscillated between subculture and mainstream, not least because it is a notoriously difficult task to describe evangelicalism in relation to the American mainstream. The methodology employed in this book cannot address the quantitative questions that many readers might ask: whether evangelicalism or evangelical millennialism varied in popularity throughout the period, or whether, in any period, evangelicals of a particular gender, or from certain social, cultural or political backgrounds, were more likely to hold millennial beliefs, or how these beliefs may have been adapted for oral or ecclesial transmission. What this book can do, nevertheless, is highlight the importance of varieties of millennialism as frequently-repeated themes and as highly flexible discourses within which believers have expressed some of the salient hopes and concerns of their evolving worldviews, and it will do so in illustrative readings of major texts and important contexts in successive periods in evangelical history.

A survey with this scope of ambition cannot help but appear impressionistic. This book will therefore aim to focus on the most important themes of its discussion, developing readings of significant texts, contexts and cultures. It is inevitable that it will reflect my own geographical bias, and perhaps use British and Irish examples to illustrate its argument of trans-Atlantic development more often than it might; some readers, recognizing the American focus of most histories of millennial ideas, might consider this a virtue. And it may also reflect my own theological bias and lived experience, which I described in the preface to *Writing the rapture* (2009). This book will certainly develop its argument sympathetically. The holders of millennial beliefs should not be carelessly dismissed: after all, as J.F.C. Harrison reminded us, there is no good reason to suppose that 'people who led apparently simple lives necessarily held simple beliefs.'[53] Nor is there any good reason to treat millennial convictions with learned irony, even though 'our sensibility to the problems of the millennium' may be 'so reduced, and our acceptance of the premises from which the millenarians started so minimal, that with the best will in the world we find it extremely difficult to see things as they did.'[54] Instead, we need to remember that millennial believers – many but not all of them evangelicals – have for many centuries found reason to retain these forms of 'alternative knowledge.'[55] Modern readers may not share the faith of the authors described in this text, but we must appreciate the commitments of the millions of evangelicals that have expected, and continue to expect, the final transformation of a slowly dying world.

1
The Emergence of Evangelical Millennialism, 1500–1600

In the late 1520s, in the immediate aftermath of the first wave of reformation iconoclasm and in situations of exceptional social distress, radical Anabaptists in and around the city states of Holland and north-west Germany revived old and revolutionary ideas. In 1532 and 1533, a number of the preachers of this foundationally unstable ideology of social change sought refuge from their persecutors in the newly Lutheran town of Münster. Among their number were disciples of Melchior Hoffmann, a wandering prophet who had gained access to significant new spheres of influence after his recent conversion to the Anabaptist cause. Hoffmann taught his followers that a short period of signs, wonders and apocalyptic woes would precede a golden age of heaven on earth which, he argued, would begin 15 centuries after the crucifixion – in 1533. In Münster, these millennial ideas were rapidly disseminated, and turned into a 'mass obsession, dominating the whole life of the poorer classes.'[1] Among the large number responding to this new message was the leader of the town's recently triumphant Lutheran party, Bernt Rothmann, who, having turned Anabaptist, added to Hoffmann's millennial discourse a smattering of the principles of communism he had learned from the recently reprinted, though spuriously attributed, Fifth Epistle of Clement.

The effect of this combination of high and popular culture was overwhelming. There 'streamed' into Münster a vast number of 'insecure and harassed proletarians,' mainly from the Dutch centres of early capitalism, suddenly attracted by the prospect of easy living; at the same time, many of the wealthy grew appalled by this 'powerful Anabaptist movement supported by a mass of unemployed and desperate foreigners.'[2] Roman Catholics and Lutherans united to outmanoeuvre the revolutionary preachers. Hoffmann was arrested, and imprisoned in a cage until his death, but the movement's leadership was assumed by a preacher who shared little of his quietist passivity. Jan Matthys, a baker turned preacher, taught his followers that their duty was not simply to wait for the millennium, but actively to prepare for it, if necessary by the violent disruption of the political status quo. He identified two visiting preachers as Enoch and Elijah – the two witnesses expected in the final days. The town erupted in mass hysteria under the impact of their preaching, and many of the wealthy made rapid plans to flee. The leadership of the now largely Anabaptist community issued proclamations which identified the town as a centre to which the godly should resort. Münster was the New Jerusalem – the only place of safety when the earth would be destroyed at Easter 1534. The results were dramatic. Streets were lit by bonfires of books, paintings and sculpture looted from the cathedral. The 'Dutch prophets,' as the two witnesses were known, dominated public life. They ordered the expulsion of all remaining Lutherans and Roman Catholics, and commanded that anyone remaining in the town who refused to be re-baptized was immediately to be put to death. By the end of February, the city was under siege. Inside, private property was abolished; all books, with the exception of the Bible, were forbidden; polygamy was established, marriages with unbelievers were broken and every woman of marriageable age was compelled to find a husband. Then the eschatological identity of the more dominant of the witnesses was revealed: Jan Bockelson, a tailor better known as John of Leiden, was proclaimed Messiah of the Last Days, the man who would become the universal king. The regime advanced his relentlessly political religion, and Bockelson and his wives lived in ostentatious luxury as Münster was plunged into a totalitarian reign of terror. But the glory and horror of the Münster millennium was not to endure. By April 1535 the town was being ravaged by famine; by June its walls had been overcome by the besieging armies of Lutheran and Roman-Catholic powers; and by January 1536 the leaders of the movement had been entirely destroyed. The millennial hopes of John of Leiden and his thousands of followers had failed.[3]

These notorious events provide an extreme example of the enduring power and appeal of medieval apocalyptic ideologies in the period of early modernity. They demonstrate both continuity and change in the patterns of eschatological belief that had extended throughout the course of the Christian centuries, demonstrating believers' continuing temptation to find doctrinal guidance outside the boundaries of the biblical canon and to combine religious and political hope in an eschatological vision of social, political and moral revolution. And yet, in the early decades of reformation, it was the evangelical opponents of the Münster revolutionaries who were most often doing something new: Anabaptists maintained and developed ideas that had circulated widely and been violently suppressed in the medieval centuries, while magisterial reformers adopted convictions that more often represented a radical disjunction in the history of Christian eschatology.[4] This chapter will trace these paradoxical patterns of continuity and change in the first generations of reformation, as theologians and commentators across Europe and across confessional divisions challenged the emergence of millennial aspiration, and, in the early seventeenth century, as evangelicals in the British Isles revived, reified and gradually popularized its theological and exegetical base.

I

In the early and middle decades of the sixteenth century, millennial expectations that had survived from the ancient and biblical worlds became a central component of multiple, popular and often radical projects for the reform of the central institutions of Christendom.[5] But these expectations – latterly haunted by the debacle at Münster – were never uncontroversial. Advocates of evangelical millennial ideologies developed key elements of these patterns of belief on a slim exegetical basis. Their opponents regularly denied the interpretive – and even the canonical – foundation of their most basic assumption, that specific biblical passages predicted the unusual conditions of a thousand-year reign of Christ within the limits of human history. But these critics were responding within orthodox theological boundaries when they indicated their concern about the possibilities of millennial belief, for ideas similar to those they were rejecting had a long if not a respectable pedigree across the Christian centuries.

Advocates of millennial belief – or 'chiliasm,' as it was often described by later writers who wished to accentuate its inherent sense of menace – appeared soon after the completion of the New Testament canon. Arguing for widely divergent and sometimes incompatible assumptions, they found the common roots of their convictions within that canon, and principally in Revelation 20:1–10, the *locus classicus* of evangelical millennial hope. This passage provided the basis for extremely material expectations of a this-worldly spiritual utopia. Many ante-Nicene texts evidenced a high regard for Revelation and embraced the possibility of an earthly millennial hope: their number included the late first-century writings of Cerinthus, the Testament of the Twelve Patriarchs and the writings of Irenaeus, Barnabas and Papias in the second century, Lactantias in the third century and Apollinaris in the fourth. But many other patristic writers disagreed, and in the longer term the effect of their critique was to be devastating. Eusebius of Caesarea admitted the canonicity of Revelation with great reluctance, but its authoritative status was entirely opposed by Dionysius of Alexandria in the third century and by Cyril of Jerusalem and John Chrysostom in the fourth.[6] Others, recognizing the increasing catholic consensus about the contents of the New Testament canon, advanced a more specific critique addressing this theology's exegetical foothold. The defenders of the Montanist heresy regarded the idea of an earthly millennium with a degree of critical caution, while most Gnostics dismissed it altogether. But among the defenders of orthodoxy, millennialism was forthrightly rejected by the Alexandrian theologians, and most importantly, in terms of the evangelical tradition, by Augustine, the hugely influential bishop of Hippo (354–430).[7]

Augustine dismissed millennial aspiration with all the zeal of a recent convert. In his earlier years as a Christian he had been sympathetic to millennial ideas but recorded his increasing disillusion with these 'ridiculous fables' in *City of God* (written 410–25), his classic exposition of historiography, providence and eschatology. He admitted that he had assumed, with many of his contemporaries, that the first resurrection of Revelation 20:4 would be a physical event, and that it might be expected around six thousand years after the world's creation. Advocates of this kind of millennial hope, he noted, were 'particularly excited by the actual number of a thousand years, taking it as appropriate that there should be a kind of Sabbath for the saints for all that time, a holy rest, that is, after the labours of the six thousand years since man's creation ... I also entertained this notion at one time.'[8] In its place, Augustine adopted the symbolical reading that his work would do so much to encourage – though there was to be some lack of clarity about its exegetical basis. Augustine did not offer a systemization of his alternative hermeneutical method, but 'spiritualized' the references to one thousand years in Revelation 20:1–10 to suggest that the reign of Christ referred to one thousand years of Christian history, a period he identified as 'the sixth millennium, the sixth day,' or, alternatively, to 'the whole period of this world's history.' Writing at the beginning of the fifth century, Augustine had no idea that history would continue long after AD 1000. He continued to read literally other references in biblical apocalyptic literature, including the three and a half years of the reign of the Antichrist, and was candid enough to admit in one place that the meaning of one detail of eschatological interpretation 'completely escapes me.'[9] Whatever its lack of clarity or consistency, nevertheless, Augustine's re-reading of Revelation 20:1–10 appeared convincing to many of his early followers.

Augustine's conclusions made an immediate impact and had enduring importance. Readers of Revelation had to wait eight centuries before the popularization of an alternative method of interpretation, the 'historicism' that would begin with Rupert of Duetz (d. 1129), who would use material from the Jewish historian Josephus and the Christian historian Eusebius to argue that the prophecies of Revelation described the history of salvation from creation to the Council of Nicaea (325).[10] But Rupert's new reading would compete in the popular imagination with the radical re-statement of millennial belief provided by Joachim of Fiore (1135–1202). His mystical reflections on Revelation proposed the existence of three distinct ages: the age of the Father, the Old Testament period; the age of the Son, from the incarnation until 1260; and the age of the Spirit, which he expected to begin in 1260, in which humanity would come into direct relationship with God and in which the church would be ruled by a new spiritual elite. Joachim's theories were adopted by groups as widely divergent as impeccably orthodox Franciscans and wildly heretical Brethren of the Free Spirit. But their influence was ultimately eclipsed. Within another century, the eschatological landscape of Christendom had been enlarged to encompass new locations for life after death – heaven and hell, the traditional destinations of the righteous and the wicked, were being discussed alongside limbo and purgatory, new destinations for those who were neither, the existence of which depended largely but not uniquely on the influence of Thomas Aquinas (c. 1225–74), whose massive and sometimes speculative *Summa Theologica* (written 1265–74) provided Christian theology with a detail of consideration that it would never again enjoy. But heretical groups continued to cogitate upon millennial themes throughout the middle ages, often, but not always, developing an idea first mooted at the beginning of the fourteenth century in the writing of Ubertino de Casale, that the Antichrist would be discovered in the papacy.[11] These medieval 'new religious movements,' so ably chronicled by Marjorie Reeves, posed as radical alternatives to the ecclesiastical status quo, but their regular recycling of early Christian heresies never mounted a serious challenge to the non-millennial presuppositions of the institutional church. They were frequently and violently suppressed. Augustine's eschatology remained paradigmatic until the middle of the sixteenth century, when it faced a new and compelling challenge.

II

Early evangelicals developed a critical reading of the eschatological tradition they had inherited. In the 1520s and 1530s, the first generation
of reformers, drawing on a relatively small number of New Testament
passages (1 John 2:18, 22; 1 John 4:3; 2 John 7), generally insisted that
the Antichrist should be recognized as the Pope. This was not an innovative conclusion. Almost one millennia before the reformation began,
around 600, Gregory I – himself a bishop of Rome – asserted that the
individual who would later assume the title of 'universal priest' would
be the forerunner of the Antichrist. Joachim of Fiore, in the twelfth century, and John Wycliffe (fl. 1320s–1384), in the fourteenth century, later
agreed. So it was perfectly appropriate that Martin Luther (1483–1546),
in his *Commentarius in Apocalypsin ante centum annos aeditus* (1528),
should refer to this pedigree of anti-papal consideration in noting that
'we are not the first to interpret the papacy to mean the reign of the
Antichrist.'[12] One generation later, John Calvin (1509–1564) continued
to defend the claim: 'anyone who has learned from Scripture what are
the things that belong particularly to God, and who on the other hand
considers well what the Pope usurps for himself, will not have much
difficulty in recognizing Antichrist, even though he were a ten year
old boy.'[13] But this firm repudiation of the authoritative foundations of
medieval Christian orthodoxy was matched by deep uncertainty about
the canonical boundaries of the Scriptures upon which the evangelical
critique of its faults had been built.[14]

Despite their biblicist reputation, many of the magisterial reformers
doubted the canonicity of Revelation. This concern about its status was
revived, for the first time since the fourth century, in the influential
New Testament *Annotationes* (1516) prepared by Erasmus of Rotterdam
(1466–1536).[15] Erasmus had two reasons to justify his caution – his own
difficulty in securing access to relevant Greek manuscripts, and the erratic
nature of those manuscripts which he eventually read. Ironically, given
the long sustention of the patristic debate on the subject, the strongest
argument he could find in favour of retaining the traditional canonical
boundaries of the New Testament was the *consensus ecclesiae*, including
the testimony of the Fathers. But that consensus – especially among the
evangelicals whose numbers Erasmus never joined – was shaken by his
claims. A number of reforming writers explicitly doubted the book's
canonical authority. Ulrich Zwingli (1484–1531), for example, denied that
Revelation should be included in Scripture, and based his argument on
traditions he traced to Jerome. Others moved from denial to ambivalence.

Luther was familiar with Erasmus' *Annotationes*, but cited more relevant reasons to question the canonicity of Revelation, including his concern that the book was insufficiently focused on Jesus Christ, and thought that in this respect the obscurity of its content might be compared to that of 4 Esdras, never the brightest star of the apocryphal firmament.[16] But he believed that Revelation still had its uses. It may not have identified a clear vision of Jesus Christ, but, as Luther enthusiastically recognized in the preface to *Commentarius in Apocalypsin ante centum annos aeditus* (1528), it did present a clear vision of the Antichrist. This new enthusiasm for Revelation marked Luther's eventual, and still somewhat ambiguous, reconciliation with its canonical authority, a changing mood evidenced by the prefaces to Revelation published in editions of his German Bible between 1522 and 1530. By the latter date, these prefaces were outlining a wider sense of the significance of the book, providing their readers with the basic parameters of an historicist interpretive method that found in the pages of the New Testament the outline of later Christian history. Luther argued that the one thousand years of Revelation 20:1–10 should be read allegorically as referring to a period stretching from the first century to the period of the reformation. The Last Judgement was the only event predicted in Revelation that remained to be fulfilled, he insisted, and, especially in his earlier writings, he appears to have expected its imminent realization. 'Leaving open the question of the book's canonicity served Luther's purpose,' one recent commentator has noted; 'resorting to allegory, he made it correspond to the chief points of his reforming program' while developing a reading of church history which, when expanded by his disciples in the *Centuries of Magdeburg* (1559–74), would come to dominate the European evangelical imagination.[17] Other reformers, without disputing the canonicity of Revelation, did not pursue its detailed exegesis. Even Calvin, who prepared commentaries on almost every New Testament book, did not deal carefully with the text. When he offered an explanation of Revelation 20:1–10 in his *Institutes* (1559), he simply highlighted that passage's references to persecution, arguing that the text 'does not apply to the eternal blessedness of the church but only to the various disturbances that awaited the church, while still toiling on earth.'[18] Millennial believers were therefore 'too childish either to need or to be worth a refutation,' he contended, for 'those who assign the children of God a thousand years in which to enjoy the inheritance of the life to come do not realise how much reproach they are casting upon Christ and his Kingdom.'[19] He traced the radical hope to the working of Satan, who, 'since he could not openly destroy the hope of the resurrection ... promised that the day was close and would soon be at hand, in order to undermine it by stealth ... Even at the present day he continually makes use of the same means of attack.'[20] But it was not to be evangelical writers who would consider that this unpicking of the canon might itself be advancing a satanic agenda. When so many of those reformers with the most commanding reputations 'either condemned the book ... or ignored it,' it was hardly implausible for Roman Catholic apologists to claim that the rhetoric of their enemies was driven by a radical rejection of the traditional biblical canon.[21]

Nevertheless, a number of significant evangelical writers did move to self-consciously rehabilitate Revelation. The first major evangelical commentary on the text was prepared by Francois Lambert (1486–1530), a French theologian, whose *Exegeseos Francisci Lamberti Auenionensis in sanctam Diui Ioannis Apocalypsim libri VII. In Academia Marpurgensi praelecti* (1528) argued that the reformation had been predicted in the pages of the New Testament.[22] John Bale (1495–1563), an English dramatist and later an Irish Reformed bishop, followed a similar method in his most influential commentary, *The image of both churches* (1547), which highlighted the importance of Revelation in the reformation agenda. Bale worked hard to recuperate the older Augustinian legacy within the new historicist consensus, for, as he argued, 'he that knoweth not this book, knoweth not what the church is whereof he is a member.' The *Image* drew on Revelation to warn those Christians who had retained their allegiance to the bishop of Rome to flee his jurisdiction and the impending judgement of God. 'After the true opinion of St. Austin,' Bale claimed, drawing on the rhetoric of *City of God*, 'we are citizens in the new Jerusalem with Jesus Christ, or else in the old superstitious Babylon with antichrist the vicar of Satan.'[23]

By 1560, it seemed, the issue of the canonicity of Revelation had been resolved, but evangelical writers continued to exorcise their literary-critical demons. Franciscus Junius (1545–1602) was a French Reformed pastor who had ministered to a number of refugee congregations before moving into a series of teaching positions in the universities of Neustadt, Heidelberg and Leiden, in which he prepared the contributions he would make to the definitive protestant Latin Bible, which he translated with Immanuel Tremellius (1590).[24] Junius turned his significant gifts to eschatological considerations, and addressed the issue of the canonicity of Revelation in his *Apocalypsis methodica analysis notisque illustrata* (1591, with second and third editions in 1599). This brief but influential book was translated into French, and an English version of the text appeared as the annotations to Revelation in the third major edition of the Geneva Bible, one of the most important English literary texts of the period (first edition, 1560; third edition, 1599). Several decades later, the German evangelical theologian David Pareus (1548–1622) still felt the need to address the arguments of Erasmus and Luther in his compendious commentary on Revelation published in 1618.[25] But by then, the verdict of the European commentators was clear: Revelation should be recognized as an essential component of holy writ, but the millennial theory it may be seen to advance was a theology that must at all costs be denied.

This concern about the dangers of millennial hope was reiterated in the most important of the early reformation creeds. Their need to rehearse Augustine's rejection of millennialism is significant, suggesting that millennial theology had lingered in the popular imagination despite the opposition of the church and the revolutionary activity of too many of its medieval and early modern adherents. The confessions of faith adopted by these early reformation communities frequently (and accurately) rejected millennial aspiration as 'Jewish.'[26] Thus the Augsburg Confession (1530), drafted by Philip Melancthon (1497–1560) and published with the approval of Luther, explicitly condemned those 'Anabaptists' who denied eternal punishment along with others, like those at Münster, who 'spread abroad Jewish opinions, that, before the resurrection of the dead, the godly shall get the sovereignty in the world, and the wicked shall be brought under in every place.'[27] The Forty-two Articles of Religion (1553), published by the Church of England, insisted that 'they that go about to renew the fable of heretics called Millenarii be repugnant to Holy Scripture, and cast themselves headlong into a Jewish dotage.'[28] The Second Helvetic Confession (1566) similarly condemned 'Jewish dreams, that before the day of judgement there shall be a golden world in the earth; and that the godly shall possess the kingdoms of the world, their wicked enemies being trodden under foot.'[29] As a confession adopted by the Reformed churches of Scotland, Hungary, Poland and Geneva, this document represented the pan-European evangelical community united in its hostility to the variety of apocalyptic extremism displayed at Münster in the early 1530s. By the end of the sixteenth century, therefore, the European evangelical consensus had been established. The text of Revelation had been returned to the biblical canon, but the foremost representatives of the Lutheran, Anglican and Calvinist reformations were resolutely opposed to any expression of millennial hope.

III

This European evangelical consensus makes all the more surprising the early seventeenth-century recovery of millennial aspiration by English and Scottish Reformed theologians.[30] The roots of this recovery can be traced to the 1550s, when many English protestants fled into temporary foreign exile to escape the persecutions of Queen Mary. These exile communities provided an environment for wide-ranging reconsideration of the cultural and political implications of English evangelical theology. In Strasbourg, Geneva and elsewhere, the exiles wrote and published texts which consolidated their emerging and fundamentally apocalyptic worldview. And yet their outlook was, in important ways, robustly conservative. In the flagship texts of the English reformation, the early editions of the Geneva Bible (1560) and the *Acts and monuments* of John Foxe (1563), these early evangelicals confirmed that the one thousand years of Revelation 20:1–10 had already been fulfilled and guarded against any interpretation that could generate a politically revolutionary application. They initiated an unprecedented publishing campaign, promoting their worldview in short tracts, dramas, and historical studies, some of which were over twice as long as Scripture. The Geneva Bible passed through three major editions from 1560 to 1599 and established itself as the foundational text of the emerging puritan movement within the British Isles and the American colonies. Between 1560 and 1644, 140 issues of its most popular edition were printed, with the second and third editions providing annotations translated from the works of Theodore Beza (1519–1605), and were 'used and pored over by three generations of English Protestants.'[31]

The exiles' publications initiated a paradigm shift in popular consciousness even as they drove the English recovery of millennial belief. Later puritan writers used Foxe's *Acts and monuments* as a principal sourcebook for their arguments from history – though they found those arguments from history challenging to their exegetical tradition, as Foxe's uncertainty about when the millennium had begun led to many of his readers' doubts as to whether it had ever begun.[32] The interpretive annotations of the Geneva Bible were of more immediate importance in the English millennial recovery. These annotations, arranged in the margins of the page around a central block of biblical text, were designed to explain the doctrinal and practical implications of the text for the benefit of the imagined 'simple reader.'[33] In its annotative format and with its advanced interpretive apparatus, the Geneva Bible appeared to consolidate a stable body of doctrine. But its annotations varied with each of its editions, and consequently so too did the nature of its eschatological concern.

The first edition of the Bible (1560) imagined its readers as being 'them that love the comming of Christ Jesus our Lord.'[34] Its dedicatory preface to Queen Elizabeth highlighted its eschatological investments, referencing Revelation 20:1–10, in its description of Satan, and Daniel 7, in its description of the history of five world empires:

> God wil fight from heaven against this great dragon, the ancient serpent, which is called the devil and Satan, til he have accomplished the whole worke and made his Churche glorious to him selfe, without spot and wrincle. For albeit all other kingdomes and monarchies, as the Babylonians, Persians, Grecians & Romains have fallen & taken end: yet the Churche of Christ even under the Crosse hath from the begynning of the worlde bene victorious, and shalbe everlastingly.[35]

That sense of impending victory was expanded upon in later editions gradually to embody Beza's distinctive reading of Romans 9–11, which emphasized a future conversion of unprecedented numbers of Jewish people and which invested in the eschatology of the Reformed tradition a sense of optimism – and, consequently, eschatological delay – it had not previously known. The annotations argued that God had temporarily blinded the Jewish nation to the truths of the Christian gospel, and that their blindness would continue until the 'fullness of the Gentiles' had embraced the evangelical faith. At that point, the annotations explained, God intended to remove their temporary blindness, and when he did, the 'whole nation of ye Jewes ... shalbe joyned to the Church of Christ.'[36] Beza's annotations anticipated the transformation of the world: 'the Jewes now remaine, as it were, in death for lacke of the Gospel: but when they & the Gentiles shal embrace Christ, ye world shalbe restored to a newe life.'[37] But this would take some time. Beza's expectations pushed the second coming into the middle distance, and allowed English evangelicals to believe that significant events might be expected to occur before its closure of human history. This apocalyptic optimism did not yet stretch to a fully millennial faith, but these notions of delay and expectation would pervade later puritan thinking, and exist as a foundational element of a great deal of later eschatological belief.

This optimism was most obviously developed in the third and final edition of the Geneva Bible (1599). This edition proved to be extremely popular, becoming so widely read that one recent commentator has suggested that its annotations were 'indicative of the climate of opinion among puritans in the first half of the seventeenth century' throughout the trans-Atlantic world.[38] The edition was published in 24 separate issues, and its New Testament was separately published on at least three occasions. It presented new annotations on Revelation which had been culled from the work of Franciscus Junius. His exegetical interests in Revelation, as we have already noted, had been demonstrated in such works as *Notae in Apocalypsim* (1589), *Apocalypsis methodica analysis notisque illustrata* (1591) and *Exposition de l'Apocalypse* (1592). Several of his texts were translated into English, and one of their number, *Apocalypsis, a brief and learned commentarie upon the Revelation of St. John* (1592), provided the source for the Geneva Bible annotations. Although Junius' notes contained significant exegetical differences from those in annotations in earlier editions of the text, the outline of a conservative Augustinian reading was still apparent. But of all the annotations on Revelation in the Geneva Bible tradition, Junius' advanced the most sceptical reading of the political status quo.

'Simple readers' could not miss the significance of Junius' text. One 1602 edition, for example, prefaced the text of Revelation with a chart describing itself as 'the order of time whereunto the contents of this booke are to be referred.'[39] This chart listed historical dates and events in relation to summaries of the ensuing annotations, and made it impossible for even the most casual of readers to misunderstand the impact of Junius' historicist method. The chart demonstrated that his annotations were rooted in scientific knowledge of the past, but moved from that historical objectivity to predict other events for which dates could not yet be provided – the dates for the church's final victory over the harlot, the two beasts, the dragon, and death itself. (Strangely, the chart did not include a reference to the conversion of the Jews that continued to be described in the edition's annotations on Romans.) Readers were being invited to insert these dates into the blank column as they noticed each prophecy being fulfilled.

But perhaps the most important contribution made by the third edition of the Geneva Bible was its re-reading of the significance of the millennium. Junius' notes teased out the implications of the references to martyrdom in Revelation 20:1–10, and their reiteration of Calvin's earlier point – that the millennium could not be a period of glory for the church – drove English puritans' reconsideration of the political implications of the biblical apocalyptic narrative. Foxe's *Acts and monuments* had assumed that the millennium should be understood as a period of ecclesiastical glory which began with the accession of Constantine, the archetypal Christian emperor, in AD 324. But Junius withdrew from this 'theology of glory' to elucidate a 'theology of the cross,' beginning the binding of Satan with the Roman destruction of Jerusalem in AD 70, with its attendant commencement of martyrdom. Although both writers agreed that the one thousand years of Revelation 20:1–10 referred to one period that was best placed in the past, their approaches contained significant differences, most notably with regard to the notion of sacral monarchy. And in this debate, it would be the conclusions of the final edition of the Geneva Bible that would win out. With its theology of eschatological delay, its expectation of impending prophetic fulfilment, and its criticism of the political status quo, the third edition of the Geneva Bible was a handbook for the final days of history.

IV

Of course, Junius' timetable was not unique. Other evangelical writers also articulated their expectation of latter-day glory within a specific chronological framework. In 1593, for example, John Napier (1550–1617) published *A plaine discovery of the whole Revelation*.[40] The text explicitly acknowledged his direct debt to the Marian exiles. As a student at St Andrews, Napier had come under the influence of one of their number, 'that worthie man of God, Maister Christopher Goodman,' who had been preaching on Revelation.[41] Goodman's ideology shared the same basis as that adopted by other evangelicals of the period, but he was never shy of criticizing existing authorities. Napier followed his lead. As a direct result of Goodman's influence, Napier pursued a life-long study of Revelation, adopting from his teacher many of the essential features of the eschatological system developed by the exiles in Geneva. His approach combined the historiography of Foxe's 'theology of glory' with the scepticism of Constantinian politico-ecclesiology that was typified in Junius' 'theology of the cross.' 'The thousand yeares that Satan was bound,' Napier wrote, 'began in An. Christi 300. or thereabout,' at exactly the same point as the beginning of the 'Antichrists universall raigne over Christians.' Thus identifying the millennium and the persecution of the Antichrist with the beginnings of a state church, Napier advanced his criticism of the political and religious assumptions that undergirded the British establishment.

Although Napier had dedicated the first edition of his book to King James – who, in 1593, was still a relatively inexperienced Scottish monarch – his cool assessment of Constantine initiated something of a re-evaluation of the role of the 'godly prince' in apocalyptic warfare. While Napier prefaced his first edition with a call for James to reform his household and his nation in preparation for a unique apocalyptic role, the second edition of the *Plaine discovery*, published in 1611, omitted any reference to his duties. In the interim, James had taken possession of the English throne and had repudiated significant elements of his Scottish Presbyterian childhood. The new translation of the Bible he had sponsored deliberately omitted the Geneva annotations, the occasionally anti-monarchical bias of which James had detested, and Napier, no doubt concerned by James's theological reversal, passed over his earlier monarchism in silence.[42] Napier's other significant contribution to the millennial tradition was his emphasis on the importance of biblical mathematics and his consequent transformation of the role of the student of biblical apocalyptic literature from exegete to prophet. His fame in history rests upon his discovery of logarithms, which he imposed upon the existing Genevan teaching to produce a chronological framework for his eschatological narrative. On the basis of his biblical-mathematical calculations, Napier concluded that the seventh trumpet, initiating God's final dealings with the earth, had already sounded, in 1541, and would complete its influence by 1786. The age, he expected, would end between 1688 and 1700.[43] Napier's conclusions were building on those of the most influential text in the emerging puritan movement. The Geneva Bible had opened up the immediate future, and Napier's mathematical theology was pushing the second coming ever further into the distance. The future had been quantified.

Others continued to emphasize an imminent prophetic fulfilment. William Perkins (1558–1602), a Cambridge pastor whose preaching exercised a profound influence upon the developing leadership of the emerging puritan movement, published his *Godly and learned exposition of the three first chapters in the Revelation* (1595), which picked up on many of Bale's themes to discuss in detail the Laodicean situation of the English church. Perkins rarely considered explicitly eschatological topics; his entry in the old *Dictionary of national biography* noted favourably that his 'sound judgement' was 'shown by the manner in which he kept clear of the all-absorbing millenarian controversy.'[44] Nevertheless Perkins' interest in predictive prophecy continued to be evident in *A digest or harmonie of the bookes of the Old and New Testament*, which listed in chronological order various biblical events and their historical situations.[45] Perkins dated Satan's binding, which marked the beginning of the millennium, in 295, and his release in 1195. Between these two events, the seals of divine judgement began to open in 795, and the four horsemen of the apocalypse had been released in 895. At the time of writing, Perkins believed that the defeat of the beast and the Babylonian whore, the saints' conquest and first resurrection were as yet unfulfilled.[46] Perkins is often cited as the father of postmillennial thought, but in *A digest* he seems uncommitted: in a series of conclusions that appeared to contradict the later amillennial / premillennial distinction, he argued that the thousand years (Revelation 20:1–10) should be located in the past, while the first resurrection (Revelation 20:4) should continue to be expected.

But Perkins' contribution to the emergence of postmillennialism should not be underestimated. His importance in establishing an optimistic eschatology is clearly evident in *A fruitfull dialogue concerning the ende of the world*, an undated dialogue between 'Christian' and 'Worldling' which appears to be set in 1587, one year before the 'protestant winds' destroyed the Spanish Armada.[47] The text castigates 'Worldling' for adhering to a pessimistic belief that the world would end within one year:

> *Worldl.* ... I am sure you knowe as much as I: they say every where, that the next yeare eightie eight Doomes day will be.
> *Christ.* They are flying tales.
> *Worldl.* Nay, I promise you: I have some skill, and I have read bookes of it that are printed; and talke goes, that there be olde prophecies of this yeare found in olde stone walls.
> *Christ.* I tell you plainely they are very lies.
> *Worldl.* ... When after Christs birth there be expired,
> of hundreds fiveteene, yeares eightie eight,
> Then comes the time of dangers to be feared,
> and all mankind with dolors it shall freight,
> For if the world in that yeare doe not fall,
> if sea and land then perish ne decay:
> Yet Empires all, and kingdomes alter shall,
> and man to ease himselfe shall have no way.
> *Christ.* For my part I make as little accompt of these verses as of Merlins drunken prophecies, or of the tales of Robinhood.[48]

Worldling's defence – somewhat ominously – refers to the prophecy of Elias and 'Anabaptisticall revelations,' a signal of the heterodox nature of the argument he was sustaining. But, Christian reminds him, 'all prophecies are not of God, and from his spirit: many are from the phantasies of wicked men, and from the suggestion of the Devill.'[49] So Worldling resorts to a more biblical defence:

> All the signes of the comming of Christ are past; Oh, what earthquakes have there been? what famine? what warres and hurliburlies among men? what signes in the Sunne and Moone? what flashing in the ayre? what blasing starres? surely, surely, the world can not

last long: there is some cause that so many men so long agoe have spoken of these times, and speciallie of the next yeare.[50]

It is this reference to the 'next yeare' which makes Perkins' intentions ambiguous, blurring the distinction between a purely didactic eschatological tract, and (assuming that *A fruitfull dialogue* was written after the event) a hint that he viewed the defeat of the Armada as a matter of apocalyptic importance. In any case, Christian replies with an argument that the signs are not all past. He lists several events which remain unfulfilled, including, most significantly, 'the conversion of the Jewes unto that religion which now they hate: as appeareth in the 11. to the Romanes.'[51] Thus the future was not entirely bleak, Perkins was teaching, and the end of the world could not be imminently expected, for there were to be better times ahead, and these better times were to be associated with the conversion of the Jews. Perkins' argument would achieve enormous influence. By the beginning of the seventeenth century, Calvin's claim that Israel as a nation had no continuing significance in the New Testament period had been successfully replaced in the minds of many European evangelicals by Beza's belief in a future calling of Abraham's physical seed – the conversion of the Jews. Adopted by Perkins, this confidence was instilled in Thomas Goodwin and Richard Sibbes, among several generations of puritan clergy who trained under his influence at Cambridge. Another Cambridge puritan, John Preston, writing in *The breastplate of faith and love* (1630), repudiated the opinions of those men who 'looke at an earthy Kingdome, (as many of the Disciples did) when they looke for great matters by Christ in this world.'[52] But there is no doubt that these hopes of the future became increasingly characteristic of seventeenth-century evangelicals, in and beyond the puritan movement.

Early seventeenth-century English evangelicals were therefore intensely conservative. With their implicit support of Elizabethan foreign policy, in attaching eschatological importance to the destruction of Roman Catholic powers, in supporting the English monarchy, and in their conservative expectation of a latter-day conversion of the Jews, they continued to reject belief in an earthly, future millennium. But in defending these convictions, these early evangelicals were preparing for a revolution in eschatological thinking.

V

By the beginning of the seventeenth century, the earlier debates about the canonicity of Revelation had almost been forgotten. The range of responses that Revelation generated demonstrated that it 'fulfilled a set of needs that manifested themselves as the reform movements progressed.'[53] For some readers, it existed as an expression of spiritual consolation; for others, it operated as a signal reminder of the imminent collapse of Roman Catholicism;[54] while to others it spoke of the conversion of the Jews and the halcyon days the godly were shortly to enjoy. Most evangelical believers embraced systems of eschatology that were decidedly optimistic without being overtly millennial, refusing to advance upon Richard Sibbes' remark that 'we are fallen into the latter end of the world.'[55] By the mid-seventeenth century, this limited expectation of latter-day glory would evolve into a fully developed millennial expectation as believers worked out the optimism of the Geneva Bible's annotations in the context of the early modern mathematical revolution and alongside notions of expected revival and the delay of the second coming. But it would take a long time for the dangers of Münster to be forgotten, and those involved in reviving the doctrine would consistently repudiate its Anabaptist past. Across Europe, believers would watch with fascination and concern the emergence of a new evangelical millennialism.

2
The Formation of Evangelical Millennialism, 1600–1660

The new evangelical millennialism emerged at the beginning of the seventeenth century, as theologians began to reassess the eschatological consequences of their creedal communities' rejection of millennial belief. Slowly, and very cautiously, they qualified widely-shared antipathies towards key eschatological ideas. Though this confessional revisionism stretched across European protestant communities, it made its most enduring impact in English and American contexts, and there, most obviously, though certainly not exclusively, among puritans. The confessions of faith that emerged out of these environments pointedly omitted the hostility to millennial theories that had marked their sixteenth-century predecessors. These confessions, and the publications they accompanied, provided the momentum for a wide and contradictory range of responses that propelled the most radical movements of the mid-century crisis, and set the parameters for patterns of conviction that would endure after the defeat of the revolutionary cause.[1]

The new interests of seventeenth-century millennial thinkers coalesced around a number of the period's most significant intellectual trends. One of the most important of these was the ongoing mathematical revolution, which was linked to the emerging 'science of order.'[2] This new habit of mind encouraged early modern evangelical writers to link their biblical, historical and chronological studies, projecting calculations into the past, in efforts to date specific events in biblical narrative, and into the future, in efforts to outline a timetable of expected events. These calculations yielded a number of unanticipated by-products, from Napier's discovery of logarithms at the end of the sixteenth century to the subversion of Britain's Gothic constitution in the middle of the seventeenth century.[3] This process of revision was assisted by the development of historical knowledge, for the intellectual revolution was driven – at least in part – by the failure of reformation historiography. Since the mid-sixteenth century, evangelical scholars had been attempting to prove that the references to one thousand years in Revelation 20:1–10 referred to a discrete period that could be identified in the past.[4] But as knowledge of the social and theological environments of the earlier Christian centuries increased and as protestant theology continued to be refined, it became obvious to many of these scholars that their search for an earlier ecclesiastical golden age was an exercise in futility. Evangelicals within and outside the puritan movement began to search for a new prophetic paradigm – one that would take history seriously, while engaging with the newly respectable activity of chronological projection and retaining the hope that a golden age could be found somewhere within the course of human history. In addition, a growing awareness of and interest in Hebraic language, literature and culture encouraged protestant theologians across confessional divisions to take seriously the wider implications of the Jewish conversions they expected in the latter days. Specifically, as they returned to detailed study of Hebrew prophetic texts, many of these writers began to moot the possibility of a Jewish return to the Promised Land.[5] And these new intellectual currents were circulating across a theological community that was broadening in its own geography, as the locus of millennial speculation moved from European contexts of intra-confessional warfare to the less contested contexts of the emerging British empire. Millennial ideas circulated across the north Atlantic through rapidly evolving networks of evangelical print. It was by means of these networks that the eschatological paradigms which developed through the British and Irish civil wars in the middle of the seventeenth century came to exercise enduring influence on the writers of the new world.[6]

While the far-reaching consequences of this revolution have been generously discussed, its causes have been 'little studied.'[7] The large amount of work that has recently been published on the evolution of the post-reformation protestant dogmatic tradition has not included any substantial discussion of its eschatological trends.[8] This chapter will therefore describe the shifting formations of evangelical millennialism in the first two-thirds of the seventeenth century. It will focus on the contexts in which that tradition's most innovative and enduring new paradigms were being developed – particularly, though not exclusively, in the cultures of English and American puritans – and it will read these paradigms within the wider context of the circulation of theological ideas across the north Atlantic in the tumultuous years of the formation of evangelical millennialism.

I

And yet, paradoxically, the evangelical millennial tradition began its consolidation in a series of texts so advanced in their revisionary instincts that they were not published in England until several decades after their author's death. *Apocalypsis apocalypseos* (Frankfurt, 1609), translated as *A revelation of the Apocalyps* (Amsterdam, 1611), was prepared by Thomas Brightman (1562–1607), a former fellow of Queens' College, Cambridge with a penchant for Presbyterian polemic.[9] Brightman's writing reacted to the 'hoch pot luckwarmnesse' of the English church, governed, as he complained, by bishops who 'love riches and honor so dearely, that they content themselvs with the losse of a full Reformation.'[10] His exegesis of Revelation 20:1–10 decisively broke with the Augustinian and reformation confessional traditions, and took the radical step of arguing that the passage referred to two periods of one thousand years each, only one of which had been completely fulfilled in the past. The first of these periods (Revelation 20:1–3) had begun in or around 304 and ended in 1300, after which the release of Satan had been made evident by the Islamic invasions of Europe. The second period of one thousand years (Revelation 20:4–10) had begun with the revival of true theology at the reformation – a revival Brightman identified as the 'first resurrection.' This beginning of the saints' rule with Christ would, he believed, result in a 'global Presbyterian utopia.'[11] But Brightman also expected the fulfilment of eschatological events in the near future. In 1650, he predicted, the power of the Turkish empire and the Roman Catholic Church would fragment and the national conversion of the Jews would begin. By the end of the century, European protestants would enjoy 'a most happy tranquillity ... the joy will be so much that it will be strange and unexpected: for in place of former troubles, there will be perpetual peace, & then Kings and Queens will be nursing fathers, and nursing mothers unto the Christian Churches.'[12] And by 2300, he concluded, the church's enemies would be finally destroyed and the eternal age would commence. In Brightman's own day, these events appeared to be far in the future. His work fell victim to censorship laws while European protestants found themselves engaged in a bloody struggle for survival. Nevertheless, his writing was influential long before its first English publication in 1641.[13] For many of his readers, Brightman would become the 'English Prophet,' the 'famous prophet of these times,' whose books made sense of the future.[14]

The broad outline of Brightman's exegesis of Revelation 20:1–10 was confirmed historically by the Irish scholar and churchman James

Ussher (1581–1656). Ussher, a professor of theology at Trinity College Dublin who was later to become archbishop of Armagh, was one of the towering intellectual figures of his day, whose 'fascination with history, chronology and the ages of Satan, the Beast ... was an effort to justify the reformation movement on a historical-theological basis.'[15] He was extremely widely read, and an avid book collector, and drove initiatives to enlarge the college library, in which Brightman's works were early represented.[16] In 1613, the same year in which Brightman's *Apocalypsis apocalypseos* appeared, Ussher published his own first book, *Gravissimae quaestionis de Christianarum ecclesiarum successione et statu*, a long and ultimately incomplete account of the history of the true church.[17] *Gravissimae quaestionis* expounded Revelation 20:1–10 to outline the course of church history and the descent of the faith that would eventually be identified with that of the reformation. Ussher's historical enquiry was rooted in his exegesis of the thousand-year binding of Satan, which, following Brightman, he referred to two distinct periods of one thousand years each. He defined the first of these millennia as that in which Satan was 'restrained [from] procuring the universal seduction.'[18] Despite the persecution of Huns, Goths, Alans, Vandals, and Persians, the true faith had been preserved, until, 'after Constantine ye great and before Mahomet ye lawgiver, Sathan was indeed so much loose, not only to vex ye churches and christian people, but also to take away and waste their provinces and kingdoms: as may be seen in ye persecutions.'[19] It was these persecutions that identified the first millennial age, Ussher contended, for 'where the state of that thousand where Sathan was bound is described, there is mention made of those who were smitten for the testimony of Jesus, and for ye word of God.'[20] The first millennium was a period of suffering, Ussher argued, following Calvin, not a period of heavenly bliss or earthly power, as Foxe had suggested; and, as a consequence, the end of the first millennium should be marked by the church's appropriation of the authority of the state. Satan's being 'newly loosed' was evidenced in the long investiture controversy, the struggles for power of the Holy Roman Emperors Henry III (1046–56) and Henry IV (1084–1105) against popes Gregory VII (1073–85) and Paschal II (1099–1118).[21] These conflicts drove the faithful remnant underground, when with 'darkness prevailing, they ... dare not preach publickly.'[22] Ussher's rewriting of Revelation 20:1–10 therefore reversed the celebration of the church's accession to temporal power in the earlier reformation tradition. Confronted with the unpromising nature of the historical record, Ussher was compelled to look elsewhere for the golden age he expected he would find. And so, following Brightman, he proposed a second millennium, a 'new binding of Satan, by the restoring of the gospel,' which had begun with the recovery of evangelical truth at the reformation, but which had not been consummated.[23] Ussher's argument, therefore, was that protestant believers, in the midst of a general European crisis, were already experiencing the conditions of the millennium, and their martyrdoms were the proof of his claim.

Ussher was never able fully to outline this radical re-thinking of evangelical eschatological expectations, for the third part of his book, addressing the period after 1370, was never published. It was not that he lost interest in the subject, for his doctoral oration, also delivered in 1613, addressed the 'reign of the saints' in Revelation 20:4. Ussher resumed his research for the third part of *Gravissimae quaestionis* but felt increasingly constrained by the changing theological environment of the English court. As late as 1625, his book agent, Thomas James, reported that he was continuing to search for 'helps necessary for the forwarding so great work,' but he found that his efforts were being stymied by those who should have been his allies.[24] This new atmosphere had been evidenced in the publication of Richard Montagu's *A gagg for the new gospel? No: a new gagg for an old goose* (1624), the first printed English denial of the reformation axiom that the Antichrist could be identified in the papacy.[25] Those holding to traditional evangelical convictions found themselves increasingly sidelined within the English church, eclipsed by representatives of the newly fashionable party of sacramental revisionists associated with William Laud, the newly appointed archbishop of Canterbury. Ussher opted for strategic silence, and sought to consolidate his eschatological interests by attempting to recruit one of Europe's leading millennial theorists as provost of Trinity College.

But others refused to be silent. The re-reading of Revelation 20:1–10 to which both Ussher and Brightman had contributed was confirmed in a series of significant European publications, some of which moved beyond their conclusions to push the church's golden age entirely into the future. Johannes Piscator (1546–1625), a professor at Herborn, one of the most important centres of European Reformed theology, had defended the notion of an entirely future millennium in a brief note in his German Bible translation (1604), but outlined his convictions in greater detail with the publication of *In Apocalypsin commentarius* (Herborn, 1613), a text reprinted in his *Commentarii in omnes libros Novi Testamenti* (Herborn, 1621).[26] The commentary staggered many of its early readers and provoked outrage across the Lutheran and German

Reformed world. In response, David Pareus (1548–1622), a professor at Heidelberg and Piscator's only rival as the most important of the German Reformed theologians, published his own commentary on Revelation, *In divinam Apocalypsin commentaries* (Heidelberg, 1618), the longest to date in the European Reformed tradition. Its defence of the Augustinian tradition explicitly repudiated Piscator's arguments and provoked an equally robust reply.[27] Johann Heinrich Alsted (1588–1638) was one of many students who found themselves caught between their mentors' competing millennial positions. Alsted was a student of Pareus who nevertheless drove forward Piscator's expectation of a future golden age for the church.[28] His *Diatribe de mille annis apocalyptics* (1627, second edition 1630) was a massive explication of Revelation 20:1–10 that was translated into German in 1630 and into English in 1643. The *Diatribe* indicated the extent to which these texts were taking their place in pan-European culture of evangelical print, for the commentary directly engaged with that of Brightman, who served as a foil to many of the most advanced of Alsted's claims. By the later 1620s, in other words, the millennial debate had begun to stretch across confessional divisions and across Europe, and, as a consequence, had begun to subvert the older denominational distinctions. And its influence was to be significant. Throughout the Thirty Years War (1618–48), a number of Lutheran theologians refused to be bound by their creedal commitments, began to consider the polemical and pastoral possibilities offered by the new millennial ideas, and adopted a robustly chiliastic faith.[29] Further east, Hungarian Calvinists continued to investigate the possibilities of millennial theology, especially in the 1650s, after sightings of new comets.[30] Across the continent, evangelicals were being driven to consider millennial ideas, and these ideas were being increasingly provided by English publications.

These English publications also reflected wider European influences – and not all of them protestant. Not all of his readers would have known it, but Brightman's work had clearly depended on conclusions already advanced by one of the most eminent defenders of Catholic reformation, Cardinal Robert Bellarmine.[31] European debates made a significant impact upon the English millennial tradition. And so, in the same year in which Alsted's *Diatribe* was published, there also appeared *Clavis Apocalyptica* (1627), the most important publication by the Cambridge philologist and biblical scholar, Joseph Mede (1586–1638). Mede's theological and ecclesiastical interests contrasted sharply with those of his partners in the millennial revolution.[32] He was certainly not a puritan. He and Brightman had taught in the same university, but they had quite different attitudes towards the hierarchical system of the Church of England. Brightman, an emerging Presbyterian, had been dismissive of the bishops' rule, but Mede found the pattern of their episcopal government described in Revelation itself.[33] Yet his work was more radical than his ecclesiological preferences might suggest. The first edition of the *Clavis* was followed by a second, enlarged, edition in 1632, and an English translation, prepared by Richard More, entitled *The key of the Revelation* (1643). The book made evident Mede's debt to the mathematical revolution. Focusing on the symbolic numbers in the biblical apocalyptic literature, he argued that 'every interpretation' should be 'tryed as it were by a square and plumb-rule' by 'the characters of Synchronismes.'[34] His commentary found a focus in apocalyptic pessimism. He admitted that 'our Brightman' had considered that references in Revelation to 'warre and slaughter' had already been fulfilled. But, he argued, the 'expectation of a future calamity conduceth more to piety, then an over-credulous security thereof, as if it were already past.'[35] And, in any case, the future promised as much blessing as woe. Mede followed Piscator in launching the millennium, 'the most abstruse of all the propheticall Scripture,' solidly into the future.[36] He denied the claims of Ussher and Brightman that the reign of the saints was one-third complete. Like Alsted, Mede argued that the text of Revelation 20:1–10 described only one period of one thousand years, and that this millennium could only be expected in the future. It was a master-stroke that made possible the radical eschatological reflections of later English evangelicals.

Mede's *Clavis* advanced a violent assault on the Augustinian and reformation tradition while modifying the conclusions of its earliest revisers. His most important book certainly had its admirers, especially among the puritans whose ranks its author never joined. In the year of its publication, Ussher invited Mede to take up the position of provost of Trinity College Dublin. Mede refused, but the men continued to correspond, regularly on eschatological issues. In 1628, Mede sent Ussher a number of copies of his new book. His covering letter clarified both his dismissal and his appropriation of medieval chronological concerns: 'I had no intent or thought, nor yet have, to avow that old conceit of the Chiliasts, That the world should as it were labour 6000. years, and in the seventh thousand should be that glorious sabbath of the reign of Christ.' Instead, he noted, he was 'inclined to think it much nearer.' Mede therefore argued in his letter that the end of the present age should be expected in 1736, 'the very year when the 1260 years of the beast's reign will expire.'[37] Ussher, in reply, expressed his appreciation for his colleague's conclusions. Ussher described the *Clavis Apocalyptica* as a 'most accurate explication,' which he 'cannot sufficiently commend,' and two years later, in 1630, he again offered Mede the role of college provost.[38] Other puritans continued to admire his scholarly contribution. Over one decade later, William Twisse, first prolocutor of the Westminster Assembly (1643–49), the most important English ecclesiastical gathering of the seventeenth century, noted in his preface to the English translation of the *Clavis* (1643) that Mede had 'exceeded in merit all others that went before him in this argument' for the millennial reign of Christ.[39] Yet the *Clavis* was a model of brevity. Twisse noted Mede's plans for a 'Larger Commentarie, which I am perswaded he hath written,' but, like's Ussher's third volume of his history, it was never published. Even in the early 1640s, Twisse admitted, when Mede's doctrine of the millennium was 'delivered with that moderation and subjection to the censure of the Church, that it can displease no man,' it was 'not received by many as Orthodox.'[40]

Nevertheless, by the 1640s the basic parameters of the emerging millennial tradition had been established. Evangelicals had entered the seventeenth century with an eschatological orientation that was apocalyptic without yet being millennial. In the early decades of the new century, evangelical writers across Europe pushed the millennium from the past to the present, explaining the text with reference to the martyrdoms of medieval 'heretics' or the revival of true religion at the reformation. But, by the 1630s, Reformed theologians in England, Ireland and the German states had begun to argue that the golden age described in Revelation 20:1–10 could only be located in the future. Their arguments would be confirmed by a number of American writers in the 1640s, including John Cotton, who argued that the millennium could be expected in 1655, Roger Williams, the defender of 'soul liberty,' Edward Johnson, the historian, Michael Wigglesworth, the poet, Samuel Sewall, the commentator, as well as Increase and Cotton Mather.[41] And by then, as it would become clear, the foundational expectation of the evangelical millennial tradition had firmly taken root.

II

Once established, this tradition mutated with remarkable speed, in both popular and scholarly publications and across the trans-Atlantic world. This trend was particularly evident among English, Scottish and American puritans, who shared a common eschatological vocabulary, but debated its proper sources and conclusions. Scottish writers were noticeably reluctant to move from assumptions of an unspecified 'latter-day glory' to embrace the fully fledged millennialism of their English and New English counterparts.[42] But, in the latter territories, these debates developed such momentum that scholars have struggled to come to terms with their breadth and significance. Much of this confusion stems from the fact that these 'hotter sort of protestants' did not confine themselves to 'the Bible only' in their search for knowledge of the future. Throughout this period, English publications demonstrated the enduring popularity of texts which advertised themselves as being the work of Merlin or Nostradamus. One recent commentator on this phenomenon has noted that the apocalyptic thought of early modernity combined Christian Cabala, Hermeticism, and angelology, as well as alchemy, astrology, and historical and textual criticism.[43] These were demanding intellectual traditions, abstruse and arcane, but they successfully entered the popular imagination and successive puritan expositors felt the need to warn their readers of the dangers inherent in dependence on these extra-Biblical sources. Thus readers of Thomas Hayne's *Christs kingdom on Earth* (1645) were advised of the 'senseless' teaching of 'Rabbi Elias,' the third-century Hebrew *midrash* projecting six thousand years of human history which had found some powerful advocates within a small coterie of the more radical millennial theorists, while others, like Thomas Hall in *A confutation of the millenarian opinion* (1657), exposed the excessive credulity of some towards the competing eschatological positions of 'Jewish Targums and Talmuds, Sibylline Oracles, the Koran, and astronomy.'[44] These writers sought to remove the influence of pagan apocalyptic and replace it with data more firmly derived from Scripture. Writers in Scotland and New England were much less likely to appeal to extra-canonical texts.

This insistence on 'the Bible only' could not silence the eschatological debate. Discussion collected around a number of key terms. Perhaps the greatest range of reference was ascribed to the term 'Antichrist.' Almost every sixteenth-century commentator who had published their conclusions on the identity of the Antichrist had pointed to the wickedness of the papacy.[45] This claim was finally granted creedal status in the Irish Articles (1615), a revision and expansion of the Thirty-nine Articles (1563) which was prepared under Ussher's guidance and adopted by the convocation of the Church of Ireland.[46] The Westminster Confession of Faith (1647) similarly concluded that the Pope 'is that Antichrist, that man of sin, and son of perdition, that exalteth himself, in the Church, against Christ and all that is called God.'[47] But this common identification presented evangelical exegetes with a genuine methodological difficulty. Early modern evangelicals knew that Jesus Christ 'shall not come, except there come a falling away first, and that man of sin be revealed, the son of perdition; who opposeth and exalteth himself above all that is called God, or that is worshipped; so that he as God sitteth in the temple of God, shewing himself that he is God' (2 Thessalonians 2:3–4). If the Antichrist were to reveal himself in the visible church – which this passage's reference to the 'temple of God' was widely believed to signify – then the Roman Catholic Church had to be recognized as being an authentic Christian denomination.[48] George Gillespie, a Scottish commissioner at the Westminster Assembly, consequently argued the case: 'If there was not a true church when Popery and Antichristianism had most universally spread itself, why is it said that Antichrist sitteth in the temple of God?'[49] But this reconsideration of the status of the Roman Catholic Church did not necessarily demand any concessions to its claims. Apocalyptic rhetoric was driving the evangelical recognition of the churchly status of the Roman communion, even as it identified the head of that communion as the eschatological enemy of true believers. But this discourse also insisted on the ongoing danger of the Roman communion: 'Rome is not to cease from being Babylon,' Ussher explained, 'till her last destruction shall come upon her; and that unto her last gasp she is to continue in her spiritual fornications, alluring all nations unto her superstition and idolatry.'[50]

Not every one of Ussher's peers could appreciate the nuance that underlay this argument. In the first half of the early seventeenth century, the eschatological role of the Roman Catholic Church was both being denied and expanded. It was being denied by many of the sacramental party within the Church of England, those followers of William Laud who attempted to answer questions of the historical validity of the Reformed faith by tracing an ecclesial succession through western catholicism – and, in so doing, qualified the assumption that evangelicals would always want to reject the legitimacy of the papal office.[51] But this definition was also being expanded, not least by an increasing number of puritans, who identified the extension of the influence of the Antichrist from the Vatican through the Church of England and into the sectarian movements of the mid-century crisis. Anglicans bore the brunt of verbal assault in this intra-puritan conflict, as radicals complained that their liturgy and theology continued to owe too much to the medieval church. James Ussher, as archbishop of Armagh, had good cause to complain that nothing was 'so familiar now a days, as to father upon Antichrist, whatsoever in church matters we do not find to suite with our own humours.'[52]

While the debate about the identification of the Antichrist tended to distinguish puritans from 'cooler' evangelicals, the debate about the proper interpretation of Revelation 20:1–10 tended to divide puritans from each other. The violence of these arguments about the millennium is a key to understanding the importance of the issues at stake: for many puritans, eschatology was an applied rather than an abstract subject, a cultural as well as a political conflict in which one was automatically involved. The tradition developed through a tangled web of publications engaged in a dynamic and impassioned debate, quoting and refuting one another with inter-textual abandon. The subtitle of Thomas Hayne's *Christs kingdom on Earth* (1645), for example, promised an examination of *What Mr. Th. Brightman, Dr. J. Alsted, Mr. J. Mede, Mr. H. Archer, The Glimpse of Sions Glory, and such as concurre in opinion with them, hold concerning the thousand years of the Saints Reign with Christ, And of Satans binding.* Similarly, Thomas Goodwin's *An exposition of the book of Revelation* (posthumously published, but based on sermons preached in 1639) referred to Theodore Beza, Thomas Brightman, Joseph Mede and John Foxe, Patrick Forbes, James Ussher, Matthew Parker, Franciscus Junius, David Pareus, William Ames, and John Napier.[53] Similarly, John Cotton, in *The churches resurrection* (1642), advanced a postmillennial apologetic that argued for an allegorical reading of the first resurrection (Revelation 20:4), which was the 'rising of men from spirituall death to spirituall life' and the revival of Independent church government, and on that basis positioned his colleagues in the Church of England with the horrors of Antichrist, arguing that 'you will finde little difference betweene Episcopacy and Popery, for they are governed by Popish Canons.'[54] Puritans were adopting competing positions, and advertising their exegetical differences.

On both sides of the Atlantic, therefore, a number of demarcated millennial positions emerged from this debate. Even in mid-century, the Augustinian tradition continued to find a few defenders. Like Calvin, these writers rejected any hope of a future 'conversion of the Jews' and consequently faced no difficulty in wondering where to place this great evangelistic advance within their eschatological scheme. *Chiliastomastix* (Rotterdam, 1644), an anti-millennial apologetic authored by the minister of a Scots congregation in the Low Countries, Alexander Petrie (c. 1594–1662), was one of a tiny number of works published to reassert Augustinian orthodoxy, in this case in response to *Israel's redemption* (1642) by Robert Maton. But Petrie's book was itself refuted in – at least in length, entirely overwhelmed by – Maton's replies in *redemption redeemed* (1646) and *A treatise of the Fifth Monarchy*

This exchange was emblematic of the larger trend. Like Maton, most puritan writers seem to have adopted a millennial theory of one kind or another, and, like Maton's texts, these defences of millennial theory dominated in the literary marketplace. Believing that this period of one thousand years had some relationship to the church in a more glorious future state, their notion of the 'blessed hope' increasingly combined evangelistic, ecclesiastical, missiological and political aspirations.

There were, of course, hugely significant disagreements among these millennial believers. Modern distinctions between pre- and postmillennialism find their roots in this period, as theologians sought to isolate and arrange the various elements of prophetic discourse. Some exegetes advanced their view of radical disjunction between this age and the next. They argued that Christ would return before the millennium, and often (though not always) added that he would remain in person with his church during that period. Some of these premillennialists were not slow to realize that their position actually demanded two future comings of Christ. For some, no doubt, this proved embarrassing, but others were keen to capitalize on the novelty. John Archer, in 1643, made the point with some force: 'Christ hath three comings,' he declared; 'the first was when he came to take our nature, and make satisfaction for sin. The second is, when hee comes to receive his Kingdome; ... A third is, that when hee comes to judge all, and end the world: the latter commings are two distinct commings.'[55] Not many of his premillennial brethren were as emphatic. Other postmillennial theologians postulated a more gradual movement into the new age, as increasingly reformed societies paved the way for Christ's return after the millennium. Some of these theorists called for radical intervention in the political status quo – the Fifth Monarchists engaged in a series of violent attempts to destabilize successive governments through the 1650s and early 1660s, for example – but others assumed a much more obviously divine movement in the conditions of the new age.[56]

The existence of this debate as to the relationship between the second coming and the millennium should not be understood as indicating that these competing millennial traditions had become clearly distinguished. The discussion has become particularly pointed as scholars have sought to define the eschatological teaching of the most important seventeenth-century creedal statement in the trans-Atlantic world, the Westminster Confession of Faith (1647). Modern scholars have struggled to reach consensus on the significance of its teaching. R.G. Clouse argued that the Confession is 'clearly' amillennial;[57] LeRoy Froom viewed the Confession as 'the strongest premillennialist symbol of Protestantism';[58] and James de Jong argued that its statements 'must be seen as a deliberate choice of mild, unsystemized, postmillennial expectations.'[59] But, recognizing the fluidity and occasional obscurity of early modern evangelical discourses, we should not impose a-, pre- or postmillennial paradigms without proper qualification. There was significant latitude both between and within these competing positions as they continued to be defined throughout this period.

Of course, with so much polemical advantage at stake, millennial ideologies could not remain static. Apocalyptic imagery and themes were too potent to remain safely within the control of careful exegetes. The tradition continued to mutate, develop, and divest itself of external controls, spiralling into confusion, chaos, and, eventually, outright opposition to the conservative political parameters upon which it had been established, culminating in the dramatic execution of Charles I in January 1649. But the seeds of this revolution were sown in the slow and cautious formation of evangelical millennial belief.

III

Seventeenth-century commentators revolutionized existing patterns of millennial belief. Three discernable paradigms emerged from the mid-century debate. Those theories that did not conform to these three paradigms were increasingly regarded as eccentric – even the double millennium motif, advanced exegetically by Brightman, defended on an historical basis by Ussher, and later adopted by Dutch Reformed theologians, including Johannes Cocceius (1603–1669).[60] In the later 1620s, Joseph Mede had proposed a scholarship characterized by pious modesty, reminding his readers that 'we shall ... enquire in vaine of those things which God would have kept secret and to be reserved for their owne times.'[61] But in succeeding decades, as English and American puritans advanced upon his conclusions, and began to take the most significant roles in the advance of evangelical millennialism, the Augustinian tradition continued to be challenged, and the staple elements of the older ideology broke down completely in the free market of ideas created by the collapse of censorship in the 1640s and in the theological turbulence of the British and Irish civil wars. Publications by Brightman, Mede and Cotton drove the three kingdoms and their North American colonies into the vortex of revolution and swept away their latent Augustinianism.[62] Later seventeenth-century commentators constructed enduring paradigms of evangelical millennial belief. Those millennial positions that did not conform to these three paradigms were increasingly regarded as eccentric. By the end of the 1650s, theologians on both sides of the Atlantic and within and beyond the puritan movement had abandoned the apocalyptic but not yet millennial eschatological schemes proposed by the first generation of evangelical scholarship, and were developing theories that addressed with the utmost seriousness the possibility of an earthly millennial hope.

3
The Consolidation of Evangelical Millennialism, 1660–1789

The debates that were generated by this millennial revival were not easily resolved. Writing in 1691, the English nonconformist Richard Baxter complained that these disputes, which had consumed the energies of evangelicals throughout most of the preceding century, had failed to reach any consensus about the most basic issues at stake. Discussion continued to focus on the number of periods of time referred to in Revelation 20:1–10 ('some hold but one Thousand years, and some two'), the location of the reign of Christ ('some of them say, The Thousand years are on Earth; and some say, They are … in Heaven: Some say, They are both in Heaven, or in the Air, and on Earth at once'), the geographical and political implications of these expected events ('some say, That there shall be a Jewish Monarchy at Jerusalem, and some, That it shall be of the godly all over the World'), and the character of the presence of the Messiah ('some say, Christ will reign there visibly in his Humane Nature; Others, that he will only sometime appear, as he did after his Resurrection: And some, That he will Rule there only by Reforming Christian Princes'). Baxter's analysis listed a long series of theological differences that were, he believed, concealed by the debaters' shared rhetorical commitment to the 'bare name of a Thousand years Reign.' 'It is a marvel,' he lamented, after the 'great disagreement of the Millenaries among themselves,' that they continued to 'cry up the Thousand years Reign, though most of them know not what the words mean.'[1] In fact, he concluded, these debates, which had continued since the reformation, had produced 'no consensus' as to whether the 'golden age would be literal or spiritual, in heaven or on earth, or, indeed, about whether the millennium was to occur in the past, present, or future.'[2]

Baxter's comments reflected the ambiguity of his times. This retreat from revolutionary expectancy, which appears to have begun during the growing conservatism of the later 1650s, was institutionalized at the Restoration, when Charles II returned to the throne. The collapse of the Commonwealth and the resurrection of a modified form of the ancient Gothic constitution led to the bloody repression of civil war radicals and their sympathizers throughout England, Scotland and Ireland. As a consequence, 'millenarianism went underground, most Dissenters acquiesced in political marginalisation, and intellectual scepticism grew.'[3] But the exit of several thousand clergymen from the Church of England during the 'great ejection' in 1662 gave a much-needed boost to religious dissent. The ejected clergy were often among the most outspoken of the clerical body, but as they slipped into nonconformity and generally withdrew from radical millennial hope their activities were regulated and carefully monitored under the terms of restrictive legislation pushed through successive Restoration parliaments.[4]

It is generally true that much of the literature produced during the later seventeenth and eighteenth centuries demonstrates a withdrawal from the religious and political debates of the civil wars. Some of those writers who had contributed most to those debates showed increasing hesitance in prophetic discussion. Even as he criticized his froward colleagues, for example, Baxter admitted that he was 'not thoroughly studied in these prophetical parts of the scriptures,' and remained unconcerned by his ignorance: he had better things to do while 'hasting ... to the world of light, where all divine mysteries are unveiled, and life, and light, and love are perfected; for which ... I am ... a believing and desiring expectant.'[5] The political upheavals of the later 1680s generated millennial speculation from across the denominational spectrum, within the established churches as well as in dissent, and on both sides of the Atlantic.[6] Hanserd Knollys and Benjamin Keach were among those who recognized the events of the Glorious Revolution (1688) – with the expectation of toleration for nonconformists provided by the new and staunchly protestant monarch – as either promising or actually initiating the glories of the millennium.[7] But this was, in many ways, the last hurrah of the earlier revolutionary fervour. For many writers, especially in the old world, the changing circumstances of eighteenth-century nonconformity precipitated a general collapse of confidence and a sudden and consequent retreat from the expression of millennial hope.

It is, of course, possible to overstate this argument. While, throughout the long eighteenth century, apocalyptic language did become 'calmer,' it is also true that there is 'little real evidence' that 'millennial thought and "prophetic" speculation became secularised, marginalised, or "internalised."'[8] Initially, it was Anglican theologians who were best known for maintaining the expectation of the millennium, but as the century progressed, as latitudinarian and moderate clergy dominated within the English establishment and as apocalyptic speculation was increasingly associated with the horror of the civil wars, it became clear that the intellectual trends of the Enlightenment had so generally 'diminished' the significance of eschatology in the 'mainstream of Christian thought' that its most natural home was now in evangelical dissent.[9] In the American colonies, by contrast, there was little of this marginalization. A number of the most important receptors of Enlightenment ideas were foremost among those maintaining older expectations of the latter-day glory. Their combination of high and popular culture drove a great deal of the celebratory and critical reflection on the Great Awakening, a period of unusual religious excitement that charged the life of British and American churches throughout the 1730s and 1740s. But millennial ideas were also being appropriated in secular discourse, in political terms, and perhaps most significantly during the institutional crises that precipitated the American revolutionary war (1775–83).[10] Responding to diverging social and cultural conditions, and in very different ecclesiastical contexts, evangelicals on either side of the Atlantic were using millennial rhetoric to fashion their national and denominational affiliations. For this was the period of the emergence of a self-conscious evangelical movement, David Bebbington has reminded us, a re-energising of popular protestantism that replaced the doubt and self-scrutiny so typical of puritan piety with a vibrant and often celebratory spirituality that encouraged believers' activity.[11] As the common concerns of this new evangelical movement displaced or downgraded specific denominational loyalties, and amid enormous social and political upheaval, the range of acceptable millennial positions continued to be refined. As we have already noted, the exegetical confusion of the civil war period was giving way to the delineation of three discrete eschatological paradigms: amillennialism, with its cautious conservation of reformation creedal opinions, which appeared to be the least popular of the emerging positions; premillennialism, which often retained something of its earlier political edge; and postmillennialism, which, David Bebbington has argued, would dominate the new evangelical movement, and confirm its activist mentality.[12]

These evangelical millennial paradigms were evolving in the context of wider eschatological ferment. In France, the revocation of the Edict of Nantes (1685) was followed by widespread anti-protestant violence. Shortly after the beginning of the eighteenth century, the simmering resentment of a number of Huguenots in the Cevennes broke out in a bloody insurrection. But 20 years of persecution had robbed them of much of their clerical elite, and these isolated communities turned to the lay leadership of a number of mystical prophets. The first of these Camisards arrived in London in 1706. They gained a number of important followers, as well as immediate notoriety for their contention that the New Testament gift of prophecy had finally been revived.[13] This was, of course, entirely counter to the confessional tradition of English evangelicals, but the claim would be made more frequently as the century progressed, especially around such critical moments as the Lisbon earthquake (1755) and the French revolution (1789).[14] This popular fascination with prophecy and apocalyptic ran entirely counter to the mainstream intellectual trends of the period, which witnessed the rise of a scholarly and distinctly anti-enthusiastic postmillennialism associated with Daniel Whitby (1638–1726). Whitby was an Anglican clergyman and biblical commentator whose celebrated anti-Calvinist polemic, *Discourse on the five points* (1710), drew responses by John Gill, in *The cause of God and truth* (1735), and Jonathan Edwards, in *Freedom of the will* (1754). His early and 'extreme Arminian' sentiments appear to have given way to Arian convictions, and his often anonymous interventions in theological debate appear to have encouraged a general rise of anti-Trinitarian theology among English dissenters.[15] But Whitby also drew fire for his millennial beliefs, and his expectation that human society would evolve naturally into the social, cultural and religious prosperity of the golden age he expected in the latter days, though the latter conviction proved to be extremely influential. It certainly confirmed important themes in evangelicalism's emerging postmillennial consensus.

The millennial commitments of eighteenth-century evangelicals simultaneously shaped and were shaped by wider political, theological and denominational factors. It is noteworthy, for example, that premillennialism was often favoured by high Calvinists like the Anglican Augustus Montague Toplady (1740–78) and the English Baptist John Gill (1697–1771), perhaps because of its close fit with their prior emphases upon divine intervention; and also significant that postmillennialism was often favoured by 'moderate' or evangelical Calvinists, like the American Congregationalist Jonathan Edwards (1703–58) and the English Baptist Andrew Fuller (1754–1815), perhaps because of its close fit with their activist enthusiasms for mission and revival. Other millennial theories were held in tension with, rather than because of, prior theological commitments: the Methodist leader and hymn-writer Charles Wesley (1707–88) was at least for some time a notable proponent of the premillennial faith he shared with those high Calvinist writers whose polemic he otherwise abominated. And these millennial theologies were often maintained in defiance of theological and political contexts: some high Calvinists, like Gill, ramped up their premillennial convictions as others of the same denomination embraced the new optimism of the evangelical movement and moved towards a more moderate Calvinism, a vigorous missionary ambition and a postmillennial faith.[16] There was, therefore, never any necessary link between millennial theories and the prior theological commitments or denominational contexts of those who held them. The rather shaky denominational fault lines of millennial affiliation were finally shattered in the aftermath of the collapse of the *ancien regime* in the revolutionary period of the 1780s and 1790s. Then, in the aftermath of early modern confessionalism and in the context of a lowering of denominational barriers, it appeared that shared millennial expectations could become increasingly important symbols of alternative ecclesiastical and theological communities – alternative foundations of new movements of faith.

This chapter will trace the continuing variety but gradual transformation of millennial thinking within the changing social, political and cultural contexts of the trans-Atlantic evangelical movement across the long eighteenth century. It will focus on work that reflected particular social, cultural and denominational contexts even as it circulated across the Atlantic in the emerging networks of religious print. And it will do so by paying particular attention to several of those distinctive but representative writers and preachers whose theological reflection, historians have agreed, contributed most to the new evangelical movement, including the American Congregationalist minister and philosopher, Jonathan Edwards, and Charles Wesley, the Anglican leader of Methodism.[17] This chapter will juxtapose a discussion of their significance with a description of the conclusions of other writers, most notably those of the high Calvinist Baptist John Gill, whose popularity in the eighteenth century illustrates the continuing appeal of older methods of eschatological reflection. Old intellectual habits died hard, even as new paradigms drove forward the consolidation of evangelical millennial faith.

I

'The age of enlightenment was also an age of fanaticisms,' Ronald Knox reminded modern readers in his classic investigation of *Enthusiasm* (1950).[18] And so to many early modern readers it must have seemed.

Many evangelicals in the late seventeenth and eighteenth centuries drew upon new categories of reason as they continued to express their millennial hopes in terms of the language and method of their less sophisticated forebears. At a popular level, this tradition drew upon common mythology, in which 'heaven and the angels remained just above the sky, thunder was the voice of God, and Satan could be encountered in darkness and storm.'[19] These unsophisticated cosmologies were encouraged in popular chapbooks, which continued to recycle such earlier publications as *Christ in the clouds* (1635).[20] Many of the millennial beliefs that drew upon this kind of worldview existed 'outside respectable Dissent, though sometimes embarrassingly close to it,' both in terms of the 'matter of ideas and beliefs' that constituted 'an intellectual milieu favourable to eschatological interpretations of events,' and at an institutional level, 'in that some sects (Quakers, Muggletonians, Ranters) remained as visible links with the enthusiasts and fanatics of the past' and in that some of the followers of Jacob Boehme and Jane Leade still attempted to find space within the global evangelical movement.[21] In the later eighteenth century, it became clear that early Methodist connections were among those existing on the cusp of non-respectability: these communities, which often promoted a robust premillennial vision, had strong links with disciples of Joanna Southcott and other prophets in her tradition, and, as a consequence, the 'autobiographies of most working-class millenarians and seekers in the period record contact at some stage with a local Methodist society,' and the connection was quite natural. For, as Harrison has recently noted, eighteenth-century millennialism seemed inherently enthusiastic.[22]

But millennial tradition was also being received at a scholarly level. Among its devotees there could be numbered some of the most significant Enlightenment figures. Isaac Newton (1643–1727) combined his scientific empiricism with a continuing fascination with the biblical accounts of the end of the world, on which he wrote more than he did on the natural science for which he is best remembered. William Whiston (1667–1752), Newton's successor as a Cambridge mathematician and famous as the translator of Josephus, advanced this combination of high and low cultures in his privately-expressed conviction that the Temple would be rebuilt, the Jews restored to the Promised Land, and the millennium begun by 1766 – but he also identified Mary Toft, who had given birth to 16 rabbits, as the fulfilment of a prophecy in Esdras.[23] Later in life, Whiston rejected the Trinitarian faith and abandoned the Church of England in favour of adherence to a congregation of General Baptists, but there is no evidence that he abandoned his eschatological hopes. His conversion provides a useful reminder that millennial belief was common across the theological spectrum, was not specific to denominational contexts, and thrived outside the evangelical movement.[24]

If English scholars kept their views private, their peers elsewhere had less concern about the public discussion of their opinions. In the later seventeenth century, a number of prominent Dutch Reformed theologians concentrated their minds on eschatological research, and drove forward the conclusions of earlier generations of English and Scottish puritans: scholars such as Johannes Cocceius (1603–1669) continued to defend Brightman's double millennium motif, while Wilhelmus à Brakel (1635–1711) anticipated the destruction of the Antichrist, the conversion of the Jews and their restoration to their ancient homeland, and Jacobus Koelman (1632–95) additionally expected their rebuilding of the temple.[25] Similarly, in North America, a wave of very public speculation that the millennium was imminent was unleashed by the remarkable events of the Great Awakening in the 1730s and 1740s, though the attendant discussion was much less concerned about the future state of Jews than it was about the future state of Americans. In the midst of the excitement, Jonathan Edwards (1703–58), philosopher and theologian, wondered whether the long-expected latter-day glory could actually be beginning on American soil.[26] These millennial hopes survived their eventual disconfirmation, as the colonies slipped from their heightened spirituality to the prosaic and inconsistent religiosity that had dominated in the period before the revival, and throughout the long eighteenth century they were shared by such a varied cast of characters as Edwards' grandson, Timothy Dwight (1752–1817), the eighth president of Yale College, and John Henry Livingston (1746–1825), the fourth president of the institution that would become Rutgers University, as well as such luminaries as the English Unitarian theologian and scientist Joseph Priestly (1733–1804) and the Anglican theologian George Stanley Faber (1773–1854).[27]

Of course, it is important not to overstate the division between these popular and scholarly traditions, for there is clear evidence from both sides of the Atlantic that, in the earlier part of the eighteenth century, these intellectual streams had begun to coalesce. Thus Edwards, for example, combined his rather traditional expectation of a latter-day glory (and his Calvinism) with the fashionable philosophies of the Boston academic elite. His combination of high and popular culture was 'part and parcel' of the new evangelical faith.[28] Evangelicalism, in its earliest stages, was being defined by its unlikely combinations, and these unlikely combinations were clearly expressed in the postmillennialism that dominated in the early evangelical movement. This eschatological theory attested to high hopes for the expansion of biblical Christianity even as it advanced the intellectual trends of the eighteenth century, for it 'provided a means whereby Protestants accommodated the apocalyptic hope to Enlightenment ideals of rational order and benevolence.'[29] In part this was related to the most fundamental assumptions of the new evangelical movement that was then beginning to emerge. By the early eighteenth century, these expectations had become 'the dominant eschatological teaching in England and America.'[30] Rooted in a new epistemological confidence, as Bebbington has argued, the evangelical movement shared a 'uniformly postmillennial' hope.[31]

II

The dominance of postmillennialism was especially evident in the American colonies. Millennial theories had underpinned the puritan emigration to the new world in the previous century, and had appeared to have been confirmed by the revivals of religion that had periodically swept across the American colonies, gathering ever larger numbers of new believers into the kingdom of God. In the middle of the eighteenth century these postmillennial theories found a vocal and influential spokesperson in the 'greatest artist of the apocalypse,' one of the most highly reputed colonial theologians and philosophers, the Congregationalist minister Jonathan Edwards (1703–58).[32]

Edwards returned to apocalyptic speculation throughout his long career. Revelation was the 'only book of the Bible he favoured with a separate commentary,' and his work on the topic drew upon and interacted with the publications of many of his contemporaries, including Sir Isaac Newton and William Whiston. Edwards' reading of Revelation was coloured but not limited by his admiration for puritan writers: his approach to the text balanced the scholarly rigour of his eighteenth-century peers with the chronological and religious-political fascinations of his seventeenth-century antecedents. But these political concerns reflected the peculiarities of his American context. Edwards was only too aware of the significance of Britain's ongoing war with French powers in Canada. For the inhabitants of New England, Stephen Stein has reminded us, the 'struggle with Rome had not ended in 1649 with the execution of Charles I, nor in 1689 with the accession of William and Mary to the throne; it was continuing as the enemy employed new and more dangerous weapons against the Puritans.'[33] And the most dangerous of these weapons were French soldiers and the native American populations who supported them. It was hardly surprising, therefore, that Edwards' private writings reflected upon the eschatological significance of current affairs. His journal entries regularly meditated upon the providential meaning of apparent defeats to the Catholic powers of Europe:

> If I heard the least hint of any thing that happened in any part of the world, that appear'd to me, in some respect or other, to have a favourable aspect on the interest of Christ's kingdom, my soul eagerly catch'd at it; and it would much animate and refresh me. I used to be earnest to read public news-papers, mainly for that end; to see if I could not find some news favourable to the interests of religion in the world.[34]

For Edwards, the world was an apocalyptic landscape, and the biblical data, primarily contained in Revelation, provided an indispensable key to its proper interpretation.

Edwards' interest in Revelation was sustained throughout his career. The earliest notes in his 'Theological Miscellanies' (dating from 1722) were comments on Revelation. But his interest in Revelation noticeably increased after early 1723, when he began writing his 'Notes on the Apocalypse,' which provided 'the most comprehensive analysis of the book of Revelation ever offered by Edwards, a synoptic account in which he commented chapter by chapter upon a range of textual and substantive issues.' Edwards was 'convinced that the Roman papacy was the Antichrist and that the Revelation describes the rise, reign and fall of the antichristian forces together with the interrelated fortunes of the church.'[35] And, like so many others in the puritan tradition of which he was a part, he dabbled in date-setting, arguing that the Antichrist's rule would end around 1866, when the fifth vial would be poured out and the power of the papacy would collapse; by 2000, he believed, the sixth and seventh vials would also have been fulfilled, the final blows to the power of the Antichrist would have occurred, and the millennium would have begun.[36]

Edwards' private meditations on the beneficent conditions of the millennium reflected the hopes of his puritan forebears. Like many earlier commentators, he expected that an extraordinary number of Jews would convert to Christianity and return to the Promised Land during the millennial period. But his conclusions also reflected the new aspirations of his eighteenth-century context. 'How happy will that state be, when neither divine nor human learning shall be confined and imprisoned within only two or three nations of Europe, but shall be diffused all over the world,' he considered, when 'this lower world shall be all over covered with light, the various parts of it mutually enlightening each other; when the most barbarous nations shall become as bright and polite as England; when ignorant heathen lands shall be stocked with most profound divines and most learned philosophers.' During the millennium, he continued, 'we shall ... have the most excellent books and wonderful performances brought from one end of the earth and another to surprise us—sometimes new and wondrous discoveries from Terra Australis Incognita, admirable books of devotion, the most divine and angelic strains from among the Hottentots, and the press shall groan in wild Tartary.' It would be an age in which human potential would be fulfilled, when 'we shall have the great advantage of the sentiments of men of the most distant nations, different circumstances, customs and tempers; [when] learning shall not be restrained [by] the particular humor of a nation or their singular way of treating of things.' There was something almost Miltonic about his eulogy of the divine liberty of the press. Knowledge would always increase in Edwards' millennium: 'there will continually be something new and surprising discovered in one part of the world and another [because of] the vast number of explorers, their different circumstances, their different paths to come at the truth. How many instructive and enlightening remains of antiquity will be discovered, here and there now buried amongst ignorant nations!' But Edwards expected that this knowledge would be directed towards its proper end, the worldwide expansion of protestant Christianity, ultimately realizing that day 'when the distant extremes of the world shall shake hands together and all nations shall be acquainted and they shall all join the forces of their minds in exploring the glories of the Creator, their hearts in loving and adoring him, their hands in serving him, and their voices in making the world to ring with his praise.'[37] Edwards expected the numbers involved in the worship of God to dramatically increase. He thought it possible that 'a hundred thousand times more converts will enter the church during the millennium than in all the ages since creation,' and that this would be a 'fitting end' to the drama of redemptive history.[38]

The detail and optimism of Edwards' private musings contrasted starkly with his public utterances. Although he had worked out a complex timetable of eschatological events, he did not refer to this chronology in public. Prophetic speculation is notably absent from the 66 sermons on Revelation which remain in Edwards' papers. 'Speculation in private but discretion in public came to be characteristic of him. He kept conjectures to himself in the notebook and in his sermons utilized more conventional and less controversial eschatological ideas – heaven, hell, the blessedness of one and the terror of the other.'[39] For this reason his early sermons did not dwell on millennial themes.

But his early writings certainly proved useful for other postmillennialists. While Edwards refused to claim that the revival he witnessed in 1734–35 was the beginning of the millennium, the ministers who republished his accounts in London were less cautious. Isaac Watts and John Guyse, in their preface to the first London edition of Edwards' *A faithful narrative of the surprizing work of GOD in the conversion of many hundred souls in Northampton, and the neighbouring towns and villages of New Hampshire in New-England* (1737), argued that no 'event of this kind so surprising as the present narrative hath set before us' had occurred 'since the first ages of Christianity.'[40] Furthermore, they insisted, those who 'profess the religion of Christ' should 'take notice of such astonishing exercises of his power and mercy' and 'give him the glory which is due,' especially as the revival had begun to 'accomplish ... his promises concerning the latter days.' Watts and Guyse noted their expectation that the events described by Edwards illustrated God's intention for England, and they encouraged their readers to 'pray, and wait, and hope for the like display of his power in the midst of us.'[41] These revivals were to continue, they seemed to believe, until the earth realized its millennial glory. Edwards was less convinced. The Northampton community which had become the focus of the events of the revival rapidly returned to its old ways, and its minister became increasingly embarrassed by the disparity between the reputation and reality of the spirituality of his church members.

Nevertheless, in 1742, when revival returned to Northampton in even more spectacular fashion than before, Edwards found himself less guarded. For over one century British and American evangelicals had prayed to see the latter-day glory, and for Edwards, and the trans-Atlantic community of dissenting Calvinists in which he participated, it seemed as if those hoped-for days had finally arrived. Caught up in the extraordinary events he recorded, Edwards noted his belief that ''tis not unlikely that this work of God's Spirit, that is so extraordinary and wonderful, is the dawning, or at least a prelude, of that glorious work of God, so often foretold in the Scripture, which ... shall renew the world of mankind ... there are many things that make it probable that this work will begin in America.' Nevertheless, as Stein has noted, this comment was 'neither in character with Edwards' earlier pronouncements on the revivals nor totally consistent with his own private reflections.'[42] Not surprisingly, Edwards quickly backtracked, and in a letter to his Scottish correspondent William McCulloch complained of rumours that he had categorically affirmed the idea that the millennium had actually begun in his home town.[43] Edwards had struggled to keep his speculative eschatology within the privacy of his own notebook, but after 1743 this policy of discretion looked increasingly difficult to sustain. Edwards attempted to institutionalize his postmillennial theories in his attempt to organize prayer meetings for revival that would be coordinated on both sides of the Atlantic. This 'concert of prayer' signalled the widespread appeal of these shared hopes. But it would be his descriptions of revival, and the hints that the latter-day glory might actually be witnessed, that would prove to be his most remarkable contribution to the trans-Atlantic consolidation of evangelical millennialism.

III

It was this dominance of postmillennialism among British and American believers that made the widespread retention of premillennialism so significant. An individual's decision to maintain an alternative eschatological position was often an expression of some degree of disquiet with the theological or practical emphases of the new evangelical movement. This combination of eschatological disquiet and concern about contemporary doctrinal decline was particularly marked in the writing of the most influential Baptist theologian of the eighteenth century, John Gill (1697–1771).

In a range of recent literature, Gill has become stereotyped as the 'father of hyper-Calvinism,' but this typology fails to do justice to his wider achievements or to appreciate his real significance in trans-Atlantic evangelicalism.[44] There has been a 'growing interest in Gill as a theologian,' but his eschatology has not received the attention it has deserved, despite the fact that so much of his contemporary reputation rested upon his prophetic studies.[45] John Rippon (1751–1836), his pastoral successor and first biographer, noted in his introduction to the third edition of Gill's commentary on the entire Bible, the *Exposition of the Old and New Testaments* (1746–1766; third edition, 1810), that his sermons on the prophetic subjects 'have been, of late years, some of the most popular of his works,' and their 'deserved value' has been evidenced in the 'several editions' through which they have passed. These sermons, with the 'two folio volumes on the Prophets, and his Exposition of the Revelation, have gained him unfading honours' and have compelled those who have studied prophecy to admit that 'if the works of Dr Gill pre-eminently embrace almost every branch of sacred theology, *prophecy is his forte.'*[46] And Rippon had good reason for his claim. Gill's contribution was nothing if not ambitious. His exegesis attempted to bridge pre- and postmillennialism by arguing for a latter-day glory before the second coming, and for a millennial glory thereafter.[47]

Gill's work was popular, but also extremely divisive. During the 'evangelical revival,' a period of religious excitement in British and Irish churches that paralleled the American Great Awakening, English Baptists divided between those who followed Gill and those who followed Fuller in their millennial thinking.[48] Their millennial theories were understood to have a wider significance, especially in terms of the missionary interests the English Baptists were then developing. It was too easy for contemporaries to identify postmillennialism and the moderate Calvinism with which it was often associated with the missionary zeal surrounding William Carey and the attempt to evangelize India, or the premillennialism and the high Calvinism with which it was associated with the suspicion of missionary activity that was often (and not entirely justifiably) associated with Gill.[49] In fact, Gill's reformulation of millennial theology suggests that he was more affected by the evangelical revival – and therefore by evangelicalism – than most of his readers have realized.

Gill was certainly aware of the differences of eschatological opinion that prevailed in his own denomination. He recognized the eschatological shortcomings of earlier Baptists. In the previous century, he lamented, 'some good men' had 'fixed the time of Christ's second coming, of his personal reign, and the millennium.' Their number included Benjamin Keach, his pastoral predecessor, who, as we have noted, believed the millennium had commenced with the Glorious Revolution. But, 'in which being mistaken,' Gill continued, these men had 'brought the doctrine into disgrace, and great neglect.'[50] Gill's ambition, therefore, was to succeed where they had failed. When he took over as pastor of the congregation in Horselydown Goat Yard Chapel, London, in 1697, he inherited the confession of faith which Keach had drawn up. Although Keach had advanced this creedal statement as a modification of that endorsed by the General Assembly of English Particular Baptist churches in 1689, Gill was unhappy with certain ambiguities which, he feared, could be exploited by the General Baptists, whose long-standing Arminianism and incipient Unitarianism he deplored. In 1729 he provided the church with a new doctrinal statement, the Goat Yard Declaration of Faith, which the congregation readily accepted. Reflecting the relative moderation of his early career, its article on eschatology failed to advance on the conclusions of the earlier English Baptist confessions of faith: 'We believe that there will be a resurrection of the dead, both of the just and unjust; and that Christ will come a second time to judge both quick and dead, when he will take vengeance on the wicked, and introduce his own people into his kingdom and glory, where they shall be for ever with him.'[51] But its ambiguity was a radical advance upon Keach's misplaced hopes.

Gill's eschatological orthodoxy was significantly qualified as he wrestled both with the exposition of Scripture and the less theologically conservative postmillennialism of his contemporary Daniel Whitby (1638–1726), the target of his polemic in *The cause of God and truth* (1735–38). His theological journey can be charted through the pages of his massive *Exposition of the Old and New Testaments* (1746–66), a project 'of unquestionable celebrity in the Republic of Letters,' the doctrinal teaching of which he consolidated in the first Baptist systematic theology, his *Body of divinity* (1769–70), and in *An exposition of the Revelation of S. John the Divine* (1776), which contained the relevant material from his *Exposition of the Old and New Testaments* in a separately published form.[52] These publications demonstrated that Gill had moved, against the trend of the age, to reclaim the premillennial hope, and the separate publication of his comments on Revelation provides evidence that, at the very least, a publisher was willing to gamble on their being a popular audience for them. But Gill's position was carefully qualified. He dismissed the 'gross and carnal objections which some that have borne the christian name, have entertained of the millennium ... as if their notion savoured more of a Turkish paradise, than of a kingdom of Christ.' Such doctrines, he claimed, have 'brought disgrace upon the doctrine of the kingdom, and given disgust to pious and spiritual minds.' Now, he asserted, 'the manner in which I conceive it, clears it from such absurdities, and represents it as quite unclogged, and free from such an objection.'[53]

As the conclusion of a life spent in the study, and building on the conclusions of his massive Biblical commentary, Gill's *Body of divinity* was composed as a systematic presentation of Christian practice and theology over multiple volumes. Representing the most mature expression of its author's faith, and reflecting its pastoral context, the *Body of divinity* was preached in a series of sermons to his congregation over the five years it took to compose. Its various chapters demonstrate that Gill did not simply reiterate the theological conclusions of the English reformation or of his puritan forebears, but was happy to introduce what Richard A. Muller has termed 'significant variants' into the Calvinistic Baptist movement.[54] Within his eschatological deliberations, his basic hermeneutic was simple: 'It is a rule to be observed, that a literal sense is not to be departed from without necessity.'[55]

Gill also imitated earlier puritan eschatological expositors in combining his rigorous Biblical scholarship with an interest in chronological speculation. Gill, as we have seen, noted that the failures of earlier writers in this respect had been the direct cause of the neglect of Biblical prophecy in the eighteenth century, but he reasoned that these earlier writers were often correct in principle and only erred in basing their calculations on the wrong extra-Biblical evidence. Gill, therefore, offered his own series of calculations. While admitting that no man knows 'the day nor the hour' of the second coming (Matthew 25:13), he contended that Scripture supplied sufficient data for the careful expositor to calculate the dates of those events which must signal his near return. Following the 'synchronistic' method outlined by Joseph Mede, Gill aligned the periods of 'the reign of the antichrist, the witnesses prophesying in sackcloth, the holy city being given to the Gentiles to be trodden under foot, and the church in the wilderness.'[56] These periods, he believed, were coextensive. 'Now these dates are given to exercise the minds, the study, and diligence of men,' he continued, and 'though men good and learned, have hitherto been mistaken in fixing the end of these dates, arising from the difficulty of knowing the time of their commencement, this should not discourage a modest and humble enquiry into them; for, for what end else are these dates given?' Gill believed the task was, in fact, relatively simple: 'could we find out the time when antichrist began his reign, the end of it could easily be fixed to a year.'[57] Therefore, following a standard puritan method, Gill began his 'modest and humble enquiry' by surveying the possible beginnings of the Antichrist's reign. He concluded that its inception was best represented by that period in which 'the emperor Phocas gave the grant of universal bishop to the pope of Rome' – in 606 AD.[58] This was a significant departure from the puritan tendency to point to an early date for the beginning of the Antichrist's reign. Nevertheless, in moving the beginnings of the millennium so far forward Gill was reflecting the irreversible movement from historicism to futurism within the Calvinist millennial tradition.

Developing his calculations, Gill charted the premillennial fulfilment of Biblical prophecy in robustly optimistic terms. He contended that the Antichrist's reign would end in 1866, the Jews would be converted and settled in Israel by 1896, and that by 1941 the Islamic empire would be destroyed, and the gospel would have spread throughout the world: 'therefore happy will he be that comes to this date; these will be happy, halcyon days indeed!'[59] Gill's first biographer noted that he did not fix these dates 'with positivity' and refused to adopt 'any lofty air.'[60] Gill admitted that his calculations could not be settled with 'precision,' and in any case, he continued, addressed only minor events, for 'the time of the second coming, and personal appearance of Christ, and of the millennium ... cannot be known hereby.'[61] These events were merely the signals of Christ's 'spiritual reign' and a 'halcyon' age: 'The more near signs, or what will more nearly precede Christ's second and personal coming, are the spiritual reign, and what will introduce that? the destruction of antichrist, the call of the Jews, and numerous conversions of Gentiles, through the general spread of the gospel.'[62] Despite numerous accusations of an anti-missionary bias, it seems clear that Gill expected the gospel to sweep the earth. His only doubt was as to when that would be.

This eschatological optimism was confirmed by Gill's most significant eschatological innovation – his concept of the 'spiritual reign' of Christ. Gill used the spiritual reign to confirm the eschatological optimism of puritan postmillennialists, expecting massive blessing within the gospel age and before the second coming. He expected that this period of blessing would prepare the saints for the tribulation and defection which it would signal, and point them towards the greater glory yet to come, for 'in the latter day there will be a great appearance of Christ in a spiritual manner, or a coming of him by the effusion of his Spirit upon his people, when his spiritual reign will take place ... after which will be the personal appearance of Christ to reign in a still more glorious manner.'[63] The spiritual reign would occasion spiritual as well as temporal victories: 'the everlasting gospel will be preached to all nations, by means of which the earth will be filled with the knowledge of the Lord, and gospel churches planted everywhere, and gospel worship be carried on as now, only with greater purity.' And the victories would not only be ecclesiological, for the advances of the gospel would 'open the way for the christian princes, to carry their victorious arms every where, and seize upon, and possess all the antichristian states.'[64] Thus distancing himself and his reconceived millennium from the 'set of men, called *fifth-monarchy men* ... who were levellers, and riotous persons,' Gill argued that Christian princes had nothing to fear from those who believed in the spiritual reign of Christ.[65] These believers, after all, agreed that no alteration would be made in the order of civil government during this unique time of spiritual blessing, but only that changes would be made in the persons to whom such rule was conferred. Civil government will be transmitted into truly godly hands, 'such who are not only nominal, but truly christian princes.'[66]

Of course, at the end of the eighteenth century, the impeccable virtue and evangelical faith of the English monarchy might have been open to question. But Gill's commentary sidestepped contemporary political concern to focus on the spiritual significance of the biblical text. And his admirers recognized his unusual prophetic insight: 'some of the interpretations of this part of Scripture which are properly his own, he lived to prove were not merely hypothetical,' John Rippon observed.[67] Gill proposed an alternative to the optimism of evangelicalism's dominant postmillennial hope; but he could not deny the potential significance of the events he was witnessing, and made room in his eschatological timetable for the realization of the political and social benefits of the trans-Atlantic awakening.

IV

These expectations of latter-day glory, which Edwards confirmed and Gill qualified, were robustly challenged in the writings of Charles Wesley (1707–88). Wesley, an Anglican evangelical clergyman and a leader of Methodism, advanced a species of eschatological thinking which, in its 'historicist, pre-millennial and anti-Catholic' readings of Scripture, robustly contradicted the possibility of the worldwide blessing which both Edwards and Gill expected towards the end of the church age.[68] His conclusions were powerfully influenced by the works of Sir Isaac Newton and Joseph Mede, both of whom, Wesley believed, 'come very near the truth,' and his reading of the prophecies seemed much more in tune with seventeenth-century scholarship of piety than with eighteenth-century scholarship of reason, with which both Edwards and Gill had attempted to critically interact. Wesley's denial of the optimism of his contemporaries was ironic, therefore, not least because he was so closely associated with the evangelical revival which both Edwards and Gill seemed to be attempting to explain, but also, as we noted, because his premillennialism seemed to fit better with the strongly interventionist theology of Calvinism than it did with the often synergistic theology associated with the Methodist movement. Wesley's millennial constructions therefore complicate many of the assumptions of scholars working in Methodist studies – but they have 'hitherto only received slight attention.'[69]

Nevertheless, Wesley's millennial pessimism should not come as a surprise, for the Methodist movement, to which he and his brother contributed so much, existed on the cusp of eschatological notoriety. Kenneth Newport's pioneering work on the theological cultures of early Methodism has discovered that many of the believers associated with the movement were actively engaged in millennial speculation, and, as we have noted, J.F.C. Harrison has argued that the Methodist movement attracted a large number of those believers working through their study of biblical prophecy, many of whom ended up outside evangelicalism altogether.[70]

Charles Wesley's study of biblical apocalyptic began in 1746.[71] It was an auspicious year for English Christianity, which marked the possibility of another civil war, the consequent shaking of British national self-confidence, and the dénouement of Jacobite rebellion at the Battle of Culloden. But Wesley's eschatological reflection was certainly not inextricably linked to the context in which it emerged. Newport has noted the 'substantial evidence' that Wesley's 'eschatological views and understanding of biblical prophecy were a very distinctive and vibrant force' in his thinking throughout the 1750s – and not least in the immediacy of his response to the earthquake which was experienced in London. In fact, Newport notes, Wesley's eschatological commitments are most clearly expressed during the 1750s, not least because 'much of the necessary documentary evidence is lacking' for the period thereafter.[72]

And Wesley expressed these views at length. He set out his prophetic opinions in a letter to an unknown correspondent, written on 25 April 1754.[73] God, he noted, 'has been pleased to lead me this winter, as it were by the hand, thro the labyrinth of the scripture Prophecies relative to the latter times.' Wesley believed that God had revealed to him the contents of those prophecies that had been 'shut up and sealed unto the time of the end,' for in the 1750s, he believed, 'those days are begun.' And his new knowledge was comprehensive. He was expecting the 'conversion of God's antient people the Jews, their restoration to their own land; the destruction of the Romish Antichrist and of all the other adversaries of Christ's kingdom; the inbringing of the fullness of the Gentiles, and the beginning of the long and blessed Period when peace, righteousness and felicity, are to flourish over the whole earth,' when 'Christ the Lord of Hosts shall reign in Mount Sion, and in Jerusalem and before his Elders gloriously.' Wesley was expecting a revolution in global affairs to occur in the immediate future. 'It will appear a Paradox to affirm that all these events will be accomplished in FORTY years time,' he admitted, 'and the first and second of them, viz the conversion of the Jews and their restoration to their own land, within the short space of seven or eight year time; but what with men is impossible, is both possible and easy with GOD.'

Wesley sketched out in order the events he expected to occur within his lifetime. The future glory of the millennium would, he believed, be prefaced by a 'long train of dreadful judgements coming on the earth, more dreadful than ever it yet beheld.' In particular, Babylon, by which Wesley referred to the Roman Catholic Church, would be given power to 'distress the Protestant Churches by wars and persecutions' before she was to be 'brought to her final Ruin.' And all this was to occur imminently, 'before the end of SEVEN years hence,' and would continue for the next forty years. During that period, 'two thirds of the whole number of mankind on the face of the earth will be cut off ... Yet the last judgement that is to be executed on the earth in these times shall be of such a dreadful and extraordinary nature, that none can escape being cut off by it, but by the preternatural assistance of angels, whom GOD will send forth to gather his elect from the 4 corners of the earth, unto a place of safety on the earth, where he will provide for them.' Yet Jews would be preserved through this cataclysm, and 'will have returned to their own land, and have an Anointed Prince of their own over them about the year 1771 or 1772; that they will be invaded in their own land and their Prince cut off and their city and sanctuary once more demolished, about the year 1777 or 1778.' Then would occur 'that total final Destruction which the Prophet calls *The great day of* GOD'S *wrath*, about the year 1794.' Wesley believed that the 'numbers and periods mentioned in Daniel and the Revelation, when rightly understood and compared together, do point out the time when these things shall be fully accomplished, so as it may be calculated without hazard, and without erring above a year or so.'[74]

Wesley's calculations entirely sidelined the significance of the evangelical revival to which he contributed so much. It was an ironic gesture of despair – and yet a pattern of behaviour which evangelicals have repeated throughout their history when, in moments of extraordinary cultural significance, they have chosen to imagine their own actual irrelevance.[75] But Wesley's reaffirmation of evangelical irrelevance and his imagination of the ultimate failure of his evangelical mission resonated with many of the apocalyptic theorists of the seventeenth century and paved the way for the social, political and cultural withdrawal of later premillennialists. Jonathan Edwards and John Gill wrote their eschatology to take account of the evangelical revival with which

Charles Wesley was so closely identified, but Wesley himself was much less assured of its significance.

V

The long eighteenth century was a period of disjunction, therefore, a period in which evangelical millennial aspirations consolidated around a series of new themes, including mission, revival, and organization. David Bebbington is correct to point to the dominance of postmillennialism among eighteenth-century evangelicals, but it is important to remember that alternative eschatological formulae continued to be developed, even among those whom he has identified as being in the vanguard of the new movement. The emergence of evangelicalism in the 1730s did impact the millennial tradition in the trans-Atlantic world. Believers moved beyond the mere articulation of specific eschatological paradigms to develop communities around their distinctive patterns of belief. And, as Wesley's exegesis demonstrates, they adopted millennial systems which continued to popularize theological complexities while evidencing an increasing suspicion of intellectual claims. At the end of the seventeenth century Richard Baxter may have worried that the debates had produced 'no consensus' as to whether the 'golden age would be literal or spiritual, in heaven or on earth, or, indeed, about whether the millennium was to occur in the past, present, or future.'[76] But, as Europe and the American colonies slid into the series of revolutions that marked the end of the eighteenth century, his theological descendants could recognize the steady, if inconsistent, consolidation of evangelical millennial belief.[77]

4
The Expansion of Evangelical Millennialism, 1789–1880

The uneasy postmillennial consensus, which evangelicals on both sides of the Atlantic had struggled to develop throughout the long eighteenth century, could not be sustained, and Charles Wesley's was not the only motion of dissent.[1] In the late eighteenth and early nineteenth centuries, a series of revolutions shook the *ancien regime* and, with it, the eschatological assumptions that had been based on expectations of its continuing social beneficence. The American war of independence (1775–83) and a succession of European revolutions and rebellions, beginning in France (1789–99) and progressing to Ireland (1798), Serbia (1804–17) and beyond, advanced upon a secular but often quietly postmillennial confidence in the inevitable ascent of religious and political liberty, which was sometimes believed to be divinely provided and which was at other times articulated in the vocabulary of Enlightenment scepticism or Romantic nationalism.[2] These events scuttled the assumption that, as one of the period's most celebrated conservatives put it, 'whatever is, is right.'[3] In the Atlantic world, these revolutions could be both driven by and simultaneously undermining of the certainties of millennial belief, and the evidence of social fragmentation that they provided, which evangelicals continued to trace into the middle decades of the nineteenth century, drove many believers towards a systemic rethinking of eschatological hope.[4] Evangelical scholars, for the most part, qualified or abandoned the creedal restrictions of the early modern confessions of faith, and the postmillennial optimism that had replaced it in the eighteenth century, but continued to generate distinctive patterns of denominational and theological allegiance. At a popular level, rising literacy rates encouraged widespread negotiation with scholarly eschatological positions and helped believers to organize new ecclesial communities, such as the Catholic Apostolic Church and the Millerites, around distinctive and often innovative eschatological hopes.[5] From the 1830s onwards, a new system of premillennial thinking emerged to dominate the evangelical imagination, and this new teaching, 'at least in the early stages of its growth,' attracted believers who were already committed to 'biblical literalism, social and ecclesiastical pessimism, Calvinism, anti-Catholicism, anti-radicalism, anti-rationalism,' and, in the old world, 'support for the Established Churches.'[6] The 'futurist' and 'dispensational' bias of this new theology would be a critical factor in the trans-Atlantic expansion of evangelical millennialism throughout the nineteenth century.[7]

Evangelicals developed the method and vocabulary of prophetic investigation as they responded to their sense of long-term social crisis.[8] Their most enduring legacy included the refining of the self-consciously 'literal' hermeneutic they had inherited from such eighteenth-century expositors as John Gill. But many of these believers went far beyond his scholarly approach. One of their number cited as proof of the validity of the 'literal' hermeneutic one of the most celebrated paintings of the 1820s, a 'splendid picture' which demonstrated 'a striking instance of the way in which Scripture will be understood by an unbiased mind ... where, with the Bible open before him, [the artist] has simply yielded his imagination to its guidance. How unconscious that he had such a host of learned Divines arrayed against him!'[9] This picture, 'The opening of the sixth seal' (1828), a depiction of the events described in Revelation 6:12–16 prepared by Francis Danby (1793–1861), one of the leading Irish Romantic artists, was being cited as evidence of the propriety of the 'common sense' reading of biblical texts. Evangelical interpreters could not agree on what that the results of the application of that hermeneutic actually signified, but they could debate these results in a common terminology and settled paradigms, for by the middle of the nineteenth century believers had agreed upon the language they would use to contour their competing millennial expectations. The Anglican theologian George Stanley Faber (1773–1854) appears to have been responsible for the coining of many of these terms, including 'premillennian' (1828), 'premillenarian' (1844), and 'postmillennial' (1851), and 'premillennial' first occurred in the title of a work by George Ogilvy, *Popular objections to the premillennial advent considered* (1846).[10] These lexical innovations did not solve the exegetical riddles, but they did help clarify competing eschatological positions as the influence of evangelical millennialism continued to expand. This chapter will trace the impact upon evangelical millennial theology of this contest between the simple faith of the 'unbiased mind' and the competing claims of the 'host of learned Divines.' It will describe the failure of the traditional historicist method, the spectacular collapse of its chronological project, the widespread abandonment of traditional postmillennialism, and the rise throughout the nineteenth century of a new variety of futurist premillennial faith.

I

Of course, throughout the nineteenth century, the craze for prophetic speculation was not limited to evangelical believers and neither was it limited to the English-speaking world. In the early 1790s the Roman Catholic bishop of the Dordogne, Pierre Pontard (1749–1832), under the influence of predictions made by the politically orientated mystic Suzette Labrousse (1747–1821), identified the events of the French revolution as signifying the beginning of the millennium.[11] During the same period, and with entirely alternative political sympathies, Richard Brothers (1757–1824), a nationalistic English protestant with pronounced British–Israelite opinions, argued that the events of the French revolution were evidence of God's judgement upon the European aristocratic elite, and that his own government's support for the French monarchy had identified Britain as a latter-day Babylon facing its own apocalyptic nemesis.[12] This self-styled 'Prince of the Hebrews' and 'Nephew of the Almighty' grew increasingly concerned by the fate of the Jews as the 1790s progressed, and his movement from relatively orthodox congregational life towards an individualistic prophetic eccentricity appears to have been encouraged by his contacts with the followers of the Swedish scientist and mystic Emanuel Swedenborg (1688–1772) and with members of the French hermetic and occult community, the Avignon Society.[13] But Brothers attracted some notable followers, and his millennial imagery gripped the excited imaginations of prominent members of the English and Irish elites. In 1795 Nathaniel Brassey Halhed (1751–1830) rose in the London parliament to defend the rights of this persecuted man of God. Halhed, a graduate of Christ Church, Oxford and a distinguished Orientalist, expounded before his astonished parliamentary colleagues the 'authenticity of the prophecies and mission of Richard Brothers as Prince and Prophet of the Hebrews,' and noted his 'deep sense of obligation for the light and life communicated to my soul through his inspired writings.'[14] Other members of the political elite shared this eschatological orientation, if not its appreciation of Brothers' ministry. Four years later, in 1799, Francis Dobbs (1750–1811), a maverick member of the Dublin parliament, rose to begin a speech on the most contested issue of the day. He was 'fanatically opposed' to the Act of Union then being discussed, but, he explained to his colleagues, in a speech which sold 30 000 copies, the issue was of no ultimate importance given the imminence and the geographical proximity of the second coming of Jesus Christ: his studies in chronology and etymology had convinced him that in the very near future Armagh would become the site for the battle of Armageddon.[15] Of course, these were remarkable interventions, calculated to excite the public imagination, but they were not out of character with the age. In the 1820s, for example, Roman Catholics in Ireland were being guided by the prophecies of Pastorini, which predicted the imminent end of unpopular protestant rule in the violence of a peasant rising.[16] Similarly, in the northeastern United States, the United Society of Believers in Christ's Second Appearance – a group better known as the Shakers – continued to develop a distinctive communitarian way of life, while members of the movement which became the Church of Jesus Christ of Latter-day Saints – better known as Mormons – engaged on a much more successful campaign of proselytizing on the basis of the angel Moroni's revelation to Joseph Smith, Jr.[17] Across the Atlantic world, across denominational divisions, and across the barriers of class, millennial believers outside the evangelical world demonstrated their familiarity with and expectation of the marvellous.

This combination of the marvellous and the credulous continued among many of those who adhered to the revelations given to prophets in the Richard Brothers tradition. Most of Brothers' followers recognized the new prophetic authority of Joanna Southcott (1750–1814), the servant-turned-prophet from Devon who began to hear voices in 1792 and whose success as a writer began almost a decade later with the publication of a record of her visions and their fulfilment throughout the preceding decade, *The strange effects of faith* (1801). Southcott accurately predicted the death of the bishop of Exeter in 1796 and the crop failures of 1799 and 1800, and gathered around herself a community of disciples which regarded her prophetic utterances as being of divine origin.[18] Her followers were generally conservative in terms of politics and faith, but some of their number developed claims that the Godhead was composed of four persons, and advocated a more radical programme of cultural and theological intervention which they believed could hasten the onset of the millennium.[19] And they became well-known for their views. In 1806, three years before her death by hanging on poisoning charges, Mary Bateman (1768–1809) sought to take advantage of the credulity of neighbouring followers of Joanna Southcott by exhibiting a miraculous hen which, she claimed, had been laying eggs bearing the inscription, 'Christ is coming.'[20] Later leaders in the tradition were often colourful characters: John 'Zion' Ward (1781–1837), the founder of the Shilohites, whose early religious experiences had taken him from his parents' Calvinism through membership of Methodist, Baptist, Independent and Sandemanian congregations before his eventual discovery of the writings of Joanna Southcott, by means of which he learned his true identity as an incarnation of Jesus Christ; John Wroe (1782–1863), whose early interest in Joanna Southcott and Judaism led to his founding of a complex pseudo-Jewish community of Christian Israelites based in Ashton, near Manchester, but stretching as far away as Australia; and James Elishama Smith (1801–57), a religious journalist whose loyalties passed successively from the Church of Scotland to Edward Irving, Joanna Southcott and John Wroe, and whose fictional account of *The coming man* (1873) described the compulsory beard-growing and circumcision of his days in the Christian Israelites.[21] These leaders were regarded as outré by orthodox believers, and did nothing to improve the reputation of radical millennial expectation among the godly, but their influence stretched across the Atlantic and even to the Antipodes.

Evangelicals did not develop their millennial theories in isolation from wider intellectual trends. Many of those millennial believers who remained outside the evangelical movement were vying for the attention of its members. William Blake (1757–1827), freethinker and poet, exercised an important eschatological influence on a number of evangelicals, including members of the Catholic Apostolic Church and the emerging Plymouth Brethren.[22] Less influential among evangelicals were the Mormon missionaries who entered Britain in the later 1830s and gained some 50 000 converts within 15 years.[23] But evangelicals were also influencing millennial believers outside the movement. In the same period, a Baptist preacher called William Miller (1782–1849), from upstate New York, began teaching that Christ's return could be expected between 21 March 1843 and 21 March 1844. His followers – who extended far beyond the Baptist denomination and on both sides of the Atlantic – took appropriate action. His apocalyptic deadline was postponed until 22 October 1844, but passed without significant impact on the wider world.[24] This 'great disappointment' marked the beginning of the dénouement of the date-setting tradition – at least within evangelicalism. But members of religious communities as widely disparate as the Seventh-Day Adventist Church and the Bahá'í Faith have continued to argue that something of apocalyptic significance did occur on 22 October 1844, pointing either to an invisible event, such as Christ's entering the Holy of Holies in the heavenly sanctuary to begin the 'investigative judgment,' or to something that happened elsewhere on earth, such as the simultaneous beginning of the teaching career of the Báb in Persia. Of course, others of those who dismissed Miller's conclusions continued to develop his mathematical approach to the interpretation of prophecy. Charles Taze Russell (1852–1916) was influenced by Millerite ministers to sell his clothing stores and to enter Christian ministry in advance of the resurrection of the dead, which they encouraged him to expect in April 1878. The disconfirmation of these hopes led Russell to the full-scale reconsideration of his religious opinions, after which, with a rational appeal to the significance of biblical mathematics, he began the community of Bible students that continues today as Jehovah's Witnesses.[25] Others developed their millennial schemes in non-supernatural terms. Through the 1840s Chartists and other political radicals took advantage of the evangelical enthusiasm for prophetic rhetoric by immersing their arguments in commonly held millennial expectations for the improvement of the human condition.[26] And, in the context of the social dislocation of rapid urbanization and industrial revolution that accompanied mid-century revolutionary activity, the international community of workers was offered the millennial vision of Karl Marx's *Communist manifesto* (1848), the impact of which could be compared only with that other iconic (and equally iconoclastic) text of the mid-nineteenth century, Charles Darwin's *On the origin of species* (1859). The lines of division were fiercely policed, but there was one point upon which the millennial believers and their secular critics could agree: on either side of the Atlantic, and far beyond, the nineteenth-century world was awash with millennial hope and in the grip of social crisis.

II

Evangelicals on both sides of the Atlantic developed widespread prophetic interests in response to the social crises they observed. In Britain and Ireland, in the context of conflict over Catholic emancipation, agitation leading up to the Reform Act (1832), and an outbreak of cholera that left a death toll of tens of thousands (1832), premillennial writers linked the growth of popular republicanism to the future tyranny of the Antichrist.[27] Many of these writers were convinced that the growth of secular democracy represented one of the most serious dangers facing Victorian evangelicals. One English layman later stated that the thoughtless expansion of the franchise allowed the 'greatest questions' to be 'decided by expediency, or (what is nearly the same thing) the wisdom of the majorities, with a sneer at every attempt to appeal to Scripture for guidance.' To do away with the demand that public officials should be members of established churches, he continued, was to 'frame laws by which the Roman Catholic may legislate and hold office in our Protestant community, and the Jew, too, sit in parliaments, care having been taken that his conscientious belief of our Saviour being an impostor should meet with nothing to offend it on entering there.'[28] These were calamitous days for conservative evangelicals.

Many believers interpreted these social crises through eschatological timetables established on competing interpretive systems. Throughout this period, evangelical readers continued to look for guidance to the past and continued to negotiate with the older expositions. Mede's legacy loomed large. Alexander Keith (1792–1880), a Scottish Presbyterian minister and one of the best-selling prophetic writers of the nineteenth century, referred approvingly to Mede's work in his *Evidence of the truth of the Christian religion, derived from the literal fulfilment of prophecy* (1828).[29] In the same year a clergyman of the Church of Ireland referred to Mede's authority as being 'perhaps highest' among prophetic writers.[30] Similarly, R.B. Cooper published a new English translation of *Clavis apocalyptica* in his *Commentary on the Revelation of St John ... by an humble follower of the pious and profoundly learned Joseph Mede* (1833), and, reflecting on the same period, B.W. Newton, a future leader of the Plymouth Brethren, remembered that he had carefully considered Mede's historicist arguments before he rejected them in favour of a futurist variety of premillennial faith.[31] In 1853, 20 years later, a leading Presbyterian admitted his debt to 'truly valuable' material in Mede's work, while in 1867 the Anglican bishop of Liverpool continued to refer to his work.[32] And this continuing confidence in Mede supported continuing confidence in the chronological speculations he himself had developed.

The seventeenth-century tradition remained influential – and so did the date-setting agenda it encouraged. James Hatley Frere (1779–1866), a dissenting writer described by S.T. Coleridge as a 'pious and well-meaning but gloomy and enthusiastic Calvinist,' based the contents of his six books on the significance of biblical numerology on the work of earlier prophetic writers, including, most importantly, that of Robert Fleming (1630–94), an exiled Scots Presbyterian, whose racy and eccentric exposition, published in 1701, had set dates for a number of events of apocalyptic significance, including the French revolution, which it anticipated 'at least before 1794.'[33] Frere built on these earlier arguments to claim in *A combined view of the prophecies of Daniel, Esdras and St John* (1815) and subsequent publications that the papacy would collapse in 1847 and that the millennial kingdom would commence in 1867.[34] Strangely, his popularity among evangelicals, which was especially evident during the widespread prophetic excitement of the 1830s, was not shaken by his evident interest in exploring and expounding the significance of the Old Testament apocrypha, the canonical status of which protestant theologians routinely denied.

Frere died one month before the beginning of the millennial glories he had anticipated, but not before he had witnessed the rise and fall of a new champion for his exegetical method, the Presbyterian-turned-prophet Edward Irving (1792–1834). Irving, hailed in somewhat Romantic terms as that 'misguided son of genius,' stepped forward from the pulpit of his fashionable church in London to offer an apocalyptic reading of current affairs.[35] His rapid move from relative insignificance as a pastoral assistant in Glasgow to celebrity as a lionized preacher in the English capital can be explained at least in part by his appeal to the spirit of the age. He was discussed in parliamentary debates and patronized and applauded by leading members of the aristocratic and political elite. He took a prominent role in the campaign to remove the apocrypha from the publications of the British and Foreign Bible Society, in campaigns opposing the possibility of Catholic relief and in the defence of the established churches. At the zenith of his popularity, between 1822 and 1824, he could preach for more than three hours at a time to audiences of many thousands, and, after the controversial interventions in Christology which resulted in his deposition from the ministry of the Church of Scotland (1833), his expositions of prophetic obscurities took the exegetical basis of Frere's historicist approach outside the mainstream of the evangelical movement and into a new movement of ecclesiastical primitivism. Irving's emerging denomination, the Catholic Apostolic Church, was noted for its interest in the restoration of charismatic gifts, including prophetic foretelling and 'speaking in tongues,' and was also the locus for a series of innovations in evangelical eschatological thinking. Irving's expulsion from the Church of Scotland indicated that he had been ejected from the British evangelical mainstream, but he remained committed to an historicist premillennial faith and continued the venerable protestant date-setting tradition. In *Babylon and infidelity foredoomed by God* (1826), he noted his expectations that the second coming should be expected in 1868. In 1827 he published his translation of a book by a Chilean Jesuit, Manuel de

Lacunza (1731–1801), entitled *The coming of Messiah in glory and majesty* (1827), the literalist bent of which had resulted in its being banned by Roman Catholic authorities, but which more than any other work drove the increasing respectability of premillennial thinking in southern parts of England.[36] Several years later Irving republished John Lacy's defence of the prophetic claims of the Camisards, *General delusion of Christians touching the ways of God's revealing himself* (1834; first published in 1712). Irving evidently depended upon many of those who had gone before him, but his followers had no doubt about his originality: after his burial, in Glasgow Cathedral in December 1834, a number of young women, dressed in white, remained in the crypt to await his impending resurrection. And he continued to find admirers in every social class. He was, his childhood friend Thomas Carlyle (1795–1881) later reminisced, the 'best man I have ever ... found in this world.'[37] Robert Murray McCheyne (1813–43), another celebrated Presbyterian preacher, noted his respect for Irving in an entry in his diary: 'I look back upon him with awe, as on the saints and martyrs of old. A holy man in spite of all his delusions and errors. He is now with his God and Saviour, whom he wronged so much, yet, I am persuaded, loved so sincerely.'[38]

Irving's end was a set-back, but the habit of prophetic calculation – and with it the historicist approach to prophetic exegesis – was dealt a fatal blow by the 'great disappointment' associated with the career of the New York Baptist preacher, William Miller (1782–1849). Miller's experiences as a soldier in the war of 1812 left him concerned about his eternal prospects, and after his return to his farming career he made real efforts to recover his childhood faith, beginning a systematic study of biblical evidences which eventually drove him to the conclusion that the time of Christ's second coming had in fact already been revealed. Adopting the 'year-day' theory that had been propounded by early modern evangelicals, Miller understood the 2300 days before the cleansing of the sanctuary in Daniel 8:14 to refer to 2300 years, assumed that this period had begun with the decree for the rebuilding of Jerusalem issued by Artaxerxes I in 457 BC, and consequently argued that it would end, 2300 years later, in 1843. He also assumed that this cleansing of the sanctuary was a symbol for the purification of the earth by fire. Miller's apocalyptic conclusions were settled by 1818, but he initiated his preaching career only in 1831, and began more widely to publicize his calculations with a series of articles in a Baptist newspaper, the *Vermont Telegraph*, over the summer of 1832. His claims met with an unusual degree of interest, and, unable to meet the demand for speaking engagements, Miller published his *Evidence from Scripture and history of the second coming of Christ, about the year 1843* (1834). With his publishing managed by a well-connected Boston clergyman, Miller's fame grew, and he attracted around himself a number of other preachers eager to share his latter-day ministry. Miller himself refused to set any specific date for the second coming; instead he set deadlines, arguing that Christ's return could be expected between 21 March 1843 and 21 March 1844. When the deadline passed without incident, he reconfigured his calculations for another date in April. But in late summer, another of his preachers, Samuel S. Snow, who had been converted from atheism through one of Miller's publications, identified the final deadline of 22 October 1844. His reasoning seemed conclusive for many in the movement. Believers sold their possessions, and waited for the final revelation of God's glory. But none of them saw Jesus Christ return.

Miller shared his date-setting interests with many of his evangelical predecessors, but differed from them in pointing to dates that were to occur within his own lifetime – and living to see them fail. Many of his followers were devastated by their disconfirmation. Some simply abandoned millennial hope. Others joined alternative Adventist groups, including the Shakers.[39] But others organized new movements around a series of competing explanations of what had happened on 22 October 1844. Some of these believers argued that the date marked the end of the moral probation of humanity, and that salvation could no longer be attained; others argued that Christ had returned, invisibly; still others argued that the expected events had occurred, but the sanctuary had been cleansed in heaven, rather than on earth, and from this party there emerged the Seventh-Day Adventist Church.[40] But, whatever the explanation, it was evident that Jesus Christ had not appeared in New England.

It took a while for English premillennialists to grasp the implications of Miller's failure. E.B. Elliott's *Horae Apocalypticae*, a sober, substantial and scholarly defence of the historicist premillennial reading of Revelation, was published in the same year as the 'great disappointment,' and almost in defiance of Miller's failure went through five English editions between 1844 and 1862. But Elliott had clearly learned a lesson about hostages to fortune. His book moved in subsequent editions to push his early prediction of the end of the age from around 1865 to around 1941.[41] Elliott's early calculations were popularized by John Cumming (1807–81), a London-based minister of the Presbyterian Church of England, who was popularly recognized as Irving's successor, and who, in such incautious works as *Signs of the times* (1854) and *The great tribulation* (1859), noted his expectation that the second coming would occur in 1864.[42] Cumming's printed sermons 'reek of unctuous self-righteousness and are riddled with the crassest of stereotypes of Jews, Roman Catholics, English Ritualists, Muslims, and atheists,' it has recently been observed.[43] And there is no doubt that his reputation suffered as a consequence of the media's discovery that he had negotiated a lease for his house that pushed far beyond the date he had set for the end of the world.[44] But his preaching, with its apocalyptic bombast, drew enormous crowds. 'The arithmetical calculations on which I must now enter may in one sense be thought dry and uninteresting as elements of a popular address, yet they are possessed of great importance,' he opined in one sermon. 'If the Spirit of God thought it was useful to direct Daniel thus to write, it is unworthy of us to say it is too dry for the minister to preach, and too dull for the hearer to investigate.' After all, he argued, 'it is not sunshine but truth we are to seek after.'[45] But, for many listeners, Cumming's calculations provided neither sunshine nor truth. The making of many of these claims – and their evident failure – cast doubt on the methodical presuppositions of his influential body of work, though date-setting expositions retained their wide appeal. In 1876, one year after Elliot's death, the London Baptist minister C.H. Spurgeon, who was never given to date-setting predictions, still felt able to describe Elliott's *Horae Apocalypticae* as the 'standard work' on the historicist premillennial approach he shared.[46] Other English Calvinistic Baptists meanwhile refuted the 'year-day' theory and the historicist approach adopted by Elliott, Cumming and 'a large part of the Nonconformists.'[47] And they were reflecting a broader evangelical trend. The date-setting tradition was clearly in decline.

Some evangelicals, realizing that date-setting calculations were discrediting the faith, did all they could to speed their departure. The Scottish Presbyterian theologian Patrick Fairbairn (1805–74) was one of many to complain that prophetic study had become a 'medley of confusion.'[48] He worried that evangelicals were tolerating the 'spirit of soothsaying,' and that at least one well-known minister had 'lived to see his most confidently-announced prognostications of great events thrice over palpably falsified.'[49] At fault, Fairbairn believed, was the habit of reading the Bible in one hand with the newspaper in the other. Prophecy is 'utterly misapplied,' he argued, 'when it is taken as a guidebook to details happening in the civil and political sphere of the world's history – as if it were intended to afford to those, who study it, an insight into the plots and movements of earthly kingdoms, to discover to them remote changes in constitutional governments, or to indicate steps of advancement in material progress.'[50] Fairbairn was calling for a new method of prophetic enquiry, one quite different from the historicism which read Scripture as a 'guide-book to details happening in the civil and political sphere of the world's history.' And the historicist interpretive approach which underlay the date-setting project was to be replaced in the popular evangelical imagination. But Fairbairn could hardly have approved of its alternative.

III

Premillennial authors, despite their competing expositions and failing predictions, did succeed in disrupting the 'fatal dream' of postmillennial progress.[51] Their successes were most clearly marked in the new variety of premillennialism that was developed by preachers and theologians who were, at first, generally associated with the established churches of Ireland, Scotland and England, but, by the century's end, were most obviously American. One of the most significant of these early 'futurist' premillennialists was William de Burgh, a minister of the Church of Ireland who grew interested in the meaning of Revelation despite his awareness of the 'prevailing opinion that this book is utterly unintelligible; so that the attempt to explain it, or even to examine its contents, is generally regarded as an indication of a spirit of curiosity and restless speculation, which will not be satisfied with the sober contemplation of those parts of Scripture which are plain and practical.'[52] De Burgh published *An exposition of the book of Revelation* (1832) despite his fears that 'the heeding of God's prophetical warnings is among us becoming more and more disreputable.'[53] His book offered a critique of the conclusions proffered by 'the best known modern writers on the Apocalypse,' among whom he included Mede, Thomas Newton (1704–82), Faber, Frere and Irving.[54] But de Burgh noted a 'wide discrepancy' between the conclusions of these authors, a confusion he explained with reference to their general hermeneutical assumptions. He explained that the historicist exegetical method, which required the expositor to relate the contents of Revelation to specific events in the history of the church, significantly limited the text's accessibility, and required readers to bring to the text a great deal of specialist knowledge. Historicist readings of Revelation therefore restricted the proper understanding of the text to the 'learned reader, whose alone, it further follows, is the Blessing on him who "reads" and "keeps" the sayings of this Book.'[55] Instead, de Burgh claimed, 'Scripture is its own interpreter' and its meaning should be available to the 'ordinary reader.'[56] Claims like these made enormous impact. They broke the link between biblical apocalyptic literature and human history – a link developed by protestant writers since the reformation – and provided for the final defeat of the historicist approach. De Burgh's work was certainly popular – it reached its fifth English edition by 1857 – but was rapidly eclipsed by that of an early and hostile reviewer, who was eventually persuaded by a number of his arguments. This convert to futurism, John Nelson Darby (1800–82), became the most celebrated exponent of an innovative prophetic system known as 'dispensationalism.'

Darby had been educated in Trinity College Dublin during a period in which the traditional postmillennialism of the British establishment was being increasingly questioned.[57] He was, he later explained, predisposed to apocalyptic pessimism: 'I, a conservative by birth, by education and by mind; a Protestant in Ireland into the bargain; I had been moved to the very depths of my soul on seeing that everything was going to be shaken. The testimony of God made me see and feel that all should be shaken.'[58] Sensing the end of the aristocratic world into which he had been born, Darby graduated with a coveted Gold Medal in Classics in 1819, was admitted to Lincoln's Inn, London, and three years later was admitted to the Irish bar. But a legal career did not attract him, and Darby worried that he should be 'selling his services to defeat justice.'[59] Much to the consternation of his father, therefore, he abandoned his legal career, and, in 1825, was ordained in the Church of Ireland.

Darby's new life as an Anglican clergyman brought him into contact with some important influences. He appears to have travelled to Paris in 1830, perhaps at the same time as Robert Daly, his rector, and Lady Powerscourt, their patron. Darby left no record of his visit – though it can be verified from other sources – but it is likely that he would have been interested in learning about the Parisian Jansenists, who, Daly noted, 'knew the truth, and, though they held many Roman Catholic errors, rejoiced in hearing the doctrines of grace.'[60] Most significantly, the movement included among its leaders two writers, the Dominican Bernard Lambert (1738–1813), and a Parisian lawyer, Pierre-Jean Agier (1748–1823), who were developing themes that would become significant in later dispensational thinking.[61] Lambert's substantial contribution to the evangelical millennial tradition was to argue that Christ would return twice: his first return would be to gather his people, and his second return would be to commence the millennium. In other words, several years before Darby pulled together the distinctive themes of dispensational premillennialism, a Parisian Dominican was already teaching a secret, pre-tribulation, rapture. Twenty years later, Samuel Prideaux Tregelles (1813–75), a New Testament textual critic, confirmed the link between Darby's eschatological innovations and those of the Parisian Jansenists: 'Lambert and Agier were the writers Mr. J. N. Darby studied earnestly before he left the Church of England. I remember his speaking much about them in 1835.'[62]

It was in the 1830s and early 1840s that Darby's eschatological thinking began to coalesce. The next event on the prophetic timetable was the 'rapture,' he argued with increasing conviction, the secret catching away of all true believers by the return of the Lord 'in the air,' of which believers should live in constant expectation; the rapture would be followed by the tribulation, the rise of the Antichrist and his bitter assaults on the new converts and Jews, he continued; and the tribulation would end with the 'glorious appearing' of Jesus Christ, divine judgement and the commencement of the millennium. His system retained its rough edges, and throughout his life Darby was much less of a dispensationalist than many of his followers and his critics have assumed.[63] But it was the system of theology that he refined which dominated in the expansion of evangelical millennialism, and that success was especially evident in North America.[64]

Of course, Darby's conclusions were to be contested. Many, believing they had gone too far, argued for the reduction of dispensationalism. B.W. Newton (1807–99), an early leader of the Plymouth Brethren, agreed with Darby's social pessimism, arguing in his commentary on Revelation (1843) that Scripture 'assumes the path of human progress to be, at present, evil; it assumes the failure of the Church's testimony; it assumes that Christ's servants will never behold the establishment of Truth in the earth, until judgement shall have first wrought its work, and they have themselves been taken to their heavenly mansions of glory,' even as he categorically denied the possibility of a pre-tribulation rapture.[65] Samuel Prideaux Tregelles, Newton's cousin, similarly complained with reference to Darby's theories that the 'errors of prophetic teaching ... have suffered no decadence, but, on the contrary, have developed ampler proportions, and extended over a wider sphere of influence than could have been supposed possible.' And yet, he continued, this pattern of failure was not surprising 'when we remember that every day is bringing us nearer to the "end of the age" – the period when right prophetic instruction will be most needed by the people of God, and when also the delusive power of the great Adversary shall be most put forth.'[66] Darby's dispensationalism, in other words, should be recognized as an element of the 'delusive power' of Satan. Others claimed to advance the dispensational faith, reifying its conclusions and further narrowing its eschatological scope. The Anglican clergyman E.W. Bullinger (1837–1913) was one of the foremost hyper-dispensationalists, for example. He redefined the duties of believers in the church age to conclude that Christians should not continue to observe the ordinances of baptism and the Lord's Supper. Bullinger's innovative methods were documented in his magnum opus, *The companion Bible* (6 vols, 1909–22), and were contested on both sides of the Atlantic by such leading writers as Harry A. Ironside (1876–1951), Brethren evangelist and pastor of the Moody Church, Chicago, in *Wrongly dividing the word of truth* (third edition, 1938).[67] Premillennial believers were distributed and divided across the denominational spectrum. But many of their number would have shared the conclusion of J.C. Ryle, the Anglican bishop of Liverpool, that 'none have injured the doctrine of the second coming so much as its overzealous friends.'[68]

IV

Not every millennial believer was preoccupied by prophetic concerns, however; others were more obviously ornaments to the wider evangelical cause. This was especially obvious in terms of mission and revival. The missionary movement in the eighteenth century may have been instigated by postmillennialists, but in the nineteenth century its greatest exponents often shared a commitment to the premillennial faith.[69] Andrew A. Bonar (1810–92) was one of a famous trio of clergymen brothers which exercised profound influence upon the piety and hymnody of evangelicals on both sides of the Atlantic throughout the later nineteenth century.[70] In 1838 he was called to the parish of Collace, in Perthshire, Scotland, where he exercised devoted pastoral care and from which he took part in the celebrated 'mission of inquiry' to Palestine, along with Robert Murray McCheyne, his close friend, and a minister in neighbouring Dundee, in 1839. Profoundly moved by McCheyne's untimely death at the age of 29, Bonar edited his friend's memoirs into one of the most popular pietistic textbooks of Victorian evangelicalism.

Millennial themes were central to Bonar's thinking throughout his literary career. Despite his subscription to the Westminster Confession of Faith (1647), the subordinate standard of the Scottish Presbyterian churches, Bonar became well-known as a defender of the premillennial faith. His interest in premillennialism preceded his evangelical conversion, coloured his sense of a call to the ministry, and pervaded the formative years of his theological training. In May 1829, for example, his diary recorded the impact of lectures on Revelation given by Edward

Irving.[71] Bonar noted that he had been 'hearing Mr. Irving's lectures all the week, and am persuaded now that his views of the Coming of Christ are truth. The views of the glory of Christ opened up in his lectures have been very impressive to me.' On 1 January 1830, struggling with his sense of call to the Christian ministry, he recorded that 'I have thought reputation much, but I see that, to one who believes the Word of God regarding the last days, such desire is folly.'[72] Exactly one year later, on 1 January 1831, he noted that 'wars and rumours of wars prepare us for things coming upon the earth. It may be, also, the sudden appearing of the Lord Jesus Christ. The nations are waking.'[73] By October of that year, Bonar's premillennial convictions were emphatic: he reported his being 'more and more convinced that the time of Christ's Coming is before the thousand years; often grieved by hearing opposition to this.'[74] On 21 January 1832 he discoursed upon the first resurrection and the reign of Christ in a paper he presented to the Exegetical Society at the University of Edinburgh.[75] By March he was grieving over his colleagues' lack of enthusiasm for foreign mission, and felt dissuaded from personal involvement in the missionary task only by his brother Horatius, who 'spoke about the need for labourers and ministers at home, and the witness for Christ's Second Coming borne by few in this land. That may be part of our work.'[76]

But Bonar's premillennial convictions were not to keep him from missionary activities, as was evidenced in the *Narrative of a mission of inquiry to the Jews from the Church of Scotland in 1839* (1842). This book was a written account of what was perhaps the most influential missionary journey of the nineteenth century.[77] McCheyne and Bonar had organized their journey with Alexander Keith, a leading exponent of premillennial views, whose exceptionally popular *Evidence of the truth of the Christian religion from the literal fulfilment of prophecy* (1828) would reach its 36th edition by 1849. As one reviewer put it, 'we cannot fail to have our confidence in the literality of the still unfulfilled word of prophecy greatly strengthened, by the perusal of such a volume of evidence on the past.'[78] Keith's work had focused on past fulfilments of biblical prophecy, and the 'mission of inquiry' was in part an experiment into the possibility of transferring his literal exegetical method into the study of the future.

The 'mission of inquiry' therefore led the men to discoveries in eschatology as much as anthropology. Bonar and McCheyne paid special attention to the apocalyptic expectations of the Jewish communities they encountered: 'The hope of Messiah's coming is strong in the hearts of many Jews here. Many believed that it would be in the year

1840, as that was the end of a period fixed in the book of Zohar.'[79] This belief was shared by Jews in Constantinople, in Austrian Poland, and in Moldavia, they reported: 'some of them expressed their belief that Messiah would come in the year 1840, and others think it is to be in the seventh-thousand year of the world, and then a time of Sabbaths is to follow.'[80] The Jewish community was in danger of such ferment, the *Narrative* recorded, that a Polish rabbi had been warning off expecting a Messiah in 1840, for fear that the ensuing discouragement would lead many of the hopeful to abandon their faith.[81] These experiences of talking to Jews had a marked influence on Bonar's thought. Long after his return to Scotland, Bonar continued to locate the Jewish people at the centre of unfulfilled prophecy.

Bonar and McCheyne shared this expectation of the imminence of apocalyptic events, and, like Keith, they argued that the basis of this expectation lay in a distinctive 'literal' hermeneutic. Its method was so fundamental, they believed, that it ought to be incorporated into the training of every missionary. Of course missionaries should have linguistic competence in Hebrew (which they believed ought to be acquired with a Spanish accent), Arabic, Spanish, German and Italian. But a missionary should also be 'well-grounded in prophecy, and he should be one who fully and thoroughly adopts the principles of literal interpretation, both in order to give him hope and perseverance, and in order to fit him for reasoning with Jews.'[82] The *Narrative* later approvingly quoted one converted Jew, then engaged in evangelism in Palestine: 'the Jews feel their dispersion to be literal; and therefore if you explain unfulfilled prophecy by saying it is spiritual, they reckon you a kind of infidel.'[83] This emphasis upon a literal hermeneutic became foundational to the discussions of the *Narrative*, and perhaps explains why the missionary team was as much engaged in the evaluation of their hermeneutic as they were in direct evangelism. As at Gaza, the missionaries tested what they saw by the expectations of what they should see if their principles of literal interpretation were correct: 'It appeared at first as if there had been no fulfilment of those distinct predictions ... But when we had completed our investigation, we found that not one word had fallen to the ground.'[84]

And others shared their conclusions, combining their preference for a literal interpretation with a growing enthusiasm to locate the Jews and the promised land at the centre of biblical prophecy. In the early 1850s, the London Presbyterian John Cumming reiterated the point, arguing that the 'present state of Palestine is proof of the fulfilment of the predictions of the overspreading abomination and its utter desolation.

I need not state what has been frequently recorded by historians, what is indicated in almost every page of the books of Moses, that Palestine was a land of unparalleled fertility and beauty in ancient times ... it was a land fitted to be the vineyard and the granary of Asia and Europe together.'[85] But it was not always to be unpopulated. 'Palestine is still the house of the Jews,' he contended. 'It is unfurnished, it is stripped of its ornaments, its glory, and its beauty; but it is their house still; and the Moslem, the Romanist, the Greek, the Arab, and the Bedouin of the desert, are simply keeping the empty house till the lawful tenant comes in, which he will do right soon.'[86] And then, Cumming concluded, the 'great Restorer' shall 'collect' the Jews from 'a thousand lands, removing what prevents their cohesion, and they shall meet and mingle in ancient and again beautiful Jerusalem, and reflect the image of him who is the Prince the Messiah.'[87] Cumming believed these times were not far off, and provided a reading of Matthew 24:32–35 that would resonate in many dispensational textbooks produced in the next 150 years: 'it is a delightful thought that the winter gives signs of closing – that the first buds of spring begin now to show themselves, that on every dry branch and stem of Judah's withered fig-tree buds at this moment are beginning to appear,' he observed. 'What is the great question of the world? The political condition of the Jew. What is the great subject of the Church? The conversion of the Jews.'[88] Even the postmillennial apologist David Brown agreed, in his study of *The restoration of the Jews: The history, principles and bearing of the question* (1861). And, each of these writers concluded, their re-gathering in Palestine would be a pre-eminent sign of the times.

Nevertheless, while many premillennial writers found their expectations of an imminent apocalypse driving them towards mission, many postmillennial writers found their expectations of the imminent onset of unusual spiritual blessing confirmed by the mid-century trans-Atlantic revivals. In the early 1830s Charles Grandison Finney, a Presbyterian minister then slipping from his Calvinistic moorings, began a campaign of preaching in Rochester, New York, 'America's first inland boom town.'[89] His sermons made an immediate – and overpowering – impact. He 'stared down from the pulpit and said flatly that if Christians united and dedicated their lives to the task, they could convert the world and bring on the millennium in three months.'[90] The clean-up of the community was spectacular: Lyman Beecher, the Presbyterian father of the noted American dynasty, declared that the events associated with Finney's preaching in the town constituted the 'greatest revival of religion that the world had ever seen.'[91] 'More than any other event,' the leading historian of the period has observed, the 1831 revival 'marked the acceptance of an activist and millennialist evangelicalism as the faith of the northern [American] middle class.'[92] In 1859, and on the other side the Atlantic, another revival was hailed in similar terms. This revival, which had emerged in the United States, began to break over northern Ireland, southern Scotland, northern England and much of Wales, was celebrated by protestant church leaders as a remarkable 'year of grace.'[93] James McCosh, a former minister of the Free Church of Scotland and future president of Princeton, endorsed its progress and reported that 'thousands and tens of thousands have been convinced or converted.'[94] For many of his peers, the revival was the precursor of a much greater work of God, the remarkable progress of which was an apocalyptic intervention heralding the promise of the millennium.[95] These patterns of events, one Irish Presbyterian minister expected, pointed onwards 'to the glories of the millennial age' and would recur 'by periodic, special, and abundant visitations of heavenly influence, until Christianity shall become the dominant power in the world.'[96] Others understood the revival to have cosmological implications, according to another commentator, who noted 'some strange appearances in the heavens, such as comets and other phenomena,' and enthused, 'thank God, the days of the millennial advent are ushering in.'[97] In America and Ireland, evangelical leaders were endorsing religious revival because it seemed to anticipate – if not to inaugurate – the millennium itself.

V

These were exciting days for many evangelical believers. In an editorial in the first issue of the *Quarterly Journal of Prophecy* (1849), Horatius Bonar declared that the 'increase of [prophetic] inquirers ... during the last five years, is most cheering,' though, he admitted, 'many who are studying "things hoped for" are by no means firmly established' in the premillennial faith.[98] He was certainly aware of the significance of the fact that ten prophetic journals had been established and more than a hundred prophetic books had been published in England between 1800 and 1840.[99] But the expansion of premillennialism did not please everyone, and important voices were raised in defence of the old ways of thinking. In 1846 the Glasgow Free Church minister David Brown, who had been assistant to Edward Irving until the outbreak of tongues-speaking in his London church, questioned his earlier premillennialism in a major work entitled *Christ's second coming: Will it be premillennial?*

The book was a theological sensation, the most thorough English-language defence of postmillennialism published to that date, and an ironic indication of the extent to which the premillennial faith had increased in influence, due in no small part to the efforts of Brown's 'estimable friend,' Andrew A. Bonar.[100] *Christ's second coming* offered a robust critique of the premillennial position as it had advanced to the mid-1840s. Following a host of seventeenth-century divines, Brown argued that the millennial age would begin abruptly, and not gradually and imperceptibly as 'liberal' postmillennialists had assumed. More obviously than any of his colleagues, Brown was aware of the sociological dynamic of the millennial debate: the 'subject handled in this volume seems periodically to agitate the Church,' he explained, and 'has its law of recurrence. In times of general excitement, of extensive change, of pervading uneasiness and trial, of mingled hope and fear – it invariably rises to the surface.'[101] But the subject was important, he insisted. 'Great mistakes have undeniably been committed by the students of prophecy from age to age, – mistakes which time, that infallible expounder of the Divine counsels, has in every case ultimately detected, but not till in many instances they had wrought confusion and every evil work.'[102] His writing against premillennialism was justified, he explained, for the new theory 'is no barren speculation – useless though true, and innocuous though false. It is a school of Scripture interpretation; it impinges upon and affects some of the most commanding points of the Christian faith; and, when suffered to work its unimpeded way, it stops not till it has pervaded with its own genius the entire system of one's theology, and the whole tone of his spiritual character.'[103]

But the progress of that postmillennial expectation of increasing social and religion benefit was rudely interrupted by the events of the American Civil War (1861–65).[104] Postmillennial ideas had been cited by clerical supporters of both sides in the run-up to the conflict, so that in some senses the struggle was one of eschatological hopes concerning the evidence of what an improving society would look like. The defeat of the Confederacy consequently led to collapse of Southern postmillennialism and the search for an alternative prophetic paradigm, which many conservatives found in a new variety of premillennial hope. It was at this point of unprecedented influence that evangelicals on both sides of the Atlantic began to question received ideas of the gradual but inevitable Christianization of the world and to embrace alternative eschatological positions which deconstructed the social expectations of the establishment and challenged believers to embrace arguments in favour of evangelical marginality. These expectations, on both sides of the Atlantic, were increasingly combined with a commitment to mission and literal interpretation. Many evangelicals were convinced by the new expectation of evangelical marginality and cultural decay, and articulated those expectations in terms of the new expansion of dispensational premillennial belief. This millennial debate precipitated a significant crisis of confessional subscription. Some premillennialists attempted to negotiate their new commitments – the *Quarterly Journal of Prophecy*, for example, argued that the 'some of the soundest and most eminent divines of the Westminster Assembly' held premillennial views – but others gave up on the confessional commitments altogether.[105] This challenge to the established orthodoxies which had patterned large parts of evangelical life since the seventeenth century eventually shattered distinctive denominational loyalties and fed into the pan-evangelical identity provided by the early Fundamentalist movement.

Throughout the first three-quarters of the nineteenth century, therefore, aspirations for millennial bliss were shared by many within and beyond the trans-Atlantic evangelical community. But, as the period came to an end, it seemed to many observers that an old world was concluding. And so, in many ways, it was. The historicist and postmillennial consensus had been disrupted, and a new faith was on the rise. These were heady days for the expansion of an evangelical millennial hope.

5
The Contest of Evangelical Millennialism, 1880–1970

The expansion of evangelical millennialism continued into the later nineteenth century, in the aftermath of the American Civil War and the late Victorian crisis of faith, as evangelical writers on both sides of the Atlantic provided the momentum for the widespread and interdisciplinary development of a literature of social despair. Evangelicals reflected in theological terms upon the crisis of the protestant establishment imagination that was marked by the trenchant cultural criticism of Thomas Carlyle and the 'possibilities of latter day belief' explored in the developing literary Gothic.[1] These publications undermined easy assumptions of national destiny, but pushed evangelicals into new and destabilizing contests of millennial belief.[2]

On both sides of the Atlantic, dispensational premillennialism grew in popularity at different speeds, for different reasons, among different theological constituencies and with different consequences. In the 1830s, Andrew A. Bonar had noted that his premillennial views were shared by few of the American clergy he encountered on his 'mission of inquiry' to Palestine.[3] By the end of the century, however, competing varieties of premillennial theology dominated evangelical communities on both sides of the Atlantic, at both popular and scholarly levels. This innovative eschatology was bolted on to theories of biblical inerrancy that had long been a staple of protestant orthodoxy but which had gained articulate new spokesmen at Princeton Theological Seminary.[4] These intellectual trends were combined to fashion a new 'Fundamentalism' that would be represented in the *Scofield reference Bible* (1909; second edition 1917), an annotated edition of the King James (Authorized) Version published by Oxford University Press that would sell tens of millions of copies in ensuing decades, and *The fundamentals: A testimony to the truth* (1910–15), a series of pamphlets which assembled more-or-less uniformly conservative voices on such increasingly contested issues as the historicity of the virgin birth or the resurrection of Jesus Christ.[5] Conservative evangelicals from a wide variety of denominations regrouped around a doctrinal platform which reduced historic protestantism to what looked to many critics like its lowest common denominator. But many adherents of this new prophetic faith believed their dispensational convictions were warranted, and the eschatological timetable their work assumed appeared to be confirmed by the events of the Russian revolution (1917), which offered prophetically inclined observers of current affairs a bogeyman whose legacy would continue until the end of the twentieth century, and the publication of the Balfour Declaration (1917), which codified politically the theological Zionism that had been developing through the latter part of the previous century, the terms of which appear to have been more than slightly influenced by the faith of the politician responsible for its existence, the British Foreign Secretary, Arthur James Balfour (1848–1930).[6]

As a movement, protestant Fundamentalism suffered an historic defeat in the media vilification surrounding the notorious Scopes Trial (1925).[7] In Britain and Ireland, Fundamentalists failed to make significant inroads in the mainstream evangelical denominations, and rapidly disappeared from the ecclesiastical landscape; but in North America, they developed an entirely new way of imagining the Christian life, its institutions, and its social and cultural responsibilities.[8] This new vision of believing activity was to be enormously influential – even in the confessional denominations.[9] In the 1930s and 1940s, American Fundamentalists retreated to the cultural margins and began to rethink their identity, creating as they did so a network of institutions which would eventually provide for the theological rearmament and cultural re-engagement of conservative evangelicals in the latter quarter of the twentieth century.[10] This chapter will describe their retreat and revival, documenting the emergence and evolution of British and American Fundamentalism in terms of the wider contest of evangelical millennial belief.

I

The cultural, literary and theological crisis of the mid-nineteenth century was represented in the equivocations of British national sentiment and in the early erosion of American expectations of 'manifest destiny.' Writing in the early 1850s, for example, the London Presbyterian John Cumming felt sure that his fellow Britons should 'never tremble about our safety' while 'our country cleaves to our country's God,' even though 'France should send forth afloat yet a mightier fleet than she has at Cherbourg, though Napoleon's military avalanches should again rush down from the Pyrenees and the Alps, though popes should send ship-loads of cardinals.' But, Cumming continued, Britain's enjoyment of peace was ultimately conditional, for if 'irreligion, pantheism, popery, and infidelity, and drunkenness, and sabbath-breaking ... gain the mastery; and let protesting voices, and pleading cries, and praying hearts be still; then our palladium is gone, the shields of the Lord are removed.'[11] And he feared that the removal of this 'palladium' was imminent. Citing calculations from Elliott's *Horae Apocalypticae* (1844) to prove that '1864 will be the close of the six thousandth year of the world,' Cumming noted his further expectation that 'our country will be surrounded by the armies of the earth as with a belt; and that the last fight for freedom and for faith may be within the silver-coasted shores of our beloved land.'[12] In fashionable churches in the world's most significant capitals, premillennial preachers could imagine that the apocalyptic destruction of British and American liberty had to occur before the latter-day glory could sweep across the earth.

It might have seemed to some British observers that the 'last fight for freedom' was to occur on the other side of the Atlantic. One decade after Cumming's remarkable sermons, evangelicals in the American south responded to the collapse of the Confederacy by rethinking the millennial exuberance of the rhetoric that had defended their culture. Postmillennial confidence had demonstrated its suitability for 'an activistic people who believed in the essential soundness of their civilization and who saw the future as an arena for its indefinite improvement and extension,' and had provided southern evangelicals with the foundation for a broad range of conservative mores.[13] Even as they entered the conflict, many of these pro-slavery evangelicals believed that they were 'riding the wave of destiny' and that providence would vindicate their cause.[14] But they lost that confidence with the final defeat of the Confederacy and the shattering impact of Reconstruction, and struggled to agree upon an eschatological position that could make sense of their experience.[15] This movement towards eschatological uncertainty was marked in the theology of a number of Southern Baptist leaders. James P. Boyce (1827–88), who had inherited his postmillennial faith from his Princeton Theological Seminary professor, Charles Hodge, developed in later career an emphasis on the imminence of the second coming that appeared quite alternative to his earlier hopes. This new perspective was shared by other Southern Baptist leaders, such as

John L. Dagg (1794–1884), president of Mercer University, and James M. Pendleton (1811–91), a founder of the controversial 'Landmarkist' grouping. John Broadus (1827–95), meanwhile, abandoned his denomination's traditional postmillennialism in favour of an idiosyncratic amillennialism.[16] The Civil War had exploded the southern millennial consensus. Northern evangelicals retained the older hopes, but the popularity of their socially advanced variety of postmillennialism ended at the Mason-Dixon Line. Even they grew uncertain of their postmillennial faith, and the fault lines of the later liberal-fundamentalist divide appeared first in the northern Presbyterian debate about the propriety of premillennialism.[17]

But premillennialism did triumph, and by the end of the century it was clear that many of the most important American dispensational authors hailed from the northern states that had been the heartland of postmillennial hope. William E. Blackstone, an Illinois Methodist with strong Zionist leanings, published *Jesus is coming* (1882), which sold one million copies by 1932.[18] Blackstone's conclusions were confirmed in more scholarly terms in *The thousand years in both Testaments* (1889), by another northerner, a Presbyterian minister called Nathaniel West, and this book became another best-selling account of the premillennial faith.[19] As a result of exposure to these and other publications, many northern evangelicals found themselves drawn away from the postmillennialism with which they had grown up.[20] One of their number was Milton H. Stine (1853 – fl. 1930), a Lutheran clergyman who had reflected in his early writing the optimistic postmillennialism of the progressive 'American' Lutheranism that was being promoted by Samuel Schmucker, the president of Gettysburg Theological Seminary, at which Stine had been a student.[21] Stine's early postmillennialism had been outlined in *Studies on the religious problem of our country* (1888), which described his expectations of the American future in exuberant terms.[22] Writing 20 years after the Civil War, his work still shared the confidence of many northern evangelicals that their postmillennial hopes had been confirmed by the conclusion of the war, for these northern believers, unlike their southern counterparts, tended to associate the abolition of slavery with the advance, rather than the decline, of the kingdom of God.[23] *Studies on the religious problem of our country* consequently argued that the 'world is surely but slowly getting better,' and that America, which Stine described as the 'hope of the world, civilly, morally, religiously' and the 'grandest country upon which God's sun ever shone,' was 'destined, in the providence of God, to lead mankind into that second Eden, where no destroying angel shall ever enter.'[24]

But Stine was shortly to abandon this confidence. His prophetic novel, *The devil's bride: A present day arraignment of formalism and doubt in the Church and in society, in the light of the Holy Scriptures: Given in the form of a pleasing story* (1910), advanced his new premillennial faith in robust, if not aesthetically gifted, terms.[25] On both sides of the Atlantic, the problems created by the Civil War and the Victorian crisis of faith were being solved by the gathering of a new theological constituency on the basis of a futurist and premillennial faith.

II

Much of the collapse of confidence in national destiny and postmillennial progress among evangelicals on both sides of the Atlantic was driven by uncertainty as to their theological situation. Many prominent evangelicals feared that the orthodoxy which they had inherited from believers in previous centuries had been critically undermined. With the rise of biblical criticism, its impact on some of the most conservative of the Scottish denominations, and rising levels of popular scepticism driven by such political and scientific publications as Marx's *Communist manifesto* (1848) and Darwin's *On the origin of species* (1859), conservative evangelicals felt suddenly outmanoeuvred in cultures and in denominations they were increasingly reluctant to recognize as their own. The apparent rapidity of this plunge into scepticism and doubt led many believers to consider whether they had entered that period of apostasy which they expected in the last days of the dispensation. It was significant in this respect that the 'Down-grade statement,' a declaration of opposition to theological modernity signed by C.H. Spurgeon and other English Baptists, concluded with the insistence that 'our hope is the Personal Pre-millennial Return of the Lord Jesus in glory.'[26] The tide of secularization that was sweeping across western Europe and North America was being interpreted through the lens of prophetic despair.

The general evangelical crisis acted as a catalyst for the formation of new inter-denominational fellowships. Many of these groups, on both sides of the Atlantic, began to consider whether the formation of organizations and the holding of events that side-stepped denominational boundaries could serve to advance the premillennial faith that concerned conservatives were increasingly beginning to share. And many believed that they could. In 1876 W.J. Erdman, Nathaniel West and a number of other Presbyterian ministers organized the first of the Believers' Meetings for Bible Study.[27] Two years later, this group had formalized its activities in the first meeting of the inter-denominational Niagara Bible Conference, the earliest and best-known of the prophecy conferences that would do so much to spread the premillennial faith throughout the United States. One of the most significant of the group's publications was *The thousand years in both Testaments* (1889), an extensive survey of biblical theology by Nathaniel West (1826–1906), an English immigrant who led Presbyterian congregations in Ohio, New York, Michigan and Kentucky, and had taught in Danville Theological Seminary, Kentucky, as well as the Moody Bible Institute, Chicago. West had been a founder member of the Niagara Conference, but his changing opinions split its leadership, for, in 1892, he concluded against the teaching of other conference leaders that Christ's return could occur at any moment, and instead began to argue that the rapture would occur after the tribulation. The ensuing controversy divided American premillennial leaders, with W.G. Moorehead (1836–1914) and W.J. Erdman (1834–1923) following West's new argument, and brought the Niagara conferences to an end in 1900.[28]

Throughout the later nineteenth century, a number of writers grew concerned by such movements away from dispensational orthodoxy. Edward Dennet (1831–1914), an English Baptist minister who had recently converted to the Plymouth Brethren, published *The blessed hope* (1879) to explain and lament the recent advances of the dispensational cause. Fifty years earlier, he explained, 'the Church had fallen into profound slumber, drugged by the opiate influences of the world, so that the doctrine of the Lord's return for His saints was forgotten, ignored, or denied.' But when Darby and other early Brethren leaders had recovered the biblical theology of the rapture, 'through the action of the Spirit of God ... thousands were startled from their sleep, and, trimming their lamps, went forth once again to meet the Bridegroom' and 'lived daily in the hope of His return.' As 'time went on,' Dennet continued, 'while the doctrine of the Second Advent has been apprehended and taught by increasing numbers, and while the truth has been undoubtedly the support and consolation of many godly souls, it is yet a question if large numbers of the saints of God have not lost its freshness and its power.' Those who had once allowed the expectation of apostasy to delineate the boundaries of their fellowship were failing to do so now – and Dennet was thinking of those believers who continued to associate with others outside the circle of the Brethren. 'Every day,' he argued, 'it is becoming ... more manifest that we are in the midst of the perilous times (2 Tim. iii.)' that Dennet expected immediately before the rapture, and 'many of us,' he feared, 'are in danger of once more falling asleep, even with the doctrine of the hope upon our lips.'[29] Despite these fears, however, it was clear that by the beginning of the twentieth century the most able and widely read defenders of dispensationalism came from outside the Brethren movement. Clarence Larkin (1850–1924), for example, was a Pennsylvania Baptist minister who put his skills in draftsmanship to prophetic use, publishing among many other items his monumental book of prophecy charts, *Dispensational truth* (1918), and a vividly illustrated commentary on Revelation (1919), which may have disappointed some readers with its insistence that 'there is nothing fantastical in this book.'[30]

Others thought that too much about premillennialism could be described as 'fantastical.' Some continued to reject its theology altogether. Among their number was Joseph Agar Beet (1840–1924), an English Methodist minister and scholar who had written numerous New Testament commentaries, all of which had been published by Hodder and Stoughton, a firm with impeccably evangelical credentials. But Beet's orthodox reputation was shaken by his study of *The last things* (1897; fifth edition, 1905).[31] The book's rejection of premillennialism was decisive.[32] But, in its pages, Beet also rejected orthodox teaching on hell. 'During the last century English opinion about the fate of the last has altogether changed,' he announced to a startled evangelical public. 'Very few can now read Wesley's sermons on "Hell" and on "Eternity" … without repudiating much of their teaching with indignation.' 'Indeed,' he continued, 'some of Spurgeon's sermons on the same subject, published less than fifty years ago, would not be tolerated now.'[33] His book was a 'protest' against the 'once-prevalent belief in the endless permanence of all human souls and the endless suffering of the lost,' and, 'as a Protestant,' Beet claimed the 'right of appeal from the traditional teaching of the Church to the supreme authority of the Bible.'[34] He lost his teaching post in a Methodist college for the opinions expressed in his book, but he was unconcerned by the controversy, for 'it is utterly vain to try, in these days of intelligent research, to defend the historic faith by suppressing contrary opinions.'[35] Despite Beet's rejection of eschatological orthodoxy, some of his views were taken up by evangelicals who had adopted the dispensational faith. The followers of E.W. Bullinger often advanced beyond the conclusions of his *The companion Bible* (1909–22) to advance arguments in favour of the annihilation of the wicked.[36] Other believers, who often used the 'Concordant Version' of the Bible (1926), combined a rather conventional dispensational system with Beet's rejection of tradition teaching on hell to argue that the punishment of the wicked would continue only until the end of the millennium, when God would restore his creation and finally be 'all in all' (1 Corinthians 15:28).[37] Of course, this position was widely denied among orthodox evangelicals, perhaps most vigorously by T.K. McCrossan, in *The Bible: Its hell and its ages* (1941), and it failed to impact the mainstream of the ranks of dispensationalists.[38]

But the dispensational system continued to be refined. Philip Mauro, in *The gospel of the kingdom: An examination of modern dispensationalism* (1927), for example, expressed his concern that the recently published Scofield Bible had 'usurped the place of authority that belongs to God's Bible alone.'[39] Its system of teaching, Mauro worried, 'is a cause of division and controversy between those followers of Christ who ought to be, at this time of crisis, solidly united against the mighty forces of unbelief and apostasy.' He feared that the Scofield Bible 'tends to bring the vital truth of our Lord's second coming unto discredit with many, because it associates that great Bible doctrine with various speculative details for which no scriptural support can be found.'[40] C.A. Chader, an American missionary in Sweden, evidently agreed, and defended his study of *God's plan through the ages* (1938) and its enclosed prophetic chart, measuring approximately three feet by one foot, on the basis that its author was 'neither Seventh Day Adventist nor Russellist [that is, a Jehovah's Witness] but an evangelical Christian with Baptist background.'[41] Meanwhile, G.H. Lang, an idiosyncratic adherent of the English Brethren movement, published the collected prophetic papers of his late mentor, G.H. Pember, in *The great prophecies of the centuries concerning Israel, the Gentiles, and the Church of God* (1941), arguing for a partial rapture. But, again, these redefinitions of dispensational theology found few adherents in the evangelical mainstream.[42]

Other evangelicals continued to reject dispensationalism altogether. Their number included former adherents of the system, such as William J. Rowlands, author of *Our Lord cometh* (1930), and Alexander Reese, a Presbyterian missionary in Brazil, who published *The approaching advent of Christ: An examination of the teaching of J.N. Darby and his followers* (1937) as 'an examination of prophetic theories that have gained a large acceptance among Evangelical Anglicans, Fundamentalists in all the Protestant Churches, Plymouth Brethren, Keswick and similar movements, free-lance Bible-teachers and evangelists, and all whose leanings are toward a realistic programme of the End, and a belief, sometimes true, that Providence is with the small battalions and the Wee Frees.'[43] Evidently in control of his writing, Reese defended his position that 'a writer is not always under obligation to suppress his amusement at his opponents' arguments.'[44] He claimed that Darby's doctrine of the secret rapture had in fact originated with a 'Mr Tweedy, from the West Indies,' and attacked two leading Brethren, C.F. Hogg and W.E. Vine, as uncritical proponents of the system.[45] But Hogg and Vine replied in *The Church and the tribulation: A review of the book entitled 'The Approaching Advent of Christ'* (1938), abominating the 'scornful phraseology' that Reese had 'adopted toward sober and earnest servants of God who have, in freedom from fundamental error, sought to set forth what they believe to be the truth, is, to say the least, not the happiest way of treating a subject.'[46] Meanwhile, *The Lord's return* (n.d.), by W. Graham Scroggie, then pastor of Spurgeon's Tabernacle in London, was a thoughtful and careful exposition of the dispensationalism that had been rejected by the Tabernacle's founder, articulated with a concern to develop a wider philosophy of history among the evangelical community he addressed.[47] These publications by Brethren and Baptists were typical of the evolution of the British dispensational movement. In North America, dispensationalism found exponents across the evangelical spectrum, but in Britain, while it continued to find able and articulate exponents, it was increasingly sidelined in the major denominations.

It was hardly surprising, therefore, that so many believers on both sides of the Atlantic frankly admitted their eschatological uncertainty. Many evangelicals wanted to engage with the millennial debate without taking a clear position. Their crisis of confidence was reflected in such publications as *The millennium Bible* (1924), by William Edward Biederwolf, a full-Bible commentary which advertised itself as 'neither a Pre-millennial, not a Post-millennial, nor a Non-millennial' volume.[48] But others retained their earlier convictions with entire hostility to any variety of premillennial faith. Even after the devastation of the First World War, prominent Reformed theologians such as B.B. Warfield (1851–1921), professor at Princeton Theological Seminary, continued to defend the old postmillennial consensus, expecting the dawn of a new age in which saving grace would be extended to every living human being.[49]

It was clear, nevertheless, that evangelicals were debating their millennial convictions in social and cultural environments in which they were growing increasingly marginal. The devastation of the Great War appeared to confound eschatological optimism, and did, to some extent, unsettle dispensationalists.[50] In 1918, a number of academics at University of Chicago issued a statement in which they argued that the millennial hopes of evangelicals were 'open to serious question. Can men today continue with confidence to expect a cataclysmic reversal of present conditions, or does the light of experience and present knowledge demand the adoption of a more constructive, though less spectacular, program for the renovation of the world?'[51] This criticism of the premillennial faith continued in the world of academic biblical studies. After 25 years of research and preparation, R.H. Charles (1855–1931), archdeacon of Westminster and a former professor at Trinity College Dublin, published his two-volume commentary on Revelation (1920) to conclude that the biblical foundation for millennial theology of any variety was no more than a jumble: the 'traditional order of the text' in the later parts of Revelation was, he felt, 'intolerably disordered and hopelessly unintelligible,' and he explained that had 'restored, so far as he can, the order of the text as it left the hand of the Seer.'[52] His radically critical approach ironically typified the conclusions of many evangelical scholars. Unable to agree on the exegesis and application of Revelation 20:1–10, prophetic enthusiasts pushed the trans-Atlantic evangelical movement into a wide-ranging contest of millennial belief.

III

And yet it was this environment of confusion, declension and contest that provided the context for the formation by conservative evangelicals of a new ecclesiological party and for the publication of the texts around which it gathered. This new movement, known as 'Fundamentalism,' was, if nothing else, an interpretive community. The principal texts it produced and consumed shaped its theology while providing sufficient ambiguity for the ultimate declension of its project for conservative evangelical union.

Fundamentalism was the boiled-down evangelical orthodoxy of protesting American pietists. Its doctrinal platform was resolutely reactive, in that it placarded a shared opposition to the liberalizing trends of the early twentieth century instead of a shared commitment to a denominational creed. But in defining itself as a conservative response to those debates, the movement rooted its identity and purpose in the cultural moment of its production rather than in the historicity of the confessional tradition it might otherwise have sought to represent. The *Scofield reference Bible* (1909; second edition, 1917) epitomized this trend. It did little to advance the broad base of conservative protestant scholarship, and instead highlighted to massive effect its editor's proclivity for prophetic speculation and ecclesiological indifference. Cyrus I. Scofield (1843–1921) was a maverick Congregational pastor who defied allegations of bigamy to become an acknowledged leader of early Fundamentalism.[53] Ironically, eyebrows have been raised by his alleged tampering with the text of the King James (Authorized) Version.[54] But his Bible was and continues to be widely respected among conservative dispensationalists, especially in North America, where in its various revisions it has sold tens of millions of copies. Scofield's contemporary reputation was such that he was invited to contribute to the other literary project which with Fundamentalism has become most closely identified. Although historians debate the origins of the movement's title, there is good evidence to suggest that it was drawn from the series of 12 paperback booklets edited by A.C. Dixon, Louis Meyer and R.A. Torrey and sponsored by two California oilmen, Lyman and Milton Stewart, entitled *The fundamentals: A testimony to the truth* (1910–15).[55] These booklets compiled short articles, a large number of which had already been published, from a wide variety of authors on such topics as the inspiration and sufficiency of Scripture, the new theories of evolution, and challenges to the orthodox Christology. The booklets were sent to 'every pastor, evangelist, missionary, theological professor, theological student, Sunday School superintendent, Y.M.C.A. and Y.W.C.A. secretary in the English speaking world, so far as the addresses of all these can be obtained.'[56] And vast numbers of recipients were evidently involved. The fourth volume reported that free copies of each of the 128-page booklets had been sent to 250 000 subscribers.[57] The fifth volume raised this total to 275 000 subscribers, and pointedly noted that Roman Catholic priests were among their number.[58] But as circulation figures began to decline, *The fundamentals* adopted a robustly protestant tone.[59] The eleventh volume offered articles on such topics as 'Is Romanism Christianity?' and, reiterating the old protestant nationalist topology, 'Rome, the antagonist of the nation.'[60] The Stewart brothers, the anonymous sponsors of the series, eventually noted that three million copies of the booklets had been printed.[61] But it was the booklets' omissions that were perhaps most significant. While later Fundamentalism became associated with the dispensationalism that had dominated in the *Scofield reference Bible*, *The fundamentals* refused to engage in prophetic speculation of any kind, and advanced the sparest of eschatological creeds. One of the rare articles on related themes was prepared by W.G. Moorehead, the founder of the Niagara Bible Conferences and an editor of the *Scofield reference Bible*, but its discussion of the theology of Jehovah's Witnesses did not take advantage of their eschatological errors to advance any kind of evangelical premillennial faith.[62] While later self-styled Fundamentalists made a priority of premillennial conviction, *The fundamentals* contained almost no reference to prophetic teaching.[63]

So perhaps it was not these publications, but rather the events of the later 1910s that did most to advance premillennial historiography among conservative evangelicals. It was, after all, with the publication of the Balfour Declaration (1917), in the same year in which the second edition of the *Scofield reference Bible* appeared, that American evangelicals rediscovered Israel and thereby drove the final nail into the coffin of their own national election and its consequent 'manifest destiny.'[64] The horrors of the Russian revolution (1917) provided evangelicals with the apocalyptic enemy they expected of a northern Eurasian Gog and Magog which would offer prophetically inclined observers of current affairs a bogeyman whose legacy would continue until the end of the twentieth century.[65] Simultaneously, the publication of the Balfour Declaration (1917) codified politically the theological Zionism that had been developing since the latter part of the previous century, the terms of which appear to have been more than slightly influenced by the faith of the politician responsible for its existence, the British Foreign Secretary, Arthur James Balfour (1848–1930).[66] The issue of the future of the Jews, which had to some degree been eclipsed in the culture wars of the earlier 1910s, was again in the forefront of evangelical consciousness. This concern was shared by evangelicals throughout the British world. In *The remarkable Jew: God's great timepiece* (1934), Leonard Sale-Harrison remembered that 'from the days of childhood' in Sydney, Australia, he had been 'taught to love the study of the great prophecies of the Bible,' and that this prophetic interest had 'never failed to be a source of inspiration and hope,' especially as it focused on the Jewish future.[67] He reminded his readers that the 'crux of the great war was not in Germany, but in Jerusalem ... the centre of Biblical geography,' and went on to defend dispensationalism, to offer a history of the Zionist movement and the British administration in Palestine, and to provide an update for its readers on the 'wonderful progress in Palestine' towards the formation of a Jewish state.[68] Sale-Harrison had no doubt about this state's significance: it was an evident 'sign of the church age closing.'[69] Many evangelicals agreed, especially in North America, and their fascination with Israel increased as they watched with unguarded excitement the tumultuous events of the mid-twentieth century.[70]

IV

Nevertheless, by the end of the 1930s, evangelicals on both sides of the Atlantic knew the bitter experience of defeat. With their social influence in eclipse, evangelicals turned in upon themselves, reifying their doctrinal standards and dividing, increasingly publicly and increasingly aggressively, between Fundamentalists and those dismissed by Fundamentalists as 'neo-evangelicals.' Fundamentalists, increasingly committed to dispensationalism, identified an ideological headquarters in the Evangelical Theological College (later to become Dallas Theological Seminary), founded in 1924 by a Scofield acolyte, Lewis Sperry Chafer. But Chafer did more than anyone else to provide American dispensationalists with a steady theological foundation. Ordained as a Presbyterian minister, Chafer eventually provided the movement with its first systematic theology, and expansive, eight-volume project (1948).[71] But even as he was preparing his text, the world went to war, and believers in both of the evangelical parties struggled to define and understand their duties to the powers that be, especially in a context in which, as many prophecy writers put it, events seemed suddenly poised for the realization of ancient hopes and fears. Of course, the Second World War was far worse than believers could have imagined, while signally failing to precipitate the apocalyptic devastation they might have been led to expect. A number of voices identified with chilling prescience the geopolitical trends that would mark the decades of the Cold War. Harry Rimmer's *The shadow of coming events* (1943) predicted the Allied victory in the war, Italy's loss of her Libyan and Ethiopian colonies, the re-establishment of Israel and Russia's new superpower status. His arguments – and, in particular, his chapter on 'The coming war with Russia' – came to influence large sections of popular and scholarly dispensationalism.[72] Events were realizing long-expected patterns. By the end of the 1940s it had become evident to many prophecy believers that the end was now at hand.

But the Fundamentalist experiment, on either side of the Atlantic, could not be sustained. The movement had, since its beginnings, advanced on a limited theological platform, and the uneasy alliances developed around that platform were not to be maintained. The theological implosion of the movement was initially evident within the world of northern Presbyterians, in which J. Gresham Machen (1881–1937) provided important if short-lived leadership.[73] But in the colourful and often hectic world of independent Bible churches, and especially in the American south, the rapid elaboration and equally sudden fragmentation of Fundamentalism was represented in the theological and cultural controversy at the Bible Institute of Los Angeles ('BIOLA') in the later 1920s, a controversy which centred on the leadership of John Murdock MacInnis (1871–1940). MacInnis had been born and raised in an immigrant family of conservative Scottish Presbyterians in the Canadian Maritimes. After informal training for the ministry at Moody Bible Institute in Chicago, he entered a series of pastorates, remaining a loyal Presbyterian throughout his life, and emerged as an important, though relatively low-profile, speaker and organizer on the Bible and Holiness Conference circuit. His appointment to BIOLA, where he oversaw a major curricular review, precipitated one of the most significant of the early Fundamentalist controversies. In part, the crisis was provoked by MacInnis's failure to uphold dispensational premillennialism. His own eschatological position owed more to historic premillennialism, but he combined that position with an expectation that believers would work for the social betterment of the world – a theological truism that provided sufficient evidence for his enemies to make the charge that he had come to support the 'social gospel.' Plymouth Brethren were drawn into the controversy. Writing from New York, one conservative leader expressed his support for MacInnis, complaining that 'the Devil likes to bring trouble' through Brethren and Scofield dispensationalists.[74] Writing from New Zealand, another leader similarly opined that opposition to MacInnis's reforms had been led by Brethren 'of a narrow type.'[75] Throughout the 1930s and 1940s the difference between dispensationalism and its amillennial and covenant theology alternative were becoming increasingly obvious.[76] The rejection of dispensationalism was particularly evident in Britain. W.J. Grier, a founder minister of the Evangelical Presbyterian Church, a body which seceded from the Presbyterian Church in Ireland in 1927, published a series of articles on the millennial question in *The momentous event: A discussion of Scripture teaching on the second advent* (1945).[77] In America, Australia and the Netherlands, his conclusions were confirmed and expanded upon by Oswald T. Allis (1880–1973), author of *Prophecy and the church* (1945),[78] Archibald Hughes, in *A new heaven and a new earth* (1958), and Herman Ridderbos, in *The coming of the kingdom* (1962).[79] And this programmatic revival of older ideas was provided with massive impetus through the celebrated preaching of Martyn Lloyd-Jones (1899–1981), and institutional support in the founding in London of the Banner of Truth Trust (1957), a publisher which, through the 1960s and beyond, would become the most important provider of the older literature of eschatological hope.[80]

These non-dispensational theologians managed to retain their convictions despite the rise in premillennial stock from the later 1940s to the later 1960s. Premillennial theology was boosted by popular evangelical response to the atomic end to the Second World War, the establishment of the modern state of Israel in 1948 and the Jewish reoccupation of Jerusalem during the Six Day War in 1967. For the significance of these events was regularly linked. In North America, dispensationalism grew in influence as it appeared to be confirmed by the moral and military bipolarity of the emerging Cold War.[81] The evangelist Billy Graham later captured the mood in his allusion to the famous words of Robert Oppenheimer:

> At 5.30 A.M. on July 16, 1945, a light brighter than a thousand suns illuminated the desert sands of New Mexico. One scientist who was watching wept. 'My God,' he exclaimed, 'we have created hell.' From that day on our world has not been the same. We entered a new era of history – perhaps the last.[82]

Premillennialists were not slow to appropriate the rhetorical potential of the atomic age. In 1955 the president of Dallas Theological Seminary and Presbyterian minister John F. Walvoord published *The return of the Lord*, an account of a normative dispensationalism that emphasized the emerging contexts of the re-establishment of Israel and the early Cold War. 'The whole world is in a state of fearful expectation,' he began; 'the advent of the atomic bomb with kindred devastating weapons has brought the world face to face with the possibility of the doom of present civilization.'[83] Writing one decade after the devastation on Japanese cities, he considered that 'our generation' was 'characterised by renewed emphasis upon future things. The world is in a state of expectancy and a key to the future is widely sought.'[84] Arthur W. Kac, author of *The rebirth of the State of Israel – Is it of God or of men?* (1958), found similar significance in the fact that Israel had 'resumed statehood at the same time with the advent of the atomic era.'[85] 'We live in a period of world history when for the first time we are witnessing the beginning of the simultaneous fulfillment of all three world events which Jesus Christ listed as those which would herald His return,' he opined, listing the 'completion of the task of the propagation of the Gospel throughout the world,' a 'time of world-wide distress,' and the 'restoration of Israel.'[86] The rise of nuclear science and the re-establishment of the state of Israel figured as events dominating the evangelical millennial imagination of the second half of the twentieth century.

These trends continued as evangelicals struggled to theorize the events of the emerging Cold War. Walvoord addressed these questions with candour, and included in his study of *The return of the Lord* (1955) chapters on 'The future of Communism according to the Bible' and 'Can we have peace in our time?' His voice was cautious, identifying prophetic trends without pointing to prophetic fulfilments. Nevertheless, he insisted that the USSR should be understood to be a 'prototype' of the godless regime yet to come: 'already its subtle, God-defying philosophy has permeated the world and awaits the release which will come when the restraint of the Holy Spirit is lifted at the translation of the church.'[87] Elsewhere Walvoord clarified that the roots of this world empire lay not in the USSR but in the revival of the European community.[88] Similarly, he believed, the trend in the United Nations towards 'centralization of power and the popular acceptance of world government as the way out of world chaos is of great importance ... Such a movement of minds and nations is the foreshadowing of the acceptance of the world government of the tribulation time and the bowing of the knee to the world dictator of that day as the unifying personality.'[89] Even the re-establishment of a Jewish state in Palestine was represented as no more than a 'prophetic trend': 'in the last ten years, there has been a movement of God among Israel which has set the stage as never before for exactly that fulfilment which is predicted in the period immediately after the translation of the church.'[90] His caution was explained by the fact that the new state possessed only half of its ancient capital: 'It is perfectly obvious that the children of Israel do not possess this land today. Until they do there cannot possibly be fulfilment of the Scripture that pertains to the millennial kingdom of Christ.'[91] His measured prose pushed irrevocably towards its expected conclusion: 'The evidence points to the conclusion that the present age is fast running its course.'[92] His excitement was shared, several years later, by his Dallas Seminary colleague, J. Dwight Pentecost (born 1915), in *Things to come* (1958), a compendious survey of protestant eschatological thought, and, at a more popular level, in his *Prophecy for today: The middle east crisis and the future of the world* (1961). This latter title, which reached its fifteenth printing by 1974, adopted a kind of quasi-scientific precision in many of its claims, including its observation that 'one mathematician has figured out, considering only the prophecies concerning the first coming of Christ, that there is only one chance in 87 plus 93 zeros that the Bible could be right on the basis of guess alone.'[93] Meanwhile *Dispensationalism today* (1965), by Charles Caldwell Ryrie (born 1925), another Dallas Seminary professor, provided the definitive statement of the old dispensational orthodoxy. American writers dominated the dispensational market, but they had no monopoly on it. Their pseudo-scientific mode of biblical exegesis was regularly adopted in the writings of F.A. Tatford (1901–86), a council member of the Prophetic Witness Movement and a director of the UK Atomic Energy Authority.[94] His *Five minutes to midnight* (1970) was typical of his approach to prophetic interpretation. It engaged with scientific advances and broad cultural themes with its continual refrain, 'it has never been so late before,' an expression Tatford would use as the title of a later book.[95] And, at the height of the Cold War, that was exactly how it looked.

But not everyone shared the pessimism of the Fundamentalists. In the United States, a large number of evangelicals continued to dissociate themselves from the perceived excesses of Fundamentalism and established a series of institutions and organizations that would provide for the cultural resurgence of conservative protestants. These 'neo-evangelicals' founded the National Association of Evangelicals (1942), the National Religious Broadcasters (1944), the Evangelical Foreign Missionary Association (1945), the World Relief Commission (1945), the National Sunday School Association (1946), the National Association of Christian Schools (1947), the Evangelical Theological Society (1949), and *Christianity Today* (1956), the premier journal of their movement of theological renaissance. Their flagship institution was Fuller Theological Seminary (established 1947).[96] Its founder, radio evangelist Charles Fuller, gathered together the intellectual cream of the evangelical crop, and pre-eminent among their number for prophetic studies was George Eldon Ladd (1911–82).[97] Ladd's objective, throughout his career, was to 'rehabilitate' evangelical scholarship within the secular academy. The historic premillennialism he defended subverted many of the assumptions of dispensational scholars. And his followers, across the evangelical spectrum, worked hard to ensure the possibility of evangelical cultural interventions. His death coincided with their certainty of success as believers emerged out of the contest and into the era of the dominance of evangelical millennialism. His series of publications made little impact outside his faith community, but among evangelicals his influence was extensive: a survey of the members of a prominent evangelical academic society, conducted two years after his death, in 1984, discovered that Ladd's influence was comparable only to that of John Calvin.[98] The Fundamentalists had attracted the headlines while the new evangelicals were setting a formidable new agenda.

V

Throughout the twentieth century, premillennial writers continued to identify their eschatology as a barometer of evangelical orthodoxy. 'There is no greater bulwark against modern liberalism than the doctrine of the premillennial return of Christ,' John Walvoord explained, for 'modernists are never premillenarians.'[99] But even as he described his faith as a 'bulwark,' Walvoord was anticipating the hermeneutic revolution that would allow dispensational writers to overturn a century of settled convictions. J.N. Darby had argued that the only fulfilment of prophecy that Scripture encouraged believers to expect was the rapture. And his followers, on both sides of the Atlantic, all agreed. Futurism had to be aggressively pursued. But the lure of historicism was baited with the establishment of the state of Israel. And Walvoord was prepared to admit that biblical prophecy could be fulfilled in the period before the rapture, that 'more prophecies have ... been fulfilled ... in our day than in all the previous centuries since the first of our era,' and the annotations in the revised Scofield Bible (1967) agreed.[100] It was a recasting of dispensationalism that would find its most significant defence in the best-selling non-fiction title of the next decade.

Dispensationalism was entering the period of its greatest commercial and literary success. Throughout the early and mid-twentieth century, while evangelicals and Fundamentalists were growing and organizing, mainstream media outlets had continued to overlook their significance.[101] In Britain and North America, dispensationalism had grown in popularity at different speeds, for different reasons, among different theological constituencies, with different degrees of institutional support, and with different consequences. Those differing consequences would be made evident in and after the 1970s, with the political re-engagement of conservative evangelicals, and, in the later 1990s, the eventual dominance of their millennial imagination. For, in the last third of the twentieth century, dispensational writers would address larger audiences than the movement's founders could ever have imagined.

6
The Dominance of Evangelical Millennialism, 1970–2000

Evangelicalism in its modern guise, and especially in North America, is very much a creation of the 1970s. By the beginning of that decade, and 'almost by sheer tenacity,' the theologians and churchmen who had attempted to create an alternative movement to the Fundamentalism that had pulled conservative protestants from the cultural mainstream had succeeded in fashioning a 'new religious identity, and *evangelical* was its designation.'[1] While this new evangelicalism claimed the lineage of historical protestant orthodoxy, it owed much to the 'neo-evangelical' attempt to reformulate the role of conservative religion in an increasingly secular America, and, like the Fundamentalism it sought to replace, fashioned itself reactively but very much in conversation with the cultural moment of its emergence. In America, the new movement's rise to prominence was so rapid and its appeal so immediate that *Newsweek* designated 1976 as the 'year of the evangelical.' And there were good reasons for this claim: in the 1976 election, 34 per cent of Americans responding to a Gallup poll identified themselves as 'born-again' or 'evangelical,' and their number included each of the major candidates in that year's presidential election.[2] These events in the mid-1970s set the pattern for the movement's continuing influence. A series of presidents, including Jimmy Carter (president, 1977–81), Ronald Reagan (president, 1981–89), Bill Clinton (president, 1993–2001), and George W. Bush (president, 2001–9), indicated their commitment to evangelical faith as they issued public confessions of sin and pursued foreign policy goals that reflected, to a greater or lesser extent, the expectations of the dispensational eschatology with which they were most familiar or to which they found it expedient to allude.[3] The movement has continued to generate wide popular support: in 1998, 47 per cent of respondents to a Gallup poll identified themselves as 'born-again' or 'evangelical,' and numbers have not much declined since.[4] Many of these believers maintain robustly millennial hopes. Hal Lindsey's pop-dispensational block-buster, *The late great planet Earth* (1970), which turned out to be the best-selling non-fiction book of the decade, set a pattern for the shape of the political re-engagement of American evangelicals in the final third of the twentieth century. In 2004 it was reported that Pat Robertson (born 1930) and Jerry Falwell (1933–2007), two televangelists who shared a commitment to a politicized premillennial worldview, were claiming to communicate with 100 million supporters every week.[5] By the first years of the twenty-first century, its critics feared, the American dispensational lobby was 'probably' the 'most powerful' grassroots coalition in the United States.[6]

But the period that marked the numerical success of North American evangelicalism also witnessed its terminal European decline. In Britain, church membership statistics peaked in the later 1950s, and ever since have continued to fall.[7] British and Irish evangelicals have none of the political clout of their American brethren, and, increasingly, have come to repudiate the eschatological tenor of their faith. Since the 1970s British believers have grown away from the premillennialism that dominated in large sections of the movement in the later nineteenth and earlier twentieth centuries, and have developed and embraced a range of eschatological positions that have drawn more clearly on the confessional formulations of the reformation. The polemical tone of a number of British interventions, such as Stephen Sizer's *Christian Zionism: Road-map to Armageddon?* (2004), would have startled many American dispensationalists, who were more used to hearing its kind of robust critique of dispensationalism and its political implications from denizens of the secular left.

The increasing difference between American and European evangelicalism should not obscure their continued interaction. There is some evidence that the European critique of dispensationalism has fed the growing instability of this quintessentially American faith. Since the 1980s a number of prominent intellectuals from within evangelicalism have reflected upon its origins, development and goals, and their criticisms have repeatedly returned to concerns about the movement's eschatological predilections. The public outcry surrounding the scandals associated with prominent televangelists in the 1980s was followed by the subtle and internal deconstruction of the movement these erring saints were believed to represent. The credibility and coherence of the evangelical faith was questioned in a series of powerful and often insightful critiques that were published on either side of the Atlantic, including David F. Wells's *No place for truth* (1993), Mark A. Noll's *The scandal of the evangelical mind* (1994), Os Guinness's *Fit bodies, fat minds* (1995), Iain H. Murray's *Evangelicalism divided* (2000), and D.G. Hart's *Deconstructing Evangelicalism* (2004). These studies agreed that the evangelical movement had failed, and offered a range of possible explanations. Their conclusions were often withering. Noll was concerned by the retreat from scientific method, believing that 'dispensationalism and creationism stamped evangelicalism with a hyper-supernaturalism that prevented born-again Protestants from appreciating the God-given character of the phenomena that most humanist, social and natural scientific scholars study.'[8] Murray, by contrast, understood the failure of evangelicalism in terms of its insufficient supernaturalism in its retreat from conservative theories of biblical inspiration, and Wells in terms of its general abandonment of theological categories of thought. Guinness, like several of the others, identified dispensationalism as a critical reason for the failure of evangelicalism.

Under the barrage of sustained critique, the new definition of 'evangelical' became 'increasingly slippery.'[9] And many within and outside the movement have found the term increasingly unhelpful. Hart concluded his series of critiques by suggested that 'instead of trying to fix evangelicalism, born-again Protestants would be better off if they abandoned the category altogether,' for evangelicalism, 'as a religious identity ... does not exist.'[10] Ironically, these critiques were being offered as many other believers celebrated the movement's greatest cross-over into popular culture. Left Behind, a series of end-time novels which dramatized and demonstrated the continuing appeal of a conservative dispensational worldview, sold over 60 million copies between 1995 and 2007 and attracted a readership of one-tenth of the American population.[11] It was an ironic gesture of defiance from a movement which critics claimed did not exist. Far from causing evangelical marginality, as its critics claimed, dispensationalism was providing for the movement's most significant entry into the American pop-cultural mainstream. The success of Left Behind provided a foil for the 'scandal of the evangelical mind,' and showed that believers were deconstructing themselves at the moment of their greatest cultural influence.[12] This chapter will comment on the public profile of evangelical millennialism in the last third of the twentieth century, and will argue that the ascent of dispensationalism provided evangelicals with a greater public profile than they had long enjoyed. But this chapter will also argue that this success marked more clearly than ever the bankruptcy of evangelical identity, in that it marked the growing differences between the American and European religious habits of mind and among American evangelicals themselves, and that it provoked a backlash and, in the later 1990s, a struggle for the destiny of the movement. At the end of the twentieth century, the dominance of one variety of evangelical millennialism could not but provide for its ultimate deconstruction.

I

The new evangelicalism that emerged in the 1970s was powerfully shaped by the cultural revolution of the previous decade, a decade that witnessed, alongside the sexual revolution with which it is most often associated, a widespread religious revival which some historians have described as America's 'fourth great awakening.'[13] In the late 1960s Biblical prophecy was a central component of the message of the 'Jesus People,' a counter-cultural movement of born-again hippies who were mainly concentrated on the west coast of the United States.[14] Their eschatological anthem – 'I wish we'd all been ready,' by the Christian rock musician Larry Norman (1947–2008) – had been written at the request of a Korean War veteran turned campus evangelist, Hal Lindsey (born 1929).[15] The imagination of these Jesus People had been fed by such texts as *World aflame* (1965), by the emerging evangelical spokesman Billy Graham (born 1918), who, by the end of the century, would preach to more people than anyone else in history.[16] *World aflame* was a tour-de-force exhibition of the new evangelical pattern of social engagement. Like many other of the movement's texts, the book appeared socially and even politically engaged and demonstrated its author's interest in preaching to the times. Graham's analysis of Western cultural decay began with an overview of the destabilizing cultural trends he identified as 'flames out of control' – lawlessness, racial struggle, the ever-present threat of Communism, and that of 'uncontrolled science.' The central message of the book was clear, and would have been familiar to anyone who had attended any of Graham's evangelistic rallies: social evils were to be countered by the conversion of the individual, and converted individuals would align themselves with churches to make significant social and political interventions. This call for Christian action sat rather uneasily with the final section of *World aflame* – an account of the 'distant trumpets' that suggested the signs of the times and the imminent and unexpected rapture, still evidently contoured by the dispensational convictions from which Graham was beginning to slip.[17] The eschatological timetable of many prophecy believers was confirmed by the Jewish capture of Jerusalem in 1967. Jerry Falwell was later prepared to admit that the reoccupation was not necessarily a fulfilment of prophecy, but others were less cautious.[18] In the same year, the *New Scofield Bible* (1967), a revision of the earlier classic, offered a significant reinterpretation of the traditional dispensational claim that the rapture was the next event on the prophetic timetable. Earlier editions of the text (1909 and 1917) had maintained this claim, arguing that the rapture was the only event that believers could expect to experience – every other fulfilment of prophecy would come after their removal from the earth. But the *New Scofield Bible* responded to the events of 1948 by arguing that the second coming should be expected after Israel's restoration to the Promised Land.[19]

This idea that the foundation of Israel had been a 'paramount prophetic sign' found its most celebrated defence in the foundational textbook of late twentieth-century popular dispensationalism.[20] In 1969, Hal Lindsey resigned from Campus Crusade for Christ to found a ministry organization entitled 'The J.C. Light and Power Company' and to begin to put together a book that would exercise immense influence in and beyond the evangelical subcultures from which it emerged. This book, *The late great planet Earth* (1970), became the best-selling non-fiction work of the decade, according to the *New York Times*, whose sales rankings did not include figures from Christian bookshops, and went on to sell over 28 million copies in 54 languages.[21] Lindsey's claim that the establishment of the state of Israel had been a 'paramount prophetic sign' was rooted in his exegesis of Matthew 24:34 ('this generation shall not pass till all these things be fulfilled').[22] Lindsey explained that 'a generation in the Bible is something like forty years.' He suggested that, 'if this is a correct deduction, then within forty years or so of 1948,' the rapture could occur. 'Many scholars who have studied Bible prophecy all their lives believe that this is so.'[23]

With its massive sales and lurid claims, *The late great planet Earth* made an immediate impact on American public life. In 1971, when he was Governor of California, Ronald Reagan, whose debt to Lindsey would later become evident, expressed his belief that the prophecies of Ezekiel pointed to a nuclear exchange with the USSR: 'the day of Armageddon isn't far off … Ezekiel says that fire and brimstone will be rained upon the enemies of God's people. That must mean that they'll be destroyed by nuclear weapons.'[24] This approach to the interpretation of current affairs through the lens of biblical prophecy was confirmed by such parallel events as the Conference on Biblical Prophecy held in Jerusalem in 1971, which attracted thousands of evangelical delegates, and by a film version of Lindsey's book narrated by Orson Welles (1979), as well as Don Thompson's series of heavily didactic feature films, *A thief in the night* (1972), *A distant thunder* (1978), *Image of the beast* (1980) and

The prodigal planet (1983). The first of these films cost a mere $68 000 to produce but was one of the most widely distributed movies of the 1970s. Within 15 years it had been translated into three languages, seen by an audience of 100 million and, its director claimed, resulted in around four million conversions to evangelical faith.[25] Lindsey's revision of dispensationalism was presented with significantly greater scholarly panache by James Montgomery Boice (1938–2000) in *The last and future world* (1974), an exposition of biblical prophecy based on a series of sermons preached in Tenth Presbyterian Church, Philadelphia, a church with a long commitment to dispensational faith.[26] Despite the sobriety of his northern Presbyterian background, and his studies at Harvard, Princeton Theological Seminary and the University of Basel, Boice was confident in his prophetic conclusions, believing that 'there is very little' in the New Testament 'that can be interpreted as optimistic regarding the course of human history.'[27] His exposition of the 'this generation' passages followed Lindsey's approach: 'these verses seem to indicate that the Lord Jesus Christ will return within one generation of the repossession of Palestine and the reconquest of Jerusalem by the Jews.' 'If that is so,' Boice continued, 'the biblical length of a generation being about forty years, then Jesus may well return with forty years of 1948 (the year of the reestablishment of the state of Israel) or of 1967 (the year in which the old city of Jerusalem once again came into Jewish hands).'[28] And others were beginning to agree. Boice's suspicions were confirmed at the highest level in 1978 when President Jimmy Carter stated that 'the establishment of the nation of Israel is the fulfilment of biblical prophecy and the very essence of its fulfilment.'[29]

It is hardly surprising therefore that by the beginning of the 1980s an estimated eight million Americans were 'firmly committed' to the dispensational system, or that they had become powerful enough to help install a president who shared their convictions in 1981.[30] *The late great planet Earth* exercised enormous influence inside Reagan's White House, and a number of cabinet members, including Attorney General Ed Meese, Secretary of Defense Caspar Weinberger, and Secretary of the Interior James Watt, shared the president's dispensational views.[31] Significantly, it was in a speech to the National Association of Evangelicals (1983) that Reagan made his apocalyptic reference to the 'evil empire' of the USSR.[32] And *The late great planet Earth* was central to this emerging political-theological platform. Lindsey appears to have briefed staff at the Pentagon, as well as military intelligence committees and staff at the State Department and the American Air War College, and there is evidence that some in the military elite were attracted to his analyses.[33]

Dispensationalism grew in public influence as an increasing number of evangelical scholars returned to older, less politically qualified, premillennial approaches. The growth of these alternatives was encouraged by such publications as the commentaries on Revelation prepared by George Eldon Ladd (1972) and Robert H. Mounce (1977), and by significant theological reflections such as Robert H. Gundry's *The church and the tribulation* (1973).[34] As more and more evangelicals embraced Lindsey's news-making eschatology, many other believers grew concerned that some among their brethren found eschatology a little too interesting. 'Thank God there is a revival of second Adventism today in the light of the momentous events of the hour,' opined Bob Stokes, an evangelist with Trans World Radio. But, he added, evangelicals should beware the temptation of eschatological certainty, for 'all too often the Christian becomes interested in fascinating details which have little relevance to his witness, and the subject of the Second Coming instead of becoming a glorious hope only serves as a sentimental speculation.'[35] These concerns were shared by such leading evangelical intellectuals as Francis Schaeffer, a missionary to Europe and counter-cultural icon whose early association with the strictly separatist Bible Presbyterian Church gave way to a theologically informed engagement with Western culture that would exercise profound influence on the emerging Christian Right.[36] Schaeffer's early dispensationalism evolved into a broader, though still premillennial, engagement with ecological and aesthetic concerns, as a number of his disciples, including Wim Rietkerk, whose *The future great planet Earth* (1989) advanced a subtle deconstruction of populist doom-saying, developed and refined his earlier approach. It was too easy, Schaeffer believed, for evangelicals who expected the destruction of the world to stand by while its ecology imploded. And Rietkerk evidently agreed. Too many evangelicals defended 'a certain kind of doomsday thinking about the future of this world [that] has weakened our resistance to pollution.'[37] But the world was not to be destroyed in an apocalyptic conflagration, he claimed, for 'just as it suffers the consequences of sin, so will it share in the blessings of man's redemption in Christ' – and its future was to be 'great.'[38]

This reconsideration of doomsday thinking was evident even in Dallas Theological Seminary, in which scholars were proposing a major restatement of the movement's doctrinal axioms. But their reification of the system – known as 'progressive' dispensationalism – horrified the movement's traditionalists and the wider community of Fundamentalists. Taking account of recent work by evangelical biblical critics, including that of a number of those who had criticized dispensationalism, the foundational text of this new theological formulation, *Progressive dispensationalism* (1993), by Craig A. Blaising and Darrell L. Bock, suggested that the dichotomy between Israel and the church which had been so central as to define earlier varieties of dispensational faith ought now to be abandoned.[39] It was a powerful restatement of opinion that significantly altered the balance of evangelical debate. The old paradigms were being redefined in a world in which prophecy was appearing to be fulfilled. As one commentator put it, 'things are happening so fast that I bet even Hal Lindsey is confused!'[40]

II

Progressive dispensationalists were revising their creed even as their more conservative brethren addressed a very different kind of threat. In 1988, H. Wayne House, a prominent spokesperson for traditional dispensationalism, suggested that the 'premillennial position is probably more on the decline at the present time' than the eschatological options it contested.[41] The text in which House made that observation, *Dominion theology: Blessing or curse?* (1988), was engaging with a newly resurgent postmillennialism, the strident political ambitions of which were proving appealing to many socially minded evangelicals. This revitalized postmillennialism had become successful because of the increasing popularity of amillennialism and the recent resurgence of Reformed theology, driven in large part by theological output of the Banner of Truth and other like-minded publishers.

This shift in theological influence drove the widespread questioning of premillennialism in British and American evangelicalism. Publishers spotted the opportunity of facilitating debates between advocates of competing eschatological parties, from *Three views on the rapture* (1984), edited by Stanley N. Gundry, to *Three views on the millennium and beyond* (1999), edited by Darrell L. Bock, 15 years later. The existence of these debates represented the influence of an important new constituency within the trans-Atlantic evangelical community. It was Dutch Reformed theologians who were most obviously committed to calling believers back to its sixteenth-century commitments. Herman Bavinck (1854–1921) prepared his *Gereformeerde dogmatiek* (*Reformed dogmatics*, 4 vols [ET, 2004]) in the early twentieth century.[42] He had been acutely aware of the competing claims in the defence of latter-day glory, but, he argued, 'the Old Testament is decidedly not chiliastic. In its depiction of the messianic kingdom it describes the completing kingdom of God that is without end and lasts forever (Dan. 2:44), preceded by judgement, resurrection, and world renewal.'[43] And he believed that Scripture had as little to offer the Christian. 'Nowhere in the New Testament is there a ray of hope that the church of Christ will again come to power and dominion on earth,' he noted. 'The most it may look for is that, under kings and all who are in high positions, it may lead a quiet and peaceable life in all godliness and dignity (Rom. 13:1; 1 Tim. 2:2).'[44] The future held little immediate promise, for 'according to the incontrovertible testimony of Scripture, the history of humankind, both in the case of culture-producing and of uncultured nations, rather ends in a general apostasy and an appalling final struggle of a coalition of all satanic forces against God and his kingdom.'[45]

Bavinck's theological reflections were developed in exegetical terms by a number of Dutch Americans. One of the most influential of their interventions was made by *More than conquerors: An interpretation of the book of Revelation* (1939), by William Hendricksen, a writer whose series of commentaries on New Testament books have gone through multiple editions. Hendricksen's contribution was to argue that the literary structure of Revelation militated against a premillennial interpretation: 'A careful reading ... of Revelation has made it clear that the book consists of seven sections, and that these seven sections run parallel to each other. Each of them spans the entire dispensation from the first to the second coming of Christ ... now from one aspect, now from another.'[46] These conclusions were confirmed in dogmatic terms by G.C. Berkouwer (1903–96), a professor at the Free University of Amsterdam, whose influential study of *De wederkomst van Christus* (2 vols, 1961, 1963) was translated into English as *The return of Christ* (1972). Berkouwer moderated the traditional rejection by millennial theory by recognizing the 'unmistakable kernel of truth' it contained, but continued to defend the older confessional position.[47]

This assault on dispensationalism drew upon the traditional confessional claims of the reformation churches and found its most able defenders in the European denominations and those American groups which most clearly shared their perspective. The conclusions of *The momentous event* (1945), by the Irish Presbyterian theologian W.J. Grier, were accompanied in North America by J. Marcellus Kik, in his preterist interpretations of *Matthew twenty-four* (1948) and *Revelation twenty* (1955), and in Scotland by James Hamilton, in his preterist *Light on the 'last days': An historical review of 'days' long past* (1962).[48] But the key text of this Reformed resistance was provided by a member of staff at the Banner of Truth, Iain H. Murray, in *The puritan hope: Revival and the interpretation of prophecy* (1971), which exercised enormous influence on a rising generation of evangelical theologians, encouraging the conclusion promulgated among others by Jon Zens, author of *Dispensationalism: A Reformed inquiry into its leading figures and features* (1978), that whatever its origins in the confessional denominations, 'dispensationalism is opposed to historic and Biblical Calvinism.'[49] The point was perhaps made most vividly in John H. Gerstner's *Wrongly dividing the word of truth: A critique of dispensationalism* (1991; second edition, 2000). The general tenor of Gerstner's claim that dispensationalism possessed 'dubious' evangelical credentials might have been predicted from the illustration on the dust-jacket of its second edition of a hatchet buried in a Scofield Bible.[50]

The challenge to premillennialism was readily adopted by British believers across and beyond the evangelical denominations. It was an approach developed at popular level in such publications as *I saw heaven opened: The message of Revelation* (1975), a contribution to IVP's widely-read and enduring series of commentaries, The Bible Speaks Today. The book's author, Michael Wilcock, a Church of England clergyman, admitted that 'most readers of the Bible have a love–hate relationship with the last of its sixty-six books,' but explained that his project emerged from midweek studies in the mysteries of Revelation in the everyday life of his congregation. His reading of Revelation 20 was strictly non-imaginative, demythologizing the conclusions of premillennial scholars to suggest instead that the chapter 'should not stand on its own as an independent framework, but should be taken as a repetition in highly coloured language of the sequence already made sufficiently clear in the non-symbolic teaching of the Gospels and Letters' – and therefore conceived of the chapter in a broadly amillennial style.[51] Bruce A. Milne, a leading British Baptist, confirmed this approach in *I want to know what the Bible says about the end of the world* (1979). Evidently thinking of *The late great planet Earth*, Milne worried that 'racily written paperbacks claiming to recount the biblical teaching on the events leading up to the end of the world have claimed sales reaching over a million copies.'[52] But, he insisted, their conclusions were too often unwarranted, for 'Jesus did not encourage a 'signs of the times' mentality,' and therefore 'our conviction concerning Christ's appearing ought not to be tied to a particular reading of the international political scene or the deep sense of crisis of our age.'[53] Indeed, 'the man who claims to have a detailing blueprint of the events of the Lord's return is suspect from the very outset. To be able to wrap it all up is in fact to miss it altogether.'[54] These kinds of texts were influential in stemming the premillennial advance – in certain sectors of evangelicalism, at least – but their deference and probity created difficulties for the development of non-speculative eschatological approaches. It was significant, for example, that the 'Contours of Christian Theology' series, published by IVP as a state-of-evangelicalism contribution to ecumenical doctrinal debate, appears to have attempted for over 20 years to find an author for the series' final volume on eschatology. British evangelicals grew increasingly suspicious of apocalyptic rhetoric, which was increasingly identified with the horrors of sectarian conflict in Northern Ireland and the perceived anti-intellectualism of American Fundamentalists.[55] It was a sign that the British evangelical mainstream was beginning to position itself at a critical distance from that of the United States.

This moment of eschatological uncertainty created its own opportunities. Throughout the 1980s, for example, a number of evangelical writers took advantage of this resurgence of non-premillennial writing to expound their own evolving political positions. These promoters of Christian Reconstruction believed that the 'false theology' of dispensationalism had caused 'many Christians' to 'abdicate their responsibilities toward economics, education, science, and civil government. This conception of the future has accelerated the debilitating doctrine that the end of all things is near, leading to further inactivity on the part of God's people.'[56] Their alternative programme of action was advanced in a series of publications including David Chilton's *Paradise restored: A biblical theology of dominion* (1985), Gary DeMar's *Something greater is here: Christian Reconstruction in biblical perspective* (1988), and Kenneth L. Gentry's *The beast of Revelation* (1989).[57] Others retained the older amillennial perspective, including O. Palmer Robertson, whose study of *The Israel of God: Yesterday, today, and tomorrow* (2000) launched a direct assault on popular Zionist assumptions.[58] 'It would seem evident that the return of the Jews to Palestine in the twentieth century ... should not be regarded as a fulfilment of Ezekiel's prophecy,' Robertson contended. 'Israel's twentieth-century rebirth as a nation did not involve any opening of graves, resurrection of the body, inpouring of the Spirit of God, or renewal of life through faith in Jesus Christ.' Therefore, he continued, 'however the establishment of the state of Israel may be viewed, it does not fulfil the expectation of Ezekiel.'[59] Robertson's work had a perceptible political subtext. His preface noted his sensitivity to the situation of Palestinians and a potential conflict of interest in Christian missions: 'how sad it would be if evangelical Christians who profess to love the Jewish people should become a tool in misdirecting their faith and expectation.'[60] Kim Riddlebarger agreed, and in *A case for amillennialism: Understanding the end times* (2003) he complained of the tendency in eschatological debate for *ad hominem* argumentation: 'dispensationalists accuse amillennialists of being anti-Semitic, liberal, or of spiritualizing the Bible by not taking the Bible literally,' while 'amillennialists accuse dispensationalists of being literalists who are prone to sensationalism.'[61] But Riddlebarger believed he understood why amillennialism remained a minority position. Amillennialists, he noted, 'do not relate current events to the Bible' and prefer to work from the basis of 'a distinctive, comprehensive Reformed theology. Therefore, amillennialism will never be as compelling a system as dispensationalism.' But it could nevertheless be more reliable, for 'in the hands of able communicators, such as Tim LaHaye and Jerry Jenkins, John Hagee, Jack Van Impe, Dave Hunt, and Hal Lindsey, the dispensational understanding of prophetic biblical texts can be applied to virtually any geopolitical crisis mentioned on the evening news ... This creates a compelling sense of urgency which makes a more theologically grounded system like amillennialism seem almost irrelevant to everyday Christian living.'[62] However less exciting it appeared, Riddlebarger concluded, amillennialism should be understood to be the 'historic Protestant understanding of the millennial age.'[63]

Of course, these charges, particularly those focusing on the prophetic relevance of Israel, precipitated counter-charges. As early as 1980, the British-born and Israeli-based evangelist Lance Lambert (born 1931) resigned himself to ongoing debate in his study of *The uniqueness of Israel* (1980): 'the bitter argument and controversy over the subject of Israel leaves me unmoved, for time itself will vindicate the truth.'[64] But others have been more forceful in their defence of the twentieth century's pre-eminent prophetic assumption. Evangelicals from across the theological spectrum have responded to this rising amillennialism and its increasingly agnostic stance towards political Zionism, from the orthodox Calvinism of Barry E. Horner's *Future Israel: Why Christian anti-Judaism must be challenged* (2007) to the politically engaged dispensationalism of Paul R. Wilkinson's *For Zion's sake: Christian Zionism and the role of John Nelson Darby* (2007). God's promises to the Jews, bound up with his promises of millennial glory, were worth defending.

III

But, in the later 1990s, not everyone was expecting the end of the world. Outside evangelicalism, some of the most prominent cultural commentators agreed on an alternative series of projections that identified in the third millennium the global dominance of liberal democracy and the economic system on which it was based. Their tone was euphoric. Francis Fukuyama, arguing from the collapse of European Communism in the later 1980s, suggested that the world was witnessing the triumph of Western political values, and with that, he argued, the 'end of history': 'what we may be witnessing is not just the end of the Cold War, or the passing of a particular period of post-war history, but the end of history as such ... that is, the end point of mankind's ideological evolution and the universalization of Western liberal democracy as the final form of human government.'[65] Others agreed, expanding the basic terms of Fukuyama's argument into a wide variety of cultural fields. Their narratives combined in a teleological theory of secularization. Historians identified the 'death of Christian Britain,' explaining that the extension of long-term patterns of ecclesiastical affiliation would lead to the disappearance of the established churches by the middle of the twenty-first century.[66] With secular liberalism on the rise and churches on the decline, it seemed that post-modernity had evacuated the West of its older religious affiliations.

None of the participants in this debate could have imagined that the significance of the millennial convictions of evangelical Christians would so quickly become apparent. But in the late 1990s evangelicals, especially in America, began to find new confidence in the public arena and to wield a cultural influence that their premillennial convictions denied could ever exist. It was in their moment of greatest influence that these American evangelicals imagined the disappearance of their movement and the destruction of their nation. For, from the mid-1990s, a series of apocalyptic novels emerged from evangelical subcultures to sell 60 million copies, to dominate best-seller lists and to call for a radical reinterpretation of the American cultural 'mainstream.'[67] The success of Left Behind was entirely unexpected – among those involved in their production, and most obviously among those who imagined that the variety of fundamentalist piety they represented had long been dismissed to the social margins.[68] Yet, as its critics have realized, the evidence from this 'alien world' is that American religion, and particularly protestant evangelicalism, is 'dumbing down' as the erstwhile liberal hegemony gives way to the 'messianic and eschatological forces of biblical faith.'[69] And the combination of those forces can wreak havoc.

The success of this cultural revolution was assisted by continuing turbulence in the middle east. In 1991, Ed Hindson, author of *End times, the middle east, and the New World Order* (1991) and Vice President of Missouri Baptist College, noted that the 'recent Gulf War was the most televised and publicized war ever ... in many ways ... a microcosm of the great end-times conflict known as the Battle of Armageddon.'[70] And, reflecting on the response to the conflict of American believers, he stated his conviction that 'most evangelicals are genuinely concerned about prophetic events and sincerely anticipate the coming of Christ.'[71] That conviction was consolidated one decade later, when the terrorist attacks on Washington and New York in September 2001 heralded the return of a new kind of 'fundamentalism' that shook the complacency of secular post-modernity to its very foundations. The post-modern has given way to the post-secular as the era of the conflict of civilizations first described by Samuel P. Huntingdon in the mid-1990s was confirmed by the attacks of 9/11. But the subsequent 'war on terror' has, its critics claim, all the hallmarks of evangelical conspiracy. In the USA, and far beyond, a rush of books, articles and documentaries has provided a series of explanations for what many critics consider to be the religiously-motivated errors of the policies and preferences of successive presidential administrations.[72] And yet the target of this polemic is much larger than it might at first appear. No one talks about the 'end of history' any more. Francis Fukuyama's brilliant study may have defined the political environment of the mid-1990s, with all its hope in the thawing of the Cold War, but the concept has been replaced, however fractiously, by Huntingdon's 'clash of civilizations.'[73] It came as no surprise to many evangelicals – their prophetic literature had long anticipated the kind of conflicts illustrated both in the Cold War and in the 'war on terror.' But what was new about the latter conflict was the perception generated by some in the mainstream media that evangelicals were now actively shaping the paradigms of military engagement – and that current affairs were beginning to replicate their apocalyptic hopes and fears.

IV

And so, at the early twenty-first century, both evangelicals and their critics have come to agree that we are living in apocalyptic times. The beginning of the third millennium has heralded a geopolitical and economic environment as unstable as that of the end of the second millennium was unexpected. But the millennial faith of evangelicals continues to speak to the culture, primarily in the United States, but consequently on both sides of the Atlantic. Paul S. Boyer, perhaps the leading historian of popular apocalyptic belief, has recently noted that the prophetic beliefs of contemporary evangelicals are in a 'shadowy but vital way ... helping mould grassroots attitudes toward current U.S. foreign policy.' After all, when George W. Bush ('our born-again president') describes his foreign-policy objective in theological terms as a 'global struggle against "evildoers,"' and when he 'casts Saddam Hussein as a demonic, quasi-supernatural figure who could unleash "a day of horror like none we have ever known,"' he was 'not only playing upon our still-raw memories of 9/11. He is also invoking a powerful and ancient apocalyptic vocabulary that for millions of prophecy believers conveys a specific and thrilling message of an approaching end – not just of Saddam, but of human history as we know it.'

Astute cultural observers – whether they are believers, sceptics or scholars – are increasingly aware of the rhetorical implications of this kind of eschatological belief. For many premillennialists, the policies of the George W. Bush administration may have appeared to be 'in harmony with God's prophetic plan: a plan that will bring human history to its apocalyptic denouement and usher in the longed-for epoch of righteousness, justice, and peace.' But many believers also expect that plan to include the annihilation of the Muslim world, the 'genocide' of which becomes the 'ultimate means of prophetic fulfilment.' Correctly, Boyer argues, 'the current political climate in the United States cannot be fully understood' without 'close attention to the prophetic scenario embraced by millions of American citizens.'[74] Darryl G. Hart may be right – evangelicalism may not exist.[75] But the millennial beliefs of many of those who identify themselves by that term are exercising enormous cultural and political significance. At the beginning of the twenty-first century evangelical millennialism may be a more important cultural force than at any other time in its history.

Conclusion

This book has described the eschatological commitments that have evolved over five centuries to dominate large and influential sections of contemporary evangelicalism in the trans-Atlantic world. It has documented the denial of evangelical millennialism in the reformation confessions of faith, the development of evangelical millennialism in the seventeenth and eighteenth centuries, and the dominance of evangelical millennialism in the modern trans-Atlantic world. But in describing that evolution, this book has also paid attention to the continual contest between competing systems of millennial ideas. It is not simply that amillennialism gave way to postmillennialism in the early eighteenth century, and that this postmillennialism was disrupted by dispensational premillennialism until the unanticipated marketability of Left Behind plunged dispensational thinking, with all of its expectations of increasing marginalization, into logical, theological and exegetical incoherence.[1] Evangelical millennial thinking has advanced along a clear trajectory but without necessarily convincing those believers who continue to adhere to the amillennialism of the reformation confessions, recently revived in popularity by Dutch and Dutch-American theologians, or to the postmillennialism that is now increasingly associated with American Reformed theologians and their charismatic and politically engaged fellow travellers. And we have also noted that the relatively late emergence of these three millennial paradigms – amillennialism, premillennialism and postmillennialism – has not negated the possibility of alternative structures of millennial belief. In its social historical survey of important elements of the print culture of this variety of popular protestantism, this book has documented the competing and contested formulations of the hopes and fears that evangelicals have developed in their reading of biblical eschatology. *Evangelical millennialism in the trans-Atlantic world, 1500–2000* has described these changes, their consequences, and their ongoing significance within the evolving theological, social, political and geographical contexts of evangelical belief.

Of course, there are obvious difficulties in drawing attention to similarities of thinking across such a broad range of evangelical texts, contexts and cultures. One of the most significant of these difficulties may be the encouragement of an assumption that the eschatological debates of evangelicals have centred on millennial themes. Throughout the tradition, however, discussions which have ranged across the lines of millennial distinction have focused on other issues. These discussions have been carried on by evangelical household names. Some have concerned the fate of the righteous. One of the most popular Baptist devotional writers of the early twentieth century was F.B. Meyer (1847–1929), whose outstanding marketability developed despite his insistence that the resurrection had occurred at the end of the first century, a fact which explained, he believed, why there were so few Christians in the second century compared with the first.[2] Others have contested the fate of the lost. Some evangelicals have pursued options that have long been considered heretical, including Andrew Jukes (1815–1901), another popular devotional writer, who drifted off into universalism with the financial assurance of a private patron, and Robin Parry, editorial director of one of the most eminent British evangelical publishers, who published *The evangelical universalist* (2008) under the pseudonym Gregory MacDonald.[3] More controversially, John Stott, an Anglican minister listed by *TIME* magazine as among the 100 most influential people in the world, defended the conditional immortality that, as we have seen, scandalized earlier generations of believers.[4] But the cautious and ambivalent response of the broader British evangelical community demonstrated that conditional immortality was now less deviant than once it had appeared. A report published by the Evangelical Alliance (2000), a coalition of churches and organizations that claims to represent over a million British Christians, confirmed the traditional teaching that the damned would be tormented, but did not insist that their torment would be eternal.[5] The fact that theologians of the calibre of Stott could even consider alternatives to traditional teaching on hell sent shockwaves through conservative evangelical communities on both sides of the Atlantic. The debate has demonstrated that new formulations of its eschatological hope continue to spring up in the most unexpected locations even as it has highlighted one aspect of evangelicalism's discontinuity from the past. These debates, with the late rise of the modern premillennial and postmillennial taxonomies,

demonstrate that the eschatological options of contemporary evangelicals are at once narrower and broader than those of the earlier centuries.
Evangelicals have continued to speculate about eschatology, but, while in
America the dispensational hegemony has been disrupted by the rise of a
politicized postmillennialism, in Britain the most contested focus of that
speculation has shifted from the communal consequences of the millennial age to the individual consequences of the rejection of the gospel.

The greatest challenge in the writing of this book – the sheer diversity
of evangelical eschatological options – is perhaps the strongest evidence
that end-times thinking remains a secondary issue in many constituencies within the modern movement. As in the seventeenth century, so in
the twenty-first, eschatology has been generally reduced to a secondary
status, and evangelicals have felt free to adopt a range of perspectives
without believing themselves to have overstepped the boundaries of the
movement. But when those perspectives begin to undermine central
tenets of the Catholic faith it is surely evidence that evangelicalism can
no longer be said to exist. This conclusion will therefore reflect upon
the degree of continuity that exists between earlier and later evangelicals by tracing the development of a number of central themes in
eschatological thinking, arguing that the discontinuities cannot always
be explained by the Enlightenment influences that much of the current
historiography links to the emergence of evangelicalism in the early
eighteenth century.

I

The slow pace of the development of evangelical millennialism is
perhaps most obvious in the area of its hermeneutics. A series of basic
hermeneutical assumptions have governed the conclusions that expositors have reached from the seventeenth century to the present day. Of
course, a number of hermeneutical assumptions have been abandoned,
especially as Enlightenment categories of interpretation fostered new
approaches to the study of Scripture. One of the grounding assumptions of apocalyptic exegesis in the early post-reformation period, as
we noticed, was historicism, the assumption that large parts of biblical prophecy referred to the broad sweep of the history of the church,
from its inception to the second coming. Early attempts at commentary
therefore combined historical and exegetical labour. This approach
elevated historical writing almost to the status of Scripture: history was
necessary for Scripture's proper interpretation. And so John Bale, reformation bishop of Ossory, claimed that the writing of history was second

in importance only to the translation of Scripture itself.[6] Writers such as John Foxe and James Ussher therefore agreed that the seal, bowl and trumpet judgements could be allocated specific instances of fulfilment within the past history of the church. As evangelical exegesis developed through the seventeenth century, both within and outside the puritan movement, this historicist approach governed the developing eschatology. God was active in history, these historicists believed, and prophecy gave an indication of his role.

But while early modern historicism was popular it was never monolithic. While most historicists used Revelation to trace the entire history of the church, certain among their number nodded towards the opinion that the book's content was primarily concerned with events surrounding the fall of Jerusalem in AD 70 and with political developments in the first century after Christ. This emerging 'preterism' was voiced, for example, in later editions of the Geneva Bible and in some of the parliamentary sermons of John Owen. It was always a minority position, however, and it took more than a century for preterist expositors to advance to the more radical claims that, as the British Congregationalist J. Stuart Russell claimed in *The parousia: A critical inquiry into the New Testament doctrine of our Lord's second coming* (1878, second edition 1887), the return of Jesus had been already figuratively completed with the destruction of Jerusalem. With claims like this, the preterist approach grew to be associated with the radical or 'liberal' fringe of protestantism.[7] But while moderate preterist ideas exercised some influence on the evangelical mainstream, the historicist approach outlined in the sixteenth and seventeenth centuries set an agenda that remained current within evangelical circles until its moment of disjunction in the immediate aftermath of the French revolution.

The historicist consensus was interrupted by the sudden popularity of prophetic 'futurism.' This interpretive approach, which insisted that Revelation dealt mainly with events at the end of the age, grew in popularity after the European revolutions generated evangelicalism's moment of profound discontinuity with its prophetic past. The rapid and widespread adoption of futurism was one of the most radical developments in nineteenth-century evangelical eschatology, and reflected to some extent the increasing popularity of an innovative premillennialism. Historicism had not required the adoption of any particular millennial theory – Jonathan Edwards had advanced a postmillennial historicism while Isaac Newton, in the late seventeenth century, and Edward Irving, in the early nineteenth century, had preferred its premillennial equivalent. But the rise of a new variety of premillennialism – the 'dispensationalism' advanced by J.N. Darby – premised the rejection of historicism as an outworking of its complex distinction between Israel and the church. Darby's rapidly-developing dispensationalism was widely disseminated, and severed one important link between nineteenth-century evangelicals and the majority of their post-reformation forebears.[8] In its most radical form, this new premillennialism contested that there could be no expected fulfilments of prophecy before the rapture – not even the emergence of the Antichrist. This futurism was popularized through prophetic conferences and journals on both sides of the Atlantic, and, despite its repudiation of the papal Antichrist motif, a founding assumption of reformation eschatology, soon became the hermeneutic of choice for the emerging Fundamentalist movement at the century's end. For futurists, the new century looked bleak.

Nevertheless, the century that seemed to validate futurism's pessimistic prophetic scenarios actually witnessed the widespread reversal of its hermeneutical approach. Twentieth-century evangelicals did continue to adhere to premillennial options, at a popular level at least, and particularly within North America. The eschatological preferences of Anglo-American Fundamentalists reiterated the basic themes of nineteenth-century futurism, and their approach was provided with classic expression in the *Scofield reference Bible* (1909; second edition, 1917). Its relative sobriety degenerated into an excessive pop-dispensationalism that was most marked by the success of Hal Lindsey's *The late great planet Earth* (1970). But Lindsey's work overturned the tradition: his 'dispen-sensationalism' modified the futurist tradition to incorporate specific references to fulfilments of prophecy in the period before the rapture.[9] Lindsey grounded his expectations in the significance of the establishment of the state of Israel in 1948, and hinted darkly that great events could be expected within 40 years of that date.[10] Events would, of course, undermine Lindsey's suggestions. But the flood of popular eschatological writing, almost always from a dispensational perspective, has not reversed his trend back towards a limited historicism with a specific interest in the setting of dates – or the identification of events in the 'church age' before the rapture as specific fulfilments of prophecy. Dispensational futurists have been happy to turn back to a limited historicism as they have come to believe that a specific event in the present age can be identified as the fulfilment of prophecy and therefore, ironically, as confirmation of the wider futurist perspective. At a popular level, at least, dispensational writers rarely explain how these purported historical fulfilments of prophecy can cohere with their repeated statements that Christ could return at any moment, and that nothing more need be fulfilled before the rapture can take place. Nevertheless, with their speculation about political events, and their interest in chronological structures, it is in the limited historicism of these pop-dispensational writers that contemporary evangelical writers show greatest continuity with their early modern peers.

More generally, at a scholarly level, evangelical scholars have tended not to be impressed by popular futurism or its revival of a limited historicism. Premillennialists in the academy – such as George E. Ladd and Robert H. Gundry – responded to this mood of 'dispensensationalism' by articulating a confident, conservative and exegetical eschatology without pandering to the mass-market expectations exploited by some of their peers.[11] Outside the ranks of premillennialists, throughout the last century, scholars in universities and mainstream seminaries have moved steadily towards the 'idealism' of the Dutch amillennial tradition. This approach – perhaps best summarized in Hendricksen's *More than conquerors* (1939) – understands Revelation to be organized as a series of pictures that teach timeless truths about the relationship between the church and the world and which resist specific historical applications. In a sense, if pop-dispensationalists take evangelicals back to the exegetical style of wild-eyed seventeenth-century fanatics, this idealism takes evangelicals back to the relative sobriety of the sixteenth-century confessions of faith. Perhaps this modern evangelical hermeneutic has less in common with the interpretive schemes of puritans than the historicism, preterism or futurism the movement had earlier preferred.

The study of the evangelical millennial tradition is therefore far from complete. This book has implicitly engaged with the debate about the origins and identity of evangelicalism. It has not disputed Bebbington's dating of the emergence of evangelicalism in the 1730s, nor his claim that the new movement added a new epistemological confidence to the theological structures of the seventeenth century. But it has noted the existence of a series of continuities and discontinuities between the eschatological positions developed in the sixteenth and seventeenth centuries and those that grew in popularity thereafter. The eschatological conclusions of early modern believers were grounded in hermeneutical approaches and a political context that looked increasingly old-fashioned as the eighteenth century waned. Yet, at the beginning of the twenty-first century, the urgent and often political prophetic enquiry of North American premillennialists can seem closer to the puritan legacy than the passivity of many of their amillennial or postmillennial cousins.

Future studies of evangelical millennialism should reconsider the development of a theology of prophetic Israel and the emergence of political Zionism: while the Geneva Bible took a lead in emphasizing the 'conversion of the Jews' motif, puritans increasingly theorized the physical return of Jews to the promised land, in a discourse that has dominated recent discussions of the relationship between certain varieties of evangelical eschatology and the foreign policies of successive American presidential administrations.[12] In a parallel concern, which has attracted significantly less scholarly interest, early modern and later evangelicals also theorized the prophetic future of Islam: the threat of Islam in puritan writing mirrored the geopolitical tensions of the early modern period, while the increasing security of western Europe in recent centuries precipitated a waning interest in the threat of Islam, which has recently revived with the 'war on terror' in the early years of the twenty-first century.[13] A sense of the danger of the Roman Catholic Church has experienced similar ebbs and flows: while Catholicism represented the nadir of protestant reformation, and puritan writers repeatedly dismissed it in apocalyptic terms, evangelicals are rethinking their traditional hostility to Rome with the rise of secularism and the 'culture wars' in the North American political landscape. In the recent Left Behind novels, perhaps most significantly, the Pope and apparently non-evangelical Catholic laity are included among those taken by the rapture.[14] Future studies of evangelical millennialism should also take account of the variously constructed relationship between the church and eschatology, the 'now' and the 'not yet,' discussing the possibility of progressive revelation and the provision of extraordinary gifts as the end of the age approached: within this context, the twentieth-century turn to biblical theology, demonstrating the influence of Geerhardus Vos, has emphasized the church's current position in the overlapping of the ages, a variant of Reformed theology now controversially developed in some of the 'kingdom now' perspectives of the charismatic movement.

II

What this book has established, however, is that trans-Atlantic evangelical millennialism has a sustained importance in its religious and cultural impact. This book has described the millennial hopes that have evolved over five centuries to dominate large and influential sections of contemporary Christianity in the trans-Atlantic world. It has traced the oscillation of influence of evangelical millennial ideas, which have sometimes emerged on one or other side of the Atlantic, sometimes to influence the other and sometimes to emerge as an independent tradition. It has argued that these hopes have developed at different speeds, for different reasons, among different theological constituencies and with different consequences among evangelicals on either side of the Atlantic. It has argued that these ideas have achieved a sustained and perhaps unmatched significance. And these ideas are more important than ever before. For, in the modern world, and reacting to its increasingly apocalyptic mood, a growing number of evangelicals wait for that time when the knowledge of God shall cover the earth 'as the waters cover the sea' (Isaiah 11:9).

Notes

Introduction

1. I assessed the theological significance of this literary genre in *Rapture fiction and the evangelical crisis* (Webster, NY: Emmaus, 2006) and traced its origins and development in *Writing the rapture: Prophecy fiction in evangelical America* (Oxford: Oxford University Press, 2009).
2. See, for example, Steve Brouwer et al., *Exporting the American Gospel: Global Christian Fundamentalism* (New York: Routledge, 1996), and Gabriel Abraham Almond et al., *Strong religion: The rise of fundamentalisms around the world* (Chicago: University of Chicago Press, 2003).
3. See, for example, Steve Bruce, *The rise and fall of the new Christian right: Conservative protestant politics in America, 1978–1988* (Oxford: Clarendon Press, 1988); Steve Bruce et al. (eds), *The rapture of politics: The Christian right as the United States approaches the year 2000* (London: Transaction Publishers, 1995); and Martin Durham, *The Christian Right, the far right and the boundaries of American conservatism* (Manchester: Manchester University Press, 2000). See also Robert Fuller, *Naming the Antichrist: The history of an American obsession* (New York: Oxford University Press, 1995), and, more generally on the political implications of religious conservatism, Terry Eagleton, *Holy terror* (Oxford: Oxford University Press, 2005).
4. See, for two most useful among the many discussions of this phenomenon, Paul Boyer, *When time shall be no more: Prophecy belief in modern American culture* (Cambridge, MA: Belknap Press of Harvard University Press, 1992), and Nicholas Guyatt, *Have a nice doomsday: Why millions of Americans are looking forward to the end of the world* (London: Ebury Press, 2007). On the political implications of evangelical prophetic belief, see, more generally, Erling Jorstad, *The politics of doomsday: Fundamentalists of the far right* (Nashville, TN: Abingdon Press, 1970); John M. Werly, 'Premillennialism and the paranoid style,' *American Studies* 18 (1977), 39–55; C.H. Lippy, 'Waiting for the end: The social context of American apocalyptic religion,' in L. Zamora (ed.), *The apocalyptic vision in America: Interdisciplinary essays on myth and culture* (Bowling Green, OH: Bowling Green University Popular Press, 1982), 37–63; Robert Clouse, 'The New Christian Right, America, and the Kingdom of God,' *Christian Scholars Review* 12 (1983), 3–16; Richard N. Ostling, 'Armageddon and the end times: Prophecies of the last days surface as a campaign issue,' *TIME* (November 5, 1984), 73; James Mills, 'The serious implications of a 1971 conversation with Ronald Reagan: A footnote to current history,' *San Diego Magazine* (August 1985), 141; Grace Halsell, *Prophecy and politics: Militant evangelists on the road to nuclear war* (Westport, CT: Lawrence Hill, 1986); Richard H. Popkin, 'The triumphant apocalypse and the catastrophic apocalypse,' in Avner Cohen and Steven Lee (eds), *Nuclear weapons and the future of humanity* (Totowa, NJ: Rowman & Allanheld, 1986), 131–49; Ed Dobson and Ed Hindson, 'Apocalypse now? What fundamentalists believe

about the end of the world,' *Policy Review* 38 (1986), 16–23; Andrew J. Weigert, 'Christian eschatological identities and the nuclear context,' *Journal for the Scientific Study of Religion* 27 (1988), 175–91; Mark G. Toulouse, 'Pat Robertson: Apocalyptic theology and American foreign policy,' *Journal of Church and State* 31:1 (1989), 73–99; Kurt Ritter, 'Reagan's 1964 TV speech for Goldwater: Millennial themes in American political rhetoric,' in Martin J. Medhurst and Thomas W. Benson (eds), *Rhetorical dimensions in media: A critical casebook*, second edition (Dubuque, IA: Kendall / Hunt, 1991), 58–72; Charles B. Strozier, *Apocalypse: On the psychology of fundamentalism in America* (Boston, MA: Beacon Press, 1994); Donald E. Wagner, *Anxious for Armageddon: A call to partnership for middle eastern and western Christians* (Scottdale, PA: Herald Press, 1995); Daniel Wojcik, 'Embracing doomsday: Faith, fatalism, and apocalyptic beliefs in the nuclear age,' *Western Folklore* 55:4 (1996), 297–330; Thomas Robbins and Susan Palmer (eds), *Millennium, messiahs and mayhem* (New York: Routledge, 1997); David Katz and Richard Popkin, *Messianic revolution: Radical religious politics to the end of the second millennium* (New York: Penguin, 1999); Philip H. Melling, *Fundamentalism in America: Millennialism, identity and militant religion* (Edinburgh: Edinburgh University Press, 1999); Orestis Lindermayer, 'Europe as Antichrist: North American pre-millenarianism,' in Stephen Hunt (ed.), *Christian millenarianism: From the early church to Waco* (Bloomington, IN: Indiana University Press, 2001), 39–49; Didi Herman, 'Globalism's "siren song": The United Nations and international law in Christian Right thought and prophecy,' *The Sociological Review* 49:1 (2001), 56–77; Gershom Gorenberg, *The end of days: Fundamentalism and the struggle for the Temple Mount* (New York: Oxford University Press, 2002); Melani McAlister, 'Prophecy, politics and the popular: The *Left Behind* series and Christian fundamentalism's New World Order,' *South Atlantic Quarterly* 102:4 (2003), 773–98; Peter Yoonsuk Paik, 'Smart bombs, serial killing, and the rapture: The vanishing bodies of imperial apocalypticism,' *Postmodern Culture* 14:1 (2003), available at http://muse.jhu.edu/journals/pmc/index.html, accessed 19 January, 2008; Mark Stover, 'A kinder, gentler teaching of contempt? Jews and Judaism in contemporary protestant evangelical children's fiction,' *Journal of Religion & Society* 7 (2005), available online at http://moses.creighton.edu/JRS/, accessed 19 January, 2008; Timothy Weber, *On the road to Armageddon: How evangelicals became Israel's best friend* (Grand Rapids, MI: Baker, 2005); Rammy M. Haija, 'The Armageddon lobby: Dispensationalist Christian Zionism and the shaping of US policy towards Israel-Palestine,' *Holy Land Studies* 5:1 (2006), 75–95; Klaus J. Milich, 'Fundamentalism hot and cold: George W. Bush and the 'Return of the Sacred",' *Cultural Critique* 62 (2006), 92–125; Kevin Phillips, *American theocracy: The peril and politics of radical religion, oil, and borrowed money in the 21st century* (New York: Viking, 2006); Joseph Purcell, 'Left Behind: Depictions of Europe as an American other in the premillennial imagination' (unpublished BA thesis, University of Manchester, 2006); Michael Standaert, *Skipping towards Armageddon: The politics and propaganda of the Left Behind novels and the LaHaye empire* (Brooklyn, NY: Soft Skull Press, 2006); Tristan Sturm, 'Prophetic eyes: The theatricality of Mark Hitchcock's premillennial geopolitics,' *Geopolitics* 11 (2006), 231–55; Hugh B. Urban, 'America, Left Behind: Bush, the neoconservatives, and evangelical Christian fiction,' *Journal of Religion & Society* 8 (2006), 1–15; Crawford Gribben, 'After *Left Behind*: The paradox of evangelical pessimism,' in Kenneth G.C. Newport and Crawford Gribben (eds), *Expecting the end: Contemporary millennialism in social and historical context* (Baylor, TX: Baylor University Press, 2006), 113–30; idem, 'Protestant millennialism, political violence and the Ulster conflict,' *Irish Studies Review* 15:1 (2007), 51–63; Molly Worthen, 'The Chalcedon problem: Rousas John Rushdoony and the origins of Christian Reconstructionism,' *Church History* (2008), 399–437; Jennie Chapman, 'Paradoxes of power: Apocalyptic agency in the Left Behind series' (unpublished PhD thesis, University of Manchester, 2010).

5. See, for example, Michael Northcott, *An angel directs the storm: Apocalyptic religion and American empire* (London: I.B. Taurus, 2004), Richard K. Fenn, *Dreams of glory: The sources of apocalyptic terror* (Aldershot: Ashgate, 2005), and, more generally, Ralph Clark Chandler, 'The wicked shall not bear rule: The fundamentalist heritage of the New Christian Right,' in David G. Bromley and Anson Shupe (eds), *New Christian politics* (Macon, GA: Mercer University Press, 1984), 41–58; Bruce Barron, *Heaven on earth? The social and political agendas of Dominion Theology* (Grand Rapids, MI: Zondervan, 1992); Michael Lienesch, *Redeeming America: Piety and politics in the new Christian right* (Chapel Hill, NC: The University of North Carolina Press, 1993); Linda Kintz and Julia Lesage (eds), *Media, culture, and the religious right* (Minneapolis, MN: University of Minnesota Press, 1998); Stefan Halper and Jonathan Clarke, *America alone: The Neo-Conservatives and the global order* (Cambridge: Cambridge University Press, 2004); Randall Balmer, *Thy kingdom come: How the religious right distorts the faith and threatens America: An evangelical's lament* (New York: Basic Books, 2006).

6. See, for example, Darryl Jones, 'The liberal Antichrist: *Left Behind* in America,' in Kenneth G.C. Newport and Crawford Gribben (eds), *Expecting the end: Millennialism in social and historical context* (Baylor, TX: Baylor University Press, 2006), 97–112.

7. See, for example, Brian E. Daley, *The hope of the early Church: Eschatology in the patristic age* (Cambridge: Cambridge University Press, 1991); Charles E. Hill, *Regnum Caelorum: Patterns of millennial thought in early Christianity*, second edition (Grand Rapids, MI: Eerdmans, 2001).

8. Augustine, *Concerning the City of God against the pagans*, trans. Henry Bettenson (London: Penguin, 1984); Michael J. Svigel, 'The phantom heresy: Did the Council of Ephesus (431) condemn chiliasm?,' *The Trinity Journal* 24 n.s. (2003), 105–12.

9. See, for a compelling account of medieval millennial movements, Norman Cohn, *The pursuit of the millennium* (1957; rpt. London: Mercury Books, 1962).

10. See, for example, Marjorie Reeves, *The influence of prophecy in the later middle ages* (Oxford: Clarendon Press, 1969).

11. Richard A. Muller, *Post-Reformation reformed dogmatics*, second edition, 4 vols (Grand Rapids, MI: Baker Academic, 2003), 4: 420.

12. D.G. Hart, *Deconstructing Evangelicalism: Conservative Protestantism in the age of Billy Graham* (Grand Rapids, MI: Baker, 2004), 28. See also Donald W. Dayton, 'Some doubts about the usefulness of the category "Evangelical",' in Donald W. Dayton and Robert K. Johnston (eds), *The variety of American*

Evangelicalism (Downers Grove, IL: InterVarsity Press, 1991), 245–51, and Harriet A. Harris, *Fundamentalism and evangelicals* (Oxford: Clarendon Press, 1998; 2008), v–x.

13. Hart, *Deconstructing Evangelicalism*, 35–6. On the culture of evangelicalism more generally, see Nancy Ammerman, *Bible believers: Fundamentalists in the modern world* (New Brunswick, NJ: Rutgers University Press, 1987); and Randall Balmer, *Mine eyes have seen the glory: A journey into the evangelical subculture in America* (1989; fourth edition, Oxford: Oxford University Press, 2006).

14. Hart, *Deconstructing Evangelicalism*, 37.

15. Hart, *Deconstructing Evangelicalism*, 48.

16. Hart, *Deconstructing Evangelicalism*, 48.

17. George M. Marsden, 'Introduction: The evangelical denomination,' in George M. Marsden (ed.), *Evangelicalism and modern America* (Grand Rapids, MI: Eerdmans, 1984), ix–xiv.

18. David W. Bebbington, *Evangelicalism in modern Britain: A history from the 1730s to the 1980s* (London: Routledge, 1989), 2–17. See also idem, 'The Advent hope in British Evangelicalism since 1800,' *Scottish Journal of Religious Studies* 9 (1988), 103–10; idem, 'Evangelical theology in the English-speaking world during the nineteenth century,' *Scottish Bulletin of Evangelical Theology* 22:2 (2004), 133–150; idem, 'Response,' in Michael A. G. Haykin and Kenneth J. Stewart (eds), *The emergence of Evangelicalism: Exploring historical continuities* (Nottingham, UK: Apollos, 2008), 417–32. Bebbington has also suggested that evangelicals developed postmillennialism as a distinctive eschatology in the eighteenth century and in the nineteenth century developed the expectation that the return of Christ would be 'personal'; *Evangelicalism in modern Britain*, passim.

19. Hart, *Deconstructing Evangelicalism*, 98.

20. Hart, *Deconstructing Evangelicalism*, 99.

21. Hart, *Deconstructing Evangelicalism*, 125.

22. Hart, *Deconstructing Evangelicalism*, 31.

23. Timothy Larsen, 'The reception given *Evangelicalism in Modern Britain* since its publication in 1989,' in Michael A.G. Haykin and Kenneth J. Stewart (eds), *The emergence of Evangelicalism: Exploring historical continuities* (Nottingham, UK: Apollos, 2008), 21–36.

24. Gribben, *Writing the rapture*, 107–28.

25. The history of the scholarly study of evangelicalism is surveyed in Hart, *Deconstructing Evangelicalism*, 35–106.

26. The American edition of the book was published as *The advent of Evangelicalism: Exploring historical continuities* (Nashville, TN: B&H Academic, 2009).

27. It has been reported that a Methodist scholar had been invited to participate in the collection; see Iain Campbell, review of *The emergence of Evangelicalism*, at http://www.reformation21.org/shelf-life/the-emergence-of-evangelicalism.php, accessed 8 May 2009.

28. Bebbington, 'Response,' 418.

29. J. F. C. Harrison, *The second coming: Popular millenarianism, 1780–1850* (New Brunswick, NJ: Rutgers University Press, 1979), 132. See also Gordon Allan, 'Southcottian sects from 1790 to the present day,' in Kenneth G. C. Newport

and Crawford Gribben (eds), *Expecting the end: Millennialism in social and historical context* (Baylor, TX: Baylor University Press, 2006), 213–36.
30. Allan, 'Southcottian sects,' 227, 232.
31. Guy Featherstone, '"Holy city": The Brethren community at Kyneton, 1900–1911,' *Brethren Historical Review* 5:1 (2008), 2–24. On B.W. Newton, see Jonathan D. Burnham, *A story of conflict: The controversial relationship between Benjamin Wills Newton and John Nelson Darby*, Studies in Evangelical History and Thought (Milton Keynes: Paternoster, 2005), and, most substantially, Nigel Pibworth, 'Benjamin Wills Newton (1807–1899): A theological biography' (unpublished manuscript, 531 pp.).
32. The followers of Joanna Southcott act as a counter-example, in that they redefine the biblical canon to include the Old Testament apocrypha and other texts; Gordon, 'Southcottian sects,' 225.
33. Andrew Pettegree, *Reformation and the culture of persuasion* (Cambridge: Cambridge University Press, 2005).
34. Diarmaid MacCulloch, *Reformation: Europe's house divided* (London: Penguin, 2004), xx, 353, 700.
35. Quoted in Christopher Burdon, *The apocalypse in England: Revelation unravelling, 1700–1834* (Basingstoke: Palgrave, 1997), 9. Of course, it is important to remember that apocalyptic was unknown as a genre in the sixteenth century; Irena Backus, *Reformation readings of the Apocalypse: Geneva, Zurich and Wittenberg* (Oxford: Oxford University Press, 2000), xi.
36. For recent theorizations of millennialism, see Leon Festinger et al., *When prophecy fails* (Minneapolis: University of Minneapolis Press, 1956); David F. Aberle, 'A note on relative deprivation theory as applied to millenarian and other cult movements,' in Sylvia Thrupp (ed.), *Millennial dreams in action: Studies in revolutionary religious movements* (New York: Schocken Books, 1970), 209–14; Graham Allan, 'A theory of millennialism: The Irvingite movement as an illustration,' *British Journal of Sociology* 25 (1974), 296–311; James West Davidson, *The logic of millennial thought: Eighteenth-century New England* (New Haven, CT: Yale University Press, 1977); Jacques Derrida, 'Of an apocalyptic tone recently adopted in philosophy,' *Semeia* 23 (1982), 63–97; Theodore Olson, *Millennialism, utopianism, and progress* (Toronto: Toronto University Press, 1982); W. Warren Wagar, *Terminal visions: The literature of last things* (Bloomington, IN: Indiana University Press, 1982); James H. Moorhead, 'Millennialism,' in Samuel S. Hill (ed.) *Encyclopaedia of religion in the South* (Macon, GA: Mercer University Press, 1984), 477–9; Barry Brummett, 'Premillennial apocalypse as a rhetorical genre,' *Central States Speech Journal* 35 (1984), 84–93; Edward A. Tiryakian, 'Modernity as an eschatological setting: A new vista for the study of religions,' *History of Religions* 25:4 (1986), 378–86; Stephen D. O'Leary, *Arguing the apocalypse: A theory of millennial rhetoric* (Oxford: Oxford University Press, 1994); Malcolm Bull (ed.), *Apocalypse theory and the ends of the world* (Oxford: Blackwell, 1995); Paul S. Fiddes, *The promised end: Eschatology in theology and literature* (Oxford: Blackwell, 2000); idem, 'Facing the end: The apocalyptic experience in some modern novels,' in John Colwell (ed.), *Called to one hope: Perspectives on the life to come* (Carlisle: Paternoster, 2000), 191–209; Stephen J. Stein, 'American millennialism: Towards construction of a new architectonic of American apocalypticism,' in Abbas Amanat and Magnus Bernhardsson (eds), *Imagining the end: Visions*

of apocalypse from the Ancient Middle East to modern America (London: I.B. Taurus, 2002), 187–211; Crawford Gribben and Timothy C.F. Stunt, 'Introduction,' in Crawford Gribben and Timothy C.F. Stunt (eds), *Prisoners of hope? Aspects of evangelical millennialism in Britain and Ireland, 1800–1880,* Studies in Evangelical history and thought (Milton Keynes: Paternoster, 2004), 1–17; David G. Bromley, 'Violence and New Religious Movements,' in James R. Lewis (ed.), *The Oxford handbook of new religious movements* (Oxford: Oxford University Press, 2004), 143–62; Richard Landes, 'Millennialism,' in James R. Lewis (ed.), *The Oxford Handbook of New Religious Movements* (Oxford: Oxford University Press, 2004), 333–58; Stephen D. O'Leary, and Glen S. McGhee (eds), *War in heaven/Heaven on earth: Theories in the apocalyptic,* Millennialism and society (London: Equinox, 2005); Brenda E. Brasher and Lee Quinby, *Gender and apocalyptic desire,* Millennialism and society (London: Equinox, 2006); Crawford Gribben, 'The future of millennial expectation,' in Newport and Gribben (eds), *Expecting the end: Millennialism in social and historical context* (Baylor, TX: Baylor University Press, 2006), 237–40; Cathy Gutierrez and Hillel Schwartz (eds), *The end that does: Art, science and millennial accomplishment,* Millennialism and society (London: Equinox, 2006); and John Wallis and Kenneth G.C. Newport (eds), *The end all around us: Apocalyptic texts and popular culture* (London: Equinox, 2008). See also, more generally, John J. Collins, Bernard McGinn, Stephen J. Stein, 'General introduction,' in Bernard McGinn (ed.), *Encyclopedia of apocalypticism,* 3 vols (New York: Continuum, 1998), 1: vii–xi; James Berger, *After the end: Representations of post-apocalypse* (Minneapolis: University of Minnesota, 1999), and Mark S. Sweetnam, 'Defining dispensationalism: A cultural studies perspective,' *Journal of Religious History* 34: 2 (2010), 191–212. For a survey of millennial studies scholarship, see David E. Smith, 'Millennial scholarship in America,' *American Quarterly* 17 (1965), 535–49; Hillel Schwartz, 'The end of the beginning: Millenarian studies, 1969–1975,' *Religious Studies Review* 2 (1976), 1–15; Leonard I. Sweet, 'Millennialism in America: Recent studies,' *Theological Studies* 40 (1979), 510–31; Douglas Shantz, 'Millennialism and apocalypticism in recent historical scholarship,' in Crawford Gribben and Timothy C.F. Stunt (eds), *Prisoners of hope? Aspects of evangelical millennialism in Britain and Ireland, 1800–1880,* Studies in Evangelical History and Thought (Milton Keynes: Paternoster, 2004), 18–43.

37. See Chapter 3 of this book; Anthony A. Hoekema, *The Bible and the future* (Grand Rapids, MI: Eerdmans, 1979), 179, commenting, perhaps inaccurately, on Norman Shepherd, 'Postmillennialism,' in *Zondervan pictorial encyclopedia of the Bible,* ed. Merrill C. Tenney (Grand Rapids, MI: Zondervan, 1975), 4: 822–3.

38. Reiner Smolinksi, 'Caveat Emptor: Pre- and postmillennialism in the late reformation period,' in James E. Force and Richard H. Popkin (eds), *Millenarianism and messianism in early modern European culture: The millenarian turn* (Dordrecht: Kluwer Academic Publishers, 2001), 146.

39. *Oxford English Dictionary,* s.v.

40. Daley, *The hope of the early Church;* Hill, *Regnum Caelorum.* On Spurgeon, see 'Spurgeon's Confession of Faith,' *The Sword and Trowel* 26 (August 1891), 446–8; S.H. Kellog, 'Christ's coming: Will it be premillennial?' in Nathaniel West (ed.), *Premillennial essays of the prophetic conference held in the Church*

of the Holy Trinity, New York City (Chicago, IL: Fleming H. Revell, 1879), 74; Lewis A. Drummond, *Spurgeon: Prince of preachers* (Grand Rapids, MI: Kregel, 1992), 650; C.W.H. Griffiths, 'Spurgeon's eschatology,' *Watching and Waiting: A publication of the Sovereign Grace Advent Testimony* 23:15 (1990), 227; Dennis M. Swanson, 'The millennial position of Spurgeon,' *The Master's Seminary Journal* 7:2 (1996), 183–212. On Ladd, see John A. D'Elia, *A place at the table: George Eldon Ladd and the rehabilitation of evangelical scholarship in America* (Oxford: Oxford University Press, 2008).

41. See Mark Sweetnam and Todd Mangum, *The Scofield Bible: Its history and impact on the evangelical church* (Milton Keynes: Paternoster, 2009); Craig A. Blaising and Darrell L. Bock, *Progressive dispensationalism* (Wheaton, IL: Victor, 1993).

42. Ernest L. Tuveson, *Redeemer nation: The idea of America's millennial role* (Chicago: University of Chicago Press, 1968), 33–4; Harrison is a prominent advocate of this distinction in *The second coming*.

43. Ernest R. Sandeen, *The roots of fundamentalism: British and American millenarianism, 1800–1930* (Chicago: University of Chicago Press, 1970), 5 n. 3.

44. Worthen, 'The Chalcedon problem,' 399–437.

45. Bryan R. Wilson, *Magic and the millennium: A sociological study of religious movements of protest among tribal and third-world peoples* (London: Harper and Row, 1973), 491.

46. Jürgen Moltmann, *The coming of God: Christian eschatology* (London: SCM, 1996), 159–92. Note that Moltmann does not deny the importance of the traditional terminology of pre- and post-millennialism, e.g. 153.

47. W.R. Ward, *Early Evangelicalism: A global intellectual history, 1670–1789* (Cambridge: Cambridge University Press, 2006), 74–5, 88, 98.

48. Philip Jenkins, *Mystics and messiahs: Cults and new religions in American history* (Oxford: Oxford University Press, 2000), 5.

49. For, as J.F.C. Harrison has noted, 'if Joseph [Smith] taught that Adam had dwelt in the Mississippi Valley and that Christ had visited the Nephites, William Blake believed that Noah and the patriarchs had lived in Britain and that the Holy Lamb of God had walked upon England's mountains. Richard Brothers' theory of British Israel linked the Anglo-Saxons with forgotten Israelite ancestors; and the Southcottians were assured that in God's providence a special place had been given to the British people ... In this respect Joseph was no more (and no less) exceptionalist than his British counterparts'; Harrison, *The second coming*, 182–3.

50. For recent surveys of scholarship on the modern trans-Atlantic world, see David Armitage and Michael J. Braddick (eds), *The British Atlantic world, 1500–1800*, second edition (Basingstoke: Palgrave Macmillan, 2009), and Alexander Murdoch, *Scotland and America, c. 1600–c. 1800* (Basingstoke: Palgrave Macmillan, 2009).

51. See, for example, Avihu Zakai, *Exile and kingdom: History and apocalypse in the puritan migration to America* (Cambridge: Cambridge University Press, 1992). This theme has been explored most recently in Joseph Chi, '"Forget not the wombe that bare you, and the brest that gave you sucke": John Cotton's sermons on Canticles and Revelation and his apocalyptic vision For England' (unpublished PhD thesis, New College, Edinburgh, 2008).

52. Harrison, *The second coming*, 163.

53. Harrison, *The second coming*, xv.
54. Harrison, *The second coming*, 131.
55. The term is used by Michael Barkun in *A culture of conspiracy: Apocalyptic visions in contemporary America* (Berkeley: University of California Press, 2003). After all, Joanna Southcott's 'record of prognostication was impressive. She foretold the war with France, the poor harvests of 1794, 1795, and 1797, and the effects of the rain in 1799 and the sun in 1800 on crops. She foretold the naval mutiny of 1797, and confounded Pomeroy by accurately predicting the death of the Bishop of Exeter'; Harrison, *The second coming*, 104.

1   The Emergence of Evangelical Millennialism, 1500–1600

1. Cohn, *Pursuit of the millennium*, 278–9. See also, more recently, Tal Howard, 'Charisma and history: The case of Münster, Westphalia, 1534–1535,' *Essays in History* 35 (1993), 48–64; Thomas Flanagan, 'The politics of the millennium,' *Terrorism and Political Violence* 7:3 (1995), 164–75; and Frederic Baumgartner, *Longing for the end: A history of millennialism in Western civilization* (New York: Palgrave, 1999).
2. Cohn, *Pursuit of the millennium*, 281.
3. Cohn, *Pursuit of the millennium*, 278–306; Ian M. Randall, *Communities of conviction: Baptist beginnings in Europe* (Schwarzenfeld, Germany: Neufeld Verlag, 2009), 8–9.
4. Muller, *Post-Reformation reformed dogmatics*, 4: 420.
5. The ancient, biblical and medieval roots of apocalyptic and millennial ideologies are generally described in Ernest Lee Tuveson, *Millennium and utopia: A study in the background of the idea of progress* (Berkeley: University of California Press, 1949); Eugene Weber, *Apocalypses: Prophecies, cults, and millennial beliefs through the ages* (Cambridge, MA: Harvard University Press, 1999); Michael Wilks (ed.), *Prophecy and eschatology: Studies in church history, Subsidia 10* (Oxford: Blackwell, 1994); and specifically described in Norman Cohn, *Cosmos, chaos and the world to come: The ancient roots of apocalyptic faith* (London: Yale University Press, 1993); Christopher Rowland and John Barton (eds), *Apocalyptic in history and tradition* (Sheffield: Sheffield Academic Press, 2002); Christopher Rowland, 'Afterword,' *Journal for the Study of the New Testament* 25:2 (2002); and Richard Landes et al. (eds), *The apocalyptic year 1000: Religious expectation and social change, 950–1050* (Oxford: Oxford University Press, 2003). For a general survey of their early modern application, see, with appropriate qualifications, L.E. Froom, *The prophetic faith of our fathers: The historical development of prophetic interpretation*, 4 vols (Washington: Review and Herald, 1948).
6. Backus, *Reformation readings of the apocalypse*, xii; Daley, *The hope of the early Church*, passim; Hill, *Regnum Caelorum*.
7. Richard Muller has noted that, during the sixteenth and seventeenth centuries, 'Reformed theology appears not as a monolithic structure – not, in short, as "Calvinism" – but as a form of Augustinian theology and piety capable of considerable variation in its form and presentation'; *Christ and the*

decree: Christology and predestination in Reformed theology from Calvin to Perkins (Durham, NC: Labyrinth, 1986), 176.

8. Augustine, *City of God*, 906–7.
9. Augustine, *City of God*, 921, 933.
10. Backus, *Reformation readings of the apocalypse*, xvi.
11. Backus, *Reformation readings of the apocalypse*, xviii.
12. Quoted in Backus, *Reformation readings of the apocalypse*, 7.
13. John Calvin, *The epistles of Paul the Apostle to the Romans and to the Thessalonians*, trans. Ross Mackenzie (Grand Rapids, MI: Eerdmans, 1972), 401.
14. For a modern example of this trend, see Fenn, *Dreams of glory*.
15. Backus, *Reformation readings of the apocalypse*, 3. On reformation millennialism more generally, see T.F. Torrance, 'The eschatology of the reformation,' *Eschatology: Scottish Journal of Theology Occasional Papers* 2 (1953), 36–62; Heinrich Quistorp, *Calvin's doctrine of the last things* (London: Lutterworth Press, 1955).
16. Backus, *Reformation readings of the apocalypse*, 6, 29.
17. Backus, *Reformation readings of the apocalypse*, 8–10.
18. John Calvin, *Institutes of the Christian religion*, eds J.T. McNeill and F.L. Battles (1559; rpt. London: SCM, 1960), iii. xxv. 5; Quistorp, *Calvin's doctrine of the last things*, passim.
19. Calvin, *Institutes*, iii. xxv. 5.
20. Calvin, *The epistles of Paul the Apostle to the Romans and to the Thessalonians*, 396.
21. Backus, *Reformation readings of the apocalypse*, 35; Irena Backus, 'The Church Fathers and the canonicity of the Apocalypse in the sixteenth century: Erasmus, Frans Titelmans, and Theodore Beza,' *Sixteenth Century Journal* 29 (1998), 662.
22. Backus, *Reformation readings of the apocalypse*, 11–13.
23. John Bale, *The image of both Churches* (1547); rpt. in *Select works of John Bale*, ed. Henry Christmas (Cambridge: University Press, 1849), 251–2.
24. Kenneth Austin, *From Judaism to Calvinism: The life and writings of Immanuel Tremellius (c. 1510–1580)*, St Andrews Studies in Reformation History (Aldershot: Ashgate, 2007).
25. Backus, *Reformation readings of the apocalypse*, 33–5.
26. On the eschatology of the reformers, see Torrance, 'The eschatology of the reformation,' 36–62; Quistorp, *Calvin's doctrine of the last things*; B.W. Ball, *A great expectation: Eschatological thought in English Protestantism to 1660* (Leiden: Brill, 1975); Paul Christianson, *Reformers and Babylon: English apocalyptic visions from the reformation to the eve of the Civil War* (Toronto: University of Toronto Press, 1978); Richard Bauckham, *Tudor apocalypse: Sixteenth-century apocalypticism, millenarianism and the English reformation: From John Bale to John Foxe and Thomas Brightman* (Appleford: Sutton Courtenay Press, 1978); Katherine Firth, *The apocalyptic tradition in Reformation Britain, 1530–1645* (Oxford: Oxford University Press, 1979); C.A. Patrides and Joseph Wittreich (eds), *The apocalypse in English Renaissance thought and literature: Patterns, antecedents and repercussions* (Manchester: Manchester University Press, 1984); Rodney L. Peterson, *Preaching in the last days: The theme of 'two witnesses' in the sixteenth and seventeenth centuries*

(Oxford: Oxford University Press, 1993); Backus, *Reformation readings of the apocalypse*; Crawford Gribben, *The puritan millennium: Literature and theology, 1550–1682* (Dublin: Four Courts, 2000); Howard Hotson, *Johann Heinrich Alsted, 1588–1638* (Oxford: Oxford University Press, 2000); idem, *Paradise postponed: Johann Heinrich Alsted and the Birth of Calvinist Millenarianism* (Dordrecht: Kluwer Academic Publishers, 2000); John Christian Laursen and Richard H. Popkin (eds), *Continental millenarians: Protestants, Catholics, heretics* (Dordrecht: Kluwer Academic Publishers, 2001); and Jeffrey K. Jue, *Heaven upon earth: Joseph Mede (1586–1638) and the legacy of millenarianism* (Dordrecht: Kluwer Academic Publications, 2006).

27. Peter Hall (ed.), *Harmony of the Protestant confessions* (1842; rpt. Edmonton: Still Waters Revival Books, 1992), 106.

28. Gerald Bray, *Documents of the English reformation* (Cambridge: James Clarke, 1995), 309–10.

29. Hall (ed.), *Harmony of the Protestant confessions*, 88.

30. On this recovery, see most recently Gribben, *The puritan millennium*; Hotson, *Paradise postponed*; and Jue, *Heaven upon earth*.

31. Christopher Hill, *Antichrist in seventeenth-century England* (London: Oxford University Press, 1971), 3–4.

32. Palle J. Olsen, 'Was John Foxe a millenarian?' *Journal of Ecclesiastical History* 45:4 (1994), 600–24.

33. Michael Jensen, '"Simply" reading the Geneva Bible: The Geneva Bible and its readers,' *Literature and Theology* 9 (1995), 30–45.

34. *Geneva Bible* (1560), sig. iii^{v}.

35. *Geneva Bible* (1560), sig. iii^{v}.

36. *Geneva Bible* (1560), note on *Romans* 11:26.

37. *Geneva Bible* (1560), note on *Romans* 11:15.

38. *Geneva Bible* (1602), 1. This issue is listed as *Hist. Cat.* number 272; STC 2902.

39. *Geneva Bible* (1602), 124^{v}.

40. See Philip Almond, 'John Napier and the mathematics of the middle future apocalypse,' *Scottish Journal of Theology* 63:1 (2010), 54–69.

41. John Napier, *A plaine discovery of the whole Revelation* (1593; 2nd ed. 1611), sig. A2r.

42. See, for an illuminating exposition of this context, Tom Furniss, 'Reading the Geneva Bible: Notes toward an English revolution?' *Prose Studies* 31:1 (2009), 1–21.

43. Napier, *Plaine discovery*, 26.

44. *DNB*, s.v. 'Perkins, William.'

45. This text has no STC entry.

46. William Perkins, *Works* (1612), 2: 817.

47. This text has no STC entry.

48. Perkins, *Works*, iii. 467.

49. Perkins, *Works*, iii. 468.

50. Perkins, *Works*, iii. 470.

51. Perkins, *Works*, 3: 470.

52. John Preston, *The breastplate of faith and love* (1630), 131.

53. Backus, *Reformation readings of the apocalypse*, 135.

54. Backus, *Reformation readings of the apocalypse*, 135–6.

55. Richard Sibbes, *Works*, ed. A.B. Grosart, 6 vols (Edinburgh: James Nichol, 1862–64), 4: 43.

2   The Formation of Evangelical Millennialism, 1600–1660

1. On the millennialism of puritan confessions of faith, see Crawford Gribben, 'The eschatology of the puritan confessions,' *Scottish Bulletin of Evangelical Theology* 20:1 (2002), 51–78. More generally, on puritan eschatology, see William Lamont, *Godly rule: Politics and religion, 1603–60* (London: Macmillan, 1969); Peter Toon (ed.), *Puritans, the millennium and the future of Israel: Puritan eschatology 1600 to 1660* (Cambridge: James Clarke, 1970); J.A. de Jong, *As the waters cover the sea: Millennial expectations in the rise of Anglo-American missions 1640–1810* (Kampen: Kok, 1970); Bernard Capp, '*Godly Rule* and English millenarianism,' *Past and Present* 52 (1971), 106–17; Hill, *Antichrist in seventeenth-century England*; B.S. Capp, *The Fifth Monarchy Men: A study in seventeenth-century millenarianism* (London: Faber and Faber, 1972); Ball, *A great expectation*; William Lamont, *Richard Baxter and the millennium: Protestant imperialism and the English revolution* (London: Croom Helm, 1979); Gribben, *The Puritan millennium*; Smolinksi, 'Caveat Emptor: Pre- and postmillennialism in the late reformation period,' 145–69; Jue, *Heaven upon earth*; Andrew Crome, 'The Jews and the literal sense: Hermeneutical approaches in the apocalyptic commentaries of Thomas Brightman (1562–1607)' (unpublished PhD thesis, University of Manchester, 2009); Chi, '"Forget not the wombe that bare you, and the brest that gave you sucke": John Cotton's Sermons on Canticles and Revelation and his apocalyptic vision for England.'
2. See the discussion in Michel Foucault, *The order of things* (1966; London: Routledge, 1989).
3. Gribben, *Puritan millennium*; Francis J. Bremer and Tom Webster (eds), *Puritans and Puritanism in Europe and America: A comprehensive encyclopedia* (Oxford: ABC-CLIO, 2006), passim. On the deconstruction of the Gothic constitution, see Allan I. MacInnes, *The British revolution, 1629–60* (Basingstoke: Palgrave Macmillan, 2004).
4. Hotson, 'Origins of Calvinist millenarianism,' passim.
5. See, for example, Richard W. Cogley, 'The fall of the Ottoman empire in the "Judeo-centric" strand of puritan millenarianism,' *Church History* 72:2 (2003), 303–32; Crome, 'The Jews and the literal sense.'
6. Philip F. Gura, *A glimpse of Sion's glory: Puritan radicalism in New England, 1620–1660* (Middletown, CT: Wesleyan University Press, 1984), 126–54; Chi, '"Forget not the wombe that bare you, and the brest that gave you sucke": John Cotton's Sermons on Canticles and Revelation and his apocalyptic vision for England.'
7. Hotson, 'Origins of Calvinist millenarianism,' 160.
8. See, for example, Muller, *Post-Reformation reformed dogmatics*, the massive of scope of which advances no further than theological prolegomena, Holy Scripture, the Trinity, and the divine essence and attributes.
9. On Brightman, see Crome, 'The Jews and the literal sense.'
10. [Anon.], *Reverend Mr. Brightmans judgement* (1642), sig. A2v–A3r.

11. *Oxford DNB*, s.v.
12. [Anon.], *Reverend Mr. Brightmans judgement*, sig. A4r.
13. Crawford Gribben, 'The Church of Scotland and the English apocalyptic imagination, 1630–1650,' *Scottish Historical Review* 88:1 (2009), 34–56.
14. Thomas Brightman, *A most comfortable exposition of … Daniel*, 895; *The art of self-deniall: or, A Christian's first lesson: By that famous Prophett of these times: Tho: Brightman* (1646).
15. Phil Kilroy, 'Sermon and pamphlet literature in the Irish Reformed Church, 1613–34,' *Archivium Hibernicum* 33 (1975), 117.
16. Elizabethanne Boran, 'The libraries of Luke Challoner and James Ussher, 1595–1608,' in Helga Robinson-Hammerstein (ed.), *European universities in the age of reformation and counter-reformation* (Dublin: Four Courts, 1998), 98–102.
17. The text was translated into English by Ambrose Ussher, James's brother, and English quotations will be taken from this unpaginated translation, Trinity College Library, Dublin, MS 2940.
18. James Ussher, *The whole works of James Ussher*, ed. C.R. Erlington and J.R. Todd, 17 vols (Dublin: Hodges and Smith, 1847–64), 2: ix: 'ligatum dici Satanum, quando ab universali seductione procuranda est cohibitus.'
19. Ussher, *Works*, 2: 6: 'Satanum ligatum asserit, ne persecutionibus amplius noceret Ecclesiæ: a Constantini videlicet Imperatoris temporibus, a quo sublatæ persecutiones, usque ad annum Domini 1300. quo Turcicum imperium in Ottomanno coepit.'
20. Ussher, *Works*, 2: 6: 'ubi status Millenarii illius, in quo vinctus erat Satanas, describitur, expressa mentio fit eorum qui securi percussi sunt propter testimonium Jesu, et propter sermonem Dei.'
21. Ussher, *Works*, 11: 417.
22. Ussher, *Works*, 2: 163–4: 'Universa sanctorum abscondetur Ecclesia. Ha enim electi Dei sapient sibi ipsis id, quod sapient; ut tamen prædicare publice (prævalentibus tenebris) non præsumant. Non quod animare fideles et secretius exhortari desistant, sed quod prædicare publice non audebunt.'
23. Ussher, *Works*, 2: xi: 'Pars tertia, deo volente, subsequeter: in qua agendum de statu rerum ab initio pontificatus Gregorii XI. usque ad initium pontificatus Leonis X. id est … De nova ligatione Satanæ per Evangelii restaurationem sub medium secundi millenari exiguo tempore fieri coepta.'
24. Ussher, *Works*, xv. 264.
25. Anthony Milton, *Catholic and Reformed: The Roman and protestant churches in English protestant thought, 1600–1640* (Cambridge: Cambridge University Press, 1995), 112.
26. *Das ander Thäil Des Newen Testaments I Darinnen … Die Episteln … und die Offenbarung S. Johannis*, trans. and annotated by Johannes Piscator (Herborn, 1604), 451; Hotson, *Johann Heinrich Alsted*, 208.
27. Hotson, *Johann Heinrich Alsted*, 212–14.
28. Hotson, *Johann Heinrich Alsted*, 130–1.
29. R.B. Barnes, *Prophecy and gnosis: Apocalypticism in the wake of the Lutheran reformation* (Stanford, CA: Stanford University Press, 1988).
30. Graeme Murdock, *Calvinism on the frontier, 1600–1660: International Calvinism and the Reformed Church in Hungary and Transylvania* (Oxford: Clarendon Press, 2000), 268–70.

31. Crome, 'The Jews and the literal sense', passim.
32. See Jue, *Heaven upon earth*; Sarah Hutton, 'The appropriation of Joseph Mede: Millenarianism in the 1640s,' in James E. Force and Richard H. Popkin (eds), *Millenarianism and messianism in early modern European culture: The millenarian turn* (Dordrecht: Kluwer Academic Publishers, 2001), 1–13.
33. Joseph Mede, *The key of the Revelation* (London, 1643), 1: 35.
34. Hill, *Antichrist in seventeenth-century England*, 27; Mede, *The key of the Revelation*, 1: 27.
35. Mede, *The key of the Revelation*, 2: 13.
36. Mede, *The key of the Revelation*, 2: 121.
37. Ussher, *Works*, 15: 407.
38. Ussher, *Works*, 15: 561; Clouse, 'The rebirth of millenarianism,' in Peter Toon (ed.), *Puritans, the millennium and the future of Israel: Puritan eschatology, 1600 to 1660* (Cambridge: James Clarke, 1970), 60.
39. Mede, *The key of the Revelation*, sig. av.
40. Mede, *The key of the Revelation*, sig. a4v.
41. Stephen J. Stein, 'Editor's introduction,' in Jonathan Edwards, *Apocalyptic writings*, ed. Stephen J. Stein, The Works of Jonathan Edwards (New Haven, CT: Yale University Press, 1977), 5, 8; John Stuart Erwin, 'Like a thief in the night: Cotton Mather's millennialism' (unpublished PhD thesis, Indiana University, 1987).
42. Gribben, 'The Church of Scotland and the English apocalyptic imagination, 1630–1650,' 34–56.
43. Firth, *The apocalyptic tradition in reformation Britain*, 5.
44. A.R. Dallison, 'Contemporary criticism of millenarianism,' in Peter Toon (ed.), *Puritans, the millennium and the future of Israel: Puritan eschatology, 1600 to 1660* (Cambridge: James Clarke, 1970), 111; John Bunyan, *Works*, ed. George Offor (Glasgow: Blackie and Son, 1860), ii: 424; Saul Leeman, 'Was Bishop Ussher's chronology influenced by a midrash?' *Semeia* 8 (1977), 127; Ussher, *Works*, vii: 45.
45. Milton, *Catholic and Reformed*, 93–127.
46. For Ussher's influence on the Irish Articles, see Amanda L. Capern, 'The Caroline Church: James Ussher and the Irish Dimension,' *Historical Journal* 39 (1996), 57–85.
47. Westminster Confession of Faith 25:6.
48. Milton, *Catholic and Reformed*, 128–72.
49. George Gillespie, *A treatise of miscellany questions* (1649); rpt. in *The Presbyterian's armoury*, ed. W.M. Hetherington (Edinburgh: Robert Ogle, and Oliver & Boyd, 1846), 27.
50. Ussher, *Works*, 12: 542–3.
51. Milton, *Catholic and Reformed*, passim.
52. Ussher, *Works*, 7: 45.
53. Thomas Goodwin, *Works*, 12 vols (Edinburgh: James Nichol, 1861–66), 3: 4, 3, 36, 88, 61, 87–8, 103–4, 178, 180, 181, 194; Christianson, *Reformers and Babylon*, 209.
54. John Cotton, *The churches resurrection* (London, 1642), 9, 19.
55. John Archer, *The personall reigne of Christ upon Earth* (London, 1643), 15.
56. Capp, *The Fifth Monarchy men*, passim.
57. Clouse, 'The rebirth of millenarianism,' 60.

58. Froom, *The prophetic faith of our fathers*, ii: 553.
59. de Jong, *As the waters cover the sea*, 38 n. 11. Along with the above texts, important studies of puritan eschatology include William Lamont, *Godly rule*; idem, *Richard Baxter and the millennium*; Capp, *The Fifth Monarchy men*; Christianson, *Reformers and Babylon*; Firth, *The apocalyptic tradition in reformation Britain*; John Coffey, *Politics, religion and the British revolutions: The mind of Samuel Rutherford* (Cambridge: Cambridge University Press, 1997).
60. W.J. Van Asselt, 'Chiliasm and Reformed eschatology in the seventeenth and eighteenth centuries,' in A. van Egmond and D. van Keulen (eds), *Christian hope in context*, Studies in Reformed Theology 4 (Zoetermeer: Meinema, 2001), 24. Cocceius would also argue for seven dispensations in redemptive history; W.J. Van Asselt, 'Structural elements in the eschatology of Johannes Cocceius,' *Calvin Theological Journal* 34 (1999), 76–104.
61. Mede, *The key of the Revelation*, 1: 121.
62. For a discussion of the eschatological conflicts of the Westminster Assembly divines, see Gribben, *The puritan millennium*, 105–19.

3   The Consolidation of Evangelical Millennialism, 1660–1789

1. Richard Baxter, *The glorious kingdom of Christ, described and clearly vindicated* (1691), 9–10.
2. Smolinksi, 'Caveat Emptor: Pre- and postmillennialism in the late reformation period,' 145–69, 147.
3. Burdon, *The Apocalypse in England*, 34.
4. See, for example, Neil H. Keeble, *The literary culture of Nonconformity in later seventeenth century England* (Leicester: Leicester University Press, 1987).
5. Richard Baxter, 'To the reader,' in Thomas Manton, *Eighteen sermons*, in *The complete works of Thomas Manton*, ed. Thomas Smith, 22 vols (London: James Nisbet & Co., 1870–75), iii: 4.
6. Warren Johnson, 'Apocalypticism in Restoration England' (unpublished PhD thesis, University of Cambridge, 2000); idem, 'The patience of the saints, the apocalypse and moderate nonconformity in Restoration England,' *Canadian Journal of History* 38 (2003), 505–16; idem, 'The Anglican apocalypse in Restoration England,' *Journal of Ecclesiastical History* 55:33 (2004), 467–501; Kenneth G.C. Newport, *Apocalypse and millennium: Studies in biblical eisegesis* (Cambridge: Cambridge University Press, 2000), passim.
7. Kenneth G.C. Newport, 'Benjamin Keach, William of Orange and the book of Revelation: A study in English prophetical exegesis,' *Baptist Quarterly* 36 (1995–96), pp. 43–51.
8. Burdon, *The Apocalypse in England*, 36. For an overview of millennial speculation in the period, see Richard H. Popkin (ed.), *Millenarianism and messianism in English literature and thought, 1650–1800* (Leiden: E.J. Brill, 1988), and James E. Force and Richard H. Popkin (eds), *The millenarian turn: Millenarian contexts of science, politics, and everyday Anglo-American life in the seventeenth and eighteenth centuries* (Dordrecht: Kluwer Academic Pubishers, 2001).
9. Van Asselt, 'Chiliasm and Reformed eschatology in the seventeenth and eighteenth centuries,' 12.

10. Nathan O. Hatch, 'The origins of civil millennialism in America: New England clergymen, war with France, and the Revolution,' *The William and Mary Quarterly*, third series 31:3 (1974), 407–30; idem, *The sacred cause of liberty: Republican thought and the millennium in revolutionary New England* (New Haven, CT: Yale University Press, 1977).

11. Bebbington, *Evangelicalism in modern Britain*, 35–8.

12. Bebbington, *Evangelicalism in modern Britain*, 62.

13. Hillel Schwartz, *The French Prophets: The history of a millenarian group in eighteenth-century England* (Los Angeles: University of California Press, 1980), 90.

14. Garnet Howard Milne, *The Westminster Confession of Faith and the cessation of special revelation: The majority puritan viewpoint on whether extra-biblical prophecy is still possible*, Studies in Christian History and Thought (Milton Keynes: Paternoster, 2007); Harrison, *The second coming*, 5.

15. *Oxford DNB*, s.v.

16. See, for example, Peter J. Morden, *Offering Christ to the world: Andrew Fuller (1754–1815) and the revival of eighteenth century Particular Baptist life* (Milton Keynes: Paternoster, 2003), passim.

17. Bebbington, *Evangelicalism in modern Britain*, 20, 47; Mark A. Noll, *The rise of evangelicalism: The age of Edwards, Whitefield, and the Wesleys*, A History of Evangelicalism (Leicester: IVP, 2004).

18. Ronald Knox, *Enthusiasm* (Oxford: Clarendon Press, 1950), 388.

19. Harrison, *The second coming*, 41.

20. Deborah M. Valenze, 'Prophecy and popular literature in eighteenth-century England,' *Journal of Ecclesiastical History* 29:1 (1978), 78–82.

21. Harrison, *The second coming*, 13–14; Ward, *Early Evangelicalism*, passim; Julie Hirst, *Jane Leade: Biography of a seventeenth-century mystic* (Aldershot: Ashgate, 2005).

22. Harrison, *The second coming*, 30, 148. On the history of Southcott and the associated sects, see G.R. Balleine, *Past finding out: The tragic story of Joanna Southcott and her successors* (London: SPCK, 1956).

23. Harrison, *The second coming*, 43; *Oxford DNB*, s.v.

24. Johnson, 'Apocalypticism in Restoration England'; idem, 'The patience of the saints, the apocalypse and moderate nonconformity in Restoration England,' 505–16; idem, 'The Anglican apocalypse in Restoration England,' 467–501.

25. Van Asselt, 'Chiliasm and Reformed eschatology in the seventeenth and eighteenth centuries,' 11–29, 25–6.

26. Edwards, *Apocalyptic writings*, 17–21, 26–9; Brandon G. Withrow, 'A future of hope: Jonathan Edwards and millennial expectations,' *Trinity Journal* 22 (2001), 75–98; George M. Marsden, *Jonathan Edwards: A life* (New Haven, CT: Yale University Press, 2003), 264–7, 335–7.

27. Harrison, *The second coming*, 5; Jack Fruchtman, *The apocalyptic politics of Richard Price and Joseph Priestly: A study in late eighteenth-century English republican millennialism* (Philadelphia, PA: American Philosophical Society, 1983).

28. Harrison, *The second coming*, 5.

29. James H. Moorhead, 'Apocalypticism in mainstream Protestantism: 1800 to the present,' in Bernard McGinn (ed.), *Encyclopedia of apocalypticism*, 3 vols (New York: Continuum, 1998), 3: 75.

30. Barry H. Howson, 'The eschatology of the Calvinistic Baptist John Gill (1697–1771) examined and compared,' *Eusebeia* 5 (2005), 33.

31. Bebbington, *Evangelicalism in modern Britain*, 62; Burdon, *The Apocalypse in England*.

32. Stein, 'Editor's introduction,' in Edwards, *Apocalyptic writings*, 8. My reading of Edwards is informed by Stein's analysis. See, more generally, C.C. Goen, 'Jonathan Edwards: A new departure in eschatology,' *Church History* 28 (1959), 25–40, and Stephen J. Stein, 'Providence and the apocalypse in the early writings of Jonathan Edwards,' *Early American Literature* 13:3 (1978–1979), 250–67.

33. Stein, 'Editor's introduction,' in Edwards, *Apocalyptic writings*, 9.

34. Quoted in David Levin (ed.), *Jonathan Edwards: A Profile* (New York: Hill & Wang, 1969), 31.

35. Stein, 'Editor's introduction,' in Edwards, *Apocalyptic writings*, 12.

36. Stein, 'Editor's introduction,' in Edwards, *Apocalyptic writings*, 18.

37. Jonathan Edwards, *The miscellanies*, ed. Amy Plantinga Pauw, The Works of Jonathan Edwards (New Haven, CT: Yale University Press, 2002), 212–13.

38. Stein, 'Editor's introduction,' in Edwards, *Apocalyptic writings*, 41.

39. Stein, 'Editor's introduction,' in Edwards, *Apocalyptic writings*, 15, 19, 23.

40. Jonathan Edwards, *The Great Awakening*, ed. C.C. Goen, The Works of Jonathan Edwards (New Haven: Yale University Press, 1972), 130.

41. Edwards, *The great awakening*, 131–2.

42. Stein, 'Editor's introduction,' in Edwards, *Apocalyptic writings*, 26.

43. Edwards, *The great awakening*, 358.

44. Gill's work was widely appreciated on both sides of the Atlantic. He was awarded an honorary doctorate from Marischal College, Aberdeen and his work was widely appreciated among American Baptists; Gregory A. Wills, *Democratic religion: Freedom, authority and church discipline in the Baptist South, 1785–1900* (Oxford: Oxford University Press, 1997), 85–6. Gill has also become a central figure in the debate about the historical origins and influence of hyper-Calvinism: see Peter Toon, *The emergence of hyper-Calvinism in English non-conformity* (London: The Olive Tree, 1967); Curt Daniel, 'Hyper-Calvinism and John Gill' (unpublished PhD thesis, University of Edinburgh, 1983); Thomas J. Nettles, *By his grace and for his glory: A historical, theological and practical study of the doctrines of grace in Baptist life* (Grand Rapids: Baker Book House, 1986), 73–107; George Ella, *John Gill and the cause of God and truth* (Eggleston: Go Publications, 1995); Iain H. Murray, *Spurgeon v. hyper-Calvinism: The battle for gospel preaching* (Edinburgh: Banner of Truth, 1995); Robert Oliver, 'John Gill: Orthodox dissenter,' *Strict Baptist Historical Society Bulletin* 23 (1996), 3–18; Michael A.G. Haykin (ed.), *The life and thought of John Gill: A tercentennial appreciation* (Leiden: E.J. Brill, 1997); George Ella, *John Gill and justification from eternity: A tercentenary appreciation* (Eggleston: Go Publications, 1998).

45. Michael A.G. Haykin, 'Introduction,' in Michael A.G. Haykin (ed.), *The life and thought of John Gill: A tercentennial appreciation*, 4–5. Among other items, Haykin is referring to Daniel, 'Hyper-Calvinism and John Gill'; Thomas Ascol, 'The doctrine of grace: A critical analysis of federalism in the theologies of John Gill and Andrew Fuller' (unpublished PhD thesis, Southwestern Baptist Theological Seminary, 1989); Timothy George, 'John Gill,' in Timothy George and David S. Dockery (eds), *Baptist theologians* (Nashville: Broadman Press,

1990), 89–94; and Ella, *John Gill and the cause of God and truth*. On Gill's eschatology, see Crawford Gribben, 'John Gill and puritan eschatology,' *Evangelical Quarterly* 73:4 (2001), 311–26, and Howson, 'The eschatology of the Calvinistic Baptist John Gill (1697–1771) examined and compared,' 33–66.

46. This biography was published separately as John Rippon, *A brief memoir of the life and writings of the late Rev. John Gill, D.D.* (1838; rpt Harrisonburg: Gano Books, 1992); see Rippon, *A brief memoir of … John Gill*, 74.

47. Howson, 'The eschatology of the Calvinistic Baptist John Gill,' 54.

48. de Jong, *As the waters cover the sea*, 202. On the evangelical revival, see G.M. Ditchfield, *The evangelical revival* (London: UCL Press, 1998).

49. Howson, 'The eschatology of the Calvinistic Baptist John Gill,' 34.

50. John Gill, *A body of divinity* (1769–70; rpt. Grand Rapids: Sovereign Grace Publishers, 1971), 623; cf. 645.

51. Quoted in Ella, *John Gill and the cause of God and truth*, 83.

52. Rippon, *A brief memoir of … John Gill*, 77; Stanley K. Fowler, 'John Gill's doctrine of believer baptism,' in Michael A.G. Haykin (ed.), *The life and thought of John Gill: A tercentennial appreciation*, 69.

53. Gill, *A body of divinity*, 644.

54. Richard A. Muller, 'John Gill and the Reformed tradition: A study in the reception of Protestant Orthodoxy in the eighteenth century,' in Michael A.G. Haykin (ed.), *The life and thought of John Gill: A tercentennial appreciation*, 51 n. 2.

55. Gill, *A body of divinity*, 638.

56. Gill, *A body of divinity*, 623.

57. Gill, *A body of divinity*, 623.

58. Gill, *A body of divinity*, 623.

59. Gill, *A body of divinity*, 624.

60. Rippon, *A brief memoir of … John Gill*, 75.

61. Gill, *A body of divinity*, 624.

62. Gill, *A body of divinity*, 625.

63. Gill, *A body of divinity*, 616.

64. Gill, *A body of divinity*, 643.

65. Gill, *A body of divinity*, 645.

66. Gill, *A body of divinity*, 645.

67. Rippon, *A brief memoir of … John Gill*, 74–75.

68. Newport, *Apocalypse and millennium*, 119.

69. Newport, *Apocalypse and millennium*, 132. The only previous substantial discussion of the Wesleys' millennialism was to be found in James Cyril Downes, 'Eschatological doctrines in the writings of John and Charles Wesley' (unpublished PhD thesis, University of Edinburgh, 1960).

70. Newport, *Apocalypse and millennium*, 91–118; Harrison, *The second coming*, 30, 148.

71. Newport, *Apocalypse and millennium*, 132.

72. Newport, *Apocalypse and millennium*, 120.

73. This letter is transcribed in full in Newport, *Apocalypse and millennium*, 144–9.

74. All references in this section are from Newport, *Apocalypse and millennium*, 144–9.

75. For a recent example of this trend, see Gribben, *Writing the rapture*, 129–44.

76. Smolinksi, 'Caveat Emptor: Pre- and postmillennialism in the late reformation period,' 145–69, 147.
77. Edward J. Ahearn, *Visionary fictions: Apocalyptic writing from Blake to the modern age* (New Haven: Yale University Press, 1996); Ruth Bloch, *Visionary republic: Millennial themes in American thought, 1756–1800* (Cambridge: Cambridge University Press, 1985); Richard Lee Rogers, 'A testimony to the whole world: Evangelicalism and millennialism in the northeastern United States, 1790–1850' (unpublished PhD thesis, Princeton University, 1996); Robert K. Whalen, '"Christians love the Jews!" The development of American philo-Semitism, 1790–1860,' *Religion and American Culture* 6:2 (1996), 225–59; C.D.A. Leighton, 'Antichrist's revolution: Some Anglican apocalypticists in the age of the French wars,' *Journal of Religious History* 24 (2000), 125–42.

4   The Expansion of Evangelical Millennialism, 1789–1880

1. W.H. Oliver, *Prophets and millennialists: The uses of Biblical prophecy in England from the 1790s to the 1840s* (Auckland, New Zealand: Auckland University Press, 1978); Timothy L. Smith, 'Righteousness and hope: Christian holiness and the millennial vision in America, 1800–1900,' *American Quarterly* 31 (1979), 21–45.
2. See, for American examples, Hatch, 'The origins of civil millennialism in America: New England clergymen, war with France, and the Revolution,' 407–30; idem, *The sacred cause of liberty*. See, for Irish examples, Patrick O'Farrell, 'Millennialism, messianism and utopianism in Irish history,' *Anglo-Irish Studies* 2 (1976), 45–68; Timothy C.F. Stunt, *From awakening to secession: Radical evangelicals in Switzerland and Britain, 1815–35* (Edinburgh: T&T Clark, 2000); Myrtle Hill, 'Watchmen in Zion: Millennial expectancy in late eighteenth-century Ulster,' in Crawford Gribben and Andrew R. Holmes (eds), *Protestant millennialism, evangelicalism and Irish society, 1790–2005* (Basingstoke: Palgrave Macmillan, 2006), 31–51.
3. Alexander Pope, 'Essay on man,' epistle 1, line 294, in *An essay on man, in four epistles, to which is added the universal prayer* (Hartford, CT: H. Benton, 1825), 19.
4. See, for example, Timothy C.F. Stunt, 'Influences in the early development of J.N. Darby,' in Crawford Gribben and Timothy C.F. Stunt (eds), *Prisoners of hope? Aspects of evangelical millennialism in Britain and Ireland, 1800–1880*, Studies in Evangelical History and Thought (Milton Keynes: Paternoster, 2004), 44–67; Crawford Gribben and Mark Sweetnam, 'J.N. Darby and the Irish origins of dispensationalism,' *Journal of the Evangelical Theological Society* 52:3 (2009), 569–77.
5. On Edward Irving and the Catholic Apostolic Church, see Gordon Strachan, *The Pentecostal theology of Edward Irving* (London: DLT, 1973); Graham Allan, 'A theory of millennialism: The Irvingite movement as an illustration,' *British Journal of Sociology* 25 (1974), 296–311; Arnold Dallimore, *The life of Edward Irving: Forerunner of the Charismatic movement* (Edinburgh: Banner of Truth, 1983); Columba Graham Flegg, *Gathered under apostles: A study of the Catholic Apostolic Church* (Oxford: Clarendon Press, 1992); Graham

W. McFarlane, *Christ and the Spirit: The doctrine of the incarnation according to Edward Irving* (Carlisle: Paternoster, 1996); Ralph Brown, 'Victorian Anglican Evangelicalism: The radical legacy of Edward Irving,' *Journal of Ecclesiastical History* 58:4 (2007), 675–704. On the Millerite movement, see David L. Rowe, *Thunder and trumpets: Millerites and dissenting religion in upstate New York, 1800–1850* (Chico, CA: Scholars Press, 1985); Michael Barkun, *Crucible of the millennium: The burned-over district of New York in the 1840s* (Syracuse: Syracuse University Press, 1986); Ruth Alden Doan, *The Miller heresy, millennialism, and American culture* (Philadelphia, PA: Temple University Press, 1987); Ronald L. Numbers and Jonathan M. Butler, *The disappointed: Millerism and millenarianism in the nineteenth century* (Bloomington, IN: Indiana University Press, 1987); and Richard Connors and Andrew Colin Gow (eds), *Anglo-American millennialism, from Milton to the Millerites* (Leiden: Brill, 2004).

6. David N. Hempton, 'Evangelicals and eschatology,' *Journal of Ecclesiastical History* 31 (1980), 191.

7. On the trajectory of nineteenth-century millennialism more generally, see Ahearn, *Visionary fictions*; Bloch, *Visionary republic*; Rogers, 'A testimony to the whole world: Evangelicalism and millennialism in the northeastern United States, 1790–1850'; Whalen, '"Christians love the Jews!" The development of American philo-Semitism, 1790–1860,' 225–59; Leighton, 'Antichrist's revolution: Some Anglican apocalypticists in the age of the French wars,' 125–42.

8. For a more general description of this period, see John Wolffe, *The expansion of evangelicalism: The age of Wilberforce, More, Chalmers and Finney*, A History of Evangelicalism (Leicester: IVP, 2007); David W. Bebbington, *The dominance of evangelicalism: The age of Spurgeon And Moody*, A History of Evangelicalism (Leicester: IVP, 2005); M.W. Carpenter and George Landow, 'Ambiguous revelations: The Apocalypse and Victorian literature,' in C.A. Patrides and J.A. Wittreich (eds), *The Apocalypse in English Renaissance thought and literature* (Manchester: Manchester University Press, 1984), 299–322.

9. William de Burgh, *An exposition of the book of Revelation,* fifth edition (Dublin: Hodges, Smith, & Co., 1857), 149, footnote.

10. *Oxford English Dictionary*, s.v.

11. Clarke Garrett, *Respectable folly: Millenarians and the French Revolution in France and England* (Baltimore, MD: Johns Hopkins University Press, 1975), 29–30.

12. Richard Brothers, *A revealed knowledge of the prophecies and times*, parts I and II (London, 1794, 1795). For the editions of Brothers's works see Harrison, *The second coming*, 241 n. 8.

13. *Oxford DNB*, s.v. On the Avignon Society, see Harrison, *The second coming*, 70.

14. Harrison, *The second coming*, 64–5.

15. Crawford Gribben, 'Introduction: Antichrist in Ireland – Protestant millennialism and Irish studies,' in Crawford Gribben and Andrew R. Holmes (eds), *Protestant millennialism, evangelicalism and Irish society, 1790–2005*, 11.

16. O'Farrell, 'Millennialism, messianism and Utopianism in Irish history,' 52.

17. Stephen J. Stein, *The Shaker experience in America: A history of the United Society of Believers* (New Haven, CT: Yale University Press, 1992); Jan Shipps, *Mormonism: The story of a new religious tradition* (Champaign, IL: University of Illinois Press, 1987).

18. *Oxford DNB*, s.v.; Balleine, *Past finding out*.

19. Allan, 'Southcottian sects.'
20. Harrison, *The second coming*, 123; *Oxford DNB*, s.v.
21. See Timothy C.F. Stunt's articles on Richard Brothers (1757–1824), John 'Zion' Ward (1781–1837), John Wroe (1782–1863), James Elishama Smith (1801–57), Henry James Prince (1811–99), Thomas Lake Harris (1823–1906), and James Jershom Jezreel (1849–85) in the *Oxford DNB*, s.v.
22. Shantz, 'Millennialism and apocalypticism in recent historical scholarship,' 41; Ahearn, *Visionary fictions*, passim.
23. Harrison, *The second coming*, 188–89.
24. See Edwin Scott Gaustad (ed.), *The rise of Adventism: A commentary on the social and religious ferment of mid-nineteenth century America* (New York: Harper and Row, 1974); Rowe, *Thunder and trumpets*; Barkun, *Crucible of the millennium*; Doan, *The Miller heresy, millennialism, and American culture*; and Numbers and Butler, *The disappointed*; and John de Patmos, *The Great Disappointment of 1844* (Brookline, MA: Miskatonic University Press, 2001).
25. M. James Penton, *Apocalypse delayed: The story of Jehovah's Witnesses* (1985; second edition, Toronto: University of Toronto Press, 1997).
26. Harrison, *The second coming*, 224; Mike Sanders, *The poetry of Chartism: Aesthetics, politics, history* (Cambridge: Cambridge University Press, 2009), passim.
27. *Quarterly Journal of Prophecy* 2 (1850), 302–3.
28. Andrew Bonar, *The development of Antichrist* (1853; rpr. Chelmsford: Sovereign Grace Advent Testimony, n.d.), 22. This Andrew Bonar, an English layman, should be distinguished from Andrew A. Bonar, the Free Church of Scotland minister, though they both held premillennial opinions in the 1850s; I regret that I did not make this distinction in Crawford Gribben, 'Andrew Bonar and the Scottish Presbyterian millennium,' in Crawford Gribben and Timothy C.F. Stunt, *Prisoners of hope? Aspects of evangelical millennialism in Britain and Ireland, 1800–1880*, 177–201, and I am grateful to Iain H. Murray for his advice in this regard.
29. Alexander Keith, *Evidence of the truth of the Christian religion, derived from the literal fulfilment of prophecy* (1828; Edinburgh: Waugh and Innes, 1832), 388, 364, 449.
30. De Burgh, *An Exposition of the Book of Revelation*, 193.
31. George H. Fromow, *Teachers of the faith and the future: B.W. Newton and Dr S.P. Tregelles*, second edition (London: Sovereign Grace Advent Testimony, 1969), 17. On Newton's theological development, see Nigel Pibworth, 'Benjamin Wills Newton (1807–1899): A theological biography' (unpublished manuscript).
32. John Cumming, *Prophetic studies; or, Lectures on the book of Daniel* (London: Arthur Hall, 1853), Iv; J.C. Ryle, *Coming events and present duties* (1867), reprinted as *Prophecy* (Fearn, Ross-shire, UK: Christian Focus, 1991), 199.
33. B.S. Frere, *A record of the family of Frere of Suffolk and Norfolk* (privately published, 1982), 192.
34. *Oxford DNB*, s.v.
35. William Reid, *Plymouth Brethrenism unveiled and refuted* (Edinburgh, 1875), 296.
36. Wilkinson, *For Zion's sake*, 184–8.
37. A.L. Drummond, *Edward Irving and his circle* (London: J. Clarke, 1937), 277.

38. Andrew A. Bonar, *Memoirs and remains of Robert Murray McCheyne* (1844; second edition, 1892; rpr. Edinburgh: Banner of Truth, 1966), 27.

39. Stein, *The Shaker experience in America*, 210–11.

40. See Rowe, *Thunder and trumpets*; Barkun, *Crucible of the millennium*; Doan, *The Miller heresy, millennialism, and American culture*; and Numbers and Butler, *The disappointed*.

41. Burdon, *The Apocalypse in England*, 36–7. *Horae Apocalypticae*, fifth edition, 4 vols (London: Seeley, Jackson and Halliday, 1862), i: xxii–xxiv; iv: 237–8.

42. On Cumming, see David Hempton, *Evangelical disenchantment: Nine portraits of faith and doubt* (New Haven, CT: Yale University Press, 2009), 19–40.

43. Hempton, *Evangelical disenchantment*, 26.

44. Hempton, *Evangelical disenchantment*, 28.

45. Cumming, *Prophetic studies*, 405.

46. Charles H. Spurgeon, *Commentating and commentaries* (London: Passmore and Alabaster, 1876), 199. Spurgeon's eschatological interests were related to the tenor of his age: Mark Hopkins, *Nonconformity's Romantic generation: Evangelical and liberal theologies in Victorian England*, Studies in Evangelical History and Thought (Milton Keynes: Paternoster, 2004).

47. C.Y. Biss, *Things which must be: Being the substance of a course of lectures* (Aylesbury: Hunt, Barnard & Co., 1880), v.

48. Patrick Fairbairn, *The interpretation of prophecy* (1865; Edinburgh: Banner of Truth, 1964), iv.

49. Fairbairn, *The interpretation of prophecy*, v, vi.

50. Fairbairn, *The interpretation of prophecy*, viii–ix.

51. B.W. Newton, *Thoughts on the Apocalypse* (1843; second edition, London: Partridge and Oakey, 1853), 6.

52. De Burgh, *An exposition of the book of Revelation*, 2.

53. De Burgh, *An exposition of the book of Revelation*, 152.

54. *Oxford DNB*, s.v. on each writer.

55. De Burgh, *An exposition of the book of Revelation*, vi.

56. De Burgh, *An exposition of the book of Revelation*, vi, 102.

57. Gary L. Nebeker, 'John Nelson Darby and Trinity College, Dublin: A study in eschatological contrasts,' *Fides et Historia* 34 (2002), 87–108. For Darby's biography, see Robert Henry Krapohl, 'A search for purity: The controversial life of John Nelson Darby' (unpublished PhD thesis, Baylor University, 1988).

58. J.N. Darby, *Letters of J.N.D.*, ed. William Kelly (London: Stow Hill Bible and Tract Depot, n.d.), ii: 254.

59. Timothy Larsen (general ed.), *Biographical dictionary of Evangelicals* (Leicester: IVP, 2003), s.v.

60. Quoted in Stunt, 'Influences in the early development of J.N. Darby,' 62.

61. Stunt, 'Influences in the early development of J.N. Darby,' 63–4.

62. S.P. Tregelles to B.W. Newton, 29 January 1857, Christian Brethren Archive, John Rylands University Library, Manchester, 7181 (7).

63. For example, Darby believed in only five dispensations; see Larry V. Crutchfield, *The origins of dispensationalism: The Darby factor* (London: University Press of America, 1992). His work was developed by his followers: see David J. MacLeod, 'Walter Scott, a link in dispensationalism between Darby and Scofield?' *Bibliotheca Sacra* 153:610 (1996), 155–76.

64. C. Norman Kraus, *Dispensationalism in America: Its rise and development* (Richmond, VA: John Knox Press, 1958).

65. Newton, *Thoughts on the Apocalypse*, 9.

66. S. P. Tregelles, *The hope of Christ's second coming* (1864; second edition, London: Samuel Bagster and Sons, 1886), 3.

67. H.A. Ironside, *Wrongly dividing the word of truth* (Neptune, NJ: Loizeaux Borthers, third edition, 1938).

68. Ryle, *Prophecy*, 33.

69. Dana L. Robert, '"The crisis of missions": Premillennial mission theory and the origins of independent evangelical missions,' in Joel A. Carpenter and Wilbert R. Shenk (eds), *Earthen vessels: American evangelicals and foreign missions, 1880–1980* (Grand Rapids, MI: Eerdmans, 1990), 29–46.

70. For Horatius Bonar, see *Horatius Bonar, D.D.: A Memorial* (London, 1890).

71. For Irving, see Strachan, *The Pentecostal theology of Edward Irving*; Dallimore, *The life of Edward Irving*; McFarlane, *Christ and the Spirit*; Clegg, *Gathered under apostles*.

72. Marjory Bonar (ed.), *Andrew A. Bonar: Diary and life* (1893; rpr. Edinburgh: Banner of Truth, 1960), 9.

73. Bonar (ed.), *Andrew A. Bonar*, 15.

74. Bonar (ed.), *Andrew A. Bonar*, 5, 17.

75. Bonar (ed.), *Andrew A. Bonar*, 19.

76. Bonar (ed.), *Andrew A. Bonar*, 20.

77. Don Chambers, 'Prelude to the last things: The Church of Scotland's mission to the Jews,' *Records of the Scottish Church History Society* 19:1 (1975), 43–58.

78. *Blackwell dictionary of evangelical biography, 1730–1860*, ed. Donald M. Lewis (Oxford: Blackwell, 1995), s.v. 'Keith, Alexander'; review of Keith's *Evidence* in *Quarterly Journal of Prophecy* 1:2 (1849), 192.

79. Andrew A. Bonar and Robert Murray McCheyne, *Narrative of a mission of inquiry to the Jews from the Church of Scotland* (Edinburgh, 1842), 1: 174.

80. Bonar and McCheyne, *Narrative*, 2: 135, 210, 237.

81. Bonar and McCheyne, *Narrative*, 2: 201.

82. Bonar and McCheyne, *Narrative*, 1: 258–9.

83. Bonar and McCheyne, *Narrative*, 1: 328.

84. Bonar and McCheyne, *Narrative*, 1: 134–5.

85. Cumming, *Prophetic studies*, 444.

86. John Cumming, *Sabbath evening readings on St Matthew* (London: Arthur Hall, 1853), 335.

87. Cumming, *Prophetic studies*, 421.

88. John Cumming, *Sabbath evening readings on St Matthew*, 346.

89. Paul E. Johnson, *A shopkeeper's millennium: Society and revivals in Rochester, New York, 1815–1837* (New York: Wang and Hill, 1978), 18.

90. Johnson, *A shopkeeper's millennium*, 3–4.

91. Johnson, *A shopkeeper's millennium*, 109.

92. Johnson, *A shopkeeper's millennium*, 5.

93. For the impact of the revival, see I.A. Muirhead, 'The revival as a dimension of Scottish church history,' *Records of the Scottish Church History Society* 20 (1980), 179–96; Kathryn Teresa Long, *The revival of 1857–58: Interpreting an American religious awakening* (Oxford: Oxford University Press, 1998); Janice

Holmes, *Religious revivals in Britain and Ireland, 1859–1905* (Dublin: Irish Academic Press, 2000); Crawford Gribben, '"The worst sect a Christian man can meet": Opposition to the Plymouth Brethren in Ireland and Scotland, 1859–1900,' *Scottish Studies Review* 3:2 (2002), 34–53; and Kenneth S. Jeffrey, *When the Lord walked the land: The 1858–62 revival in the north east of Scotland*, Studies in Evangelical History and Thought (Carlisle, 2002).

94. James McCosh, *The Ulster revival and its physiological accidents: A paper read before the Evangelical Alliance, September 22, 1859* (Belfast, 1859), 10–11. On McCosh and Princeton, see David B. Calhoun, *Princeton Seminary: The majestic testimony, 1869–1929* (Edinburgh: Banner of Truth, 1996), 7.

95. See Iain H. Murray, *The Puritan hope: Revival and the interpretation of prophecy* (Edinburgh: Banner of Truth, 1971), passim.

96. John Weir, *The Ulster awakening: Its origin, progress, and fruit: With notes of a tour of personal observation and inquiry* (London, 1860), 7, 9.

97. *Revivals and the millennial advent foretold by the prophets and the apostles* (Belfast, 1859), 5.

98. 'Preface,' *Quarterly Journal of Prophecy* 1 (1849), iv.

99. Ronald R. Nelson, 'Apocalyptic speculation and the French revolution,' *Evangelical Quarterly* 53 (1981), 205.

100. David Brown, *Christ's second coming: Will it be premillennial?* (1846; 1882 ed., rpt. Edmonton, 1990), 91.

101. Brown, *Christ's second coming*, 3.

102. Brown, *Christ's second coming*, 4.

103. Brown, *Christ's second coming*, 8.

104. James H. Moorhead, *American apocalypse: Yankee protestants and the Civil War, 1860–1869* (New Haven: Yale University Press, 1978); idem, 'The erosion of postmillennialism in American religious thought, 1865–1925,' *Church History* 53:1 (1984), 61–77.

105. *Quarterly Journal of Prophecy* 1:2 (1849), 199–200.

5 The Contest of Evangelical Millennialism, 1880–1970

1. Bram Stoker, *Dracula* (1897; rpr. Oxford: Oxford University Press, 1996), xxxviii.

2. Robert K. Whalen, 'Millenarianism and millennialism in America, 1790–1880' (unpublished PhD thesis, State University of New York, Stony Brook, 1972); Douglas W. Frank, *Less than conquerors: How evangelicals entered the twentieth century* (Grand Rapids, MI: William B. Eerdmans, 1986); Timothy Weber, *Living in the shadow of the second coming: American premillennialism, 1875–1982* (Grand Rapids, MI: Academie Books, 1983); Timothy E. Fulop, '"The future golden day of the race": Millennialism and black Americans in the Nadir, 1877–1901,' *Harvard Theological Review* 84:1 (1991), 75–99.

3. Bonar and McCheyne, *Narrative*, ii: 118.

4. Sandeen, *The roots of Fundamentalism*; George M. Marsden, *Fundamentalism and American culture: The shaping of twentieth-century Evangelicalism, 1870–1925* (Oxford: Oxford University Press, 1980; new edition, 2006); idem, *Understanding Fundamentalism and Evangelicalism* (Grand Rapids, MI: Eerdmans, 1991); idem,

'Fundamentalism as an American phenomenon,' in D.G. Hart (ed.), *Reckoning with the past: Historical essays on American evangelicalism from the Institute for the Study of American Evangelicals* (Grand Rapids: Baker, 1995), 303–21.

5. On the *Scofield reference Bible*, see Sweetnam and Mangum, *The Scofield Bible*.

6. Wilkinson, *For Zion's sake*, 226; Wilson, *Armageddon now!*, passim.

7. Ray Ginger, *Six days or forever? Tennessee vs. John Thomas Scopes* (1958; rpr. Oxford: Oxford University Press, 1974).

8. See, for example, Virginia Lieson Brereton, *Training God's army: The American Bible School, 1880–1940* (Bloomington, IN: Indiana University Press, 1990); Marsden, George M. *Understanding Fundamentalism and Evangelicalism* (Grand Rapids, MI: Eerdmans, 1991); idem, 'Fundamentalism as an American phenomenon,' 303–21.

9. Joseph H. Hall, 'The controversy over Fundamentalism in the Christian Reformed Church, 1915–1966' (unpublished ThD. thesis, Concordia Theological Seminary, 1974); Michael G. Borgert, 'Harry Bultema and the *Maranatha* controversy in the Christian Reformed Church,' *Calvin Theological Journal* 42:1 (2007), 90–109.

10. Joel A. Carpenter, *Revive us again: The reawakening of American Fundamentalism* (Oxford: Oxford University Press, 1997).

11. Cumming, *Prophetic studies*, 449–50.

12. Cumming, *Sabbath evening readings on St Matthew*, 347.

13. James H. Moorhead, 'Between progress and apocalypse: A reassessment of millennialism in American religious thought, 1800–1880,' *Journal of American History* 71:3 (1984), 541.

14. Jack Maddex, 'Proslavery millennialism: Social eschatology in Antebellum Southern Calvinism,' *American Quarterly* 31:1 (1979), 58.

15. Maddex, 'Proslavery millennialism,' 60; James Spivey, 'The millennium,' in Paul Basden (ed.), *Has our theology changed? Southern Baptist thought since 1845* (Nashville: B&H, 1994), 230–62.

16. Spivey, 'The millennium,' 238, 245, 261; Thomas J. Nettles, *James Petigru Boyce: A Southern Baptist Statesman* (Phillipsburg: P&R, 2009); see James Petigru Boyce, *Abstract of systematic theology* (1887; Cape Coral, FL: Founder Press, 2006), chapter forty.

17. David W. Shedden, 'Presbyterian premillennialism and the *Presbyterian Review*' (unpublished ThM thesis, Princeton Theological Seminary, 2007).

18. Jon Zens, *Dispensationalism: A Reformed inquiry into its leading figures and features* (Phillipsburg, NJ: P&R, 1978), 10.

19. Sandeen, *The roots of Fundamentalism*.

20. Moorhead, *American apocalypse*; idem, 'The erosion of postmillennialism in American religious thought, 1865–1925,' 61–77; idem, *World without end: Mainstream American protestant visions of the last things, 1880–1925* (Bloomington, IN: Indiana University Press, 2000).

21. Mark A. Noll, *A history of Christianity in the United States and Canada* (Grand Rapids, MI: Eerdmans, 1992), 214–15.

22. The cultural and religious impact of the Civil War has been surveyed in a series of recent publications: Edward J. Blum, *Reforging the white Republic: Race, religion, and American nationalism, 1865–1898* (2005); Mark A. Noll, *The Civil War as a theological crisis* (Chapel Hill, NC: University of North Carolina

Press, 2006); and Harry S. Stout, *Upon the altar of the nation: A moral history of the Civil War* (New York: Viking, 2006).
23. Stout, *Upon the altar of the nation*, 93. Milton H. Stine, *Studies on the religious problem of our country* (York, PA: Lutheran Printing House, 1888), 161.
24. Stine, *Studies on the religious problem of our country*, 5, 9, 16.
25. Gribben, *Writing the rapture*, 38–45.
26. Spurgeon, 'Mr. Spurgeon's Confession of Faith,' 85.
27. Sandeen, *The roots of Fundamentalism*.
28. Sandeen, *The roots of Fundamentalism*; G.S. Smith, 'West, Nathaniel (1826–1906),' in D.G. Hart (ed.), *Dictionary of the Presbyterian and Reformed tradition in America* (Downers Grove, Illinois: IVP, 1999), 273; W.V. Tollinger, 'Moorehead, William Gallogly (1836–1914),' in D.G. Hart (ed.), *Dictionary of the Presbyterian and Reformed tradition in America*, 164; C. Wilt, 'Erdman, William Jacob (1834–1923),' in D.G. Hart (ed.), *Dictionary of the Presbyterian and Reformed tradition in America*, 92.
29. Edward Dennett, *The blessed hope* (1879; rpr. Bromley, Kent: Wilson Foundation, 1969), 2.
30. Clarence Larkin, *Dispensational truth* (Glenside, PA: Clarence Larkin Estate, 1918); Clarence Larkin, *The book of Revelation* (Glenside, PA: Clarence Larkin Estate, 1919), x.
31. D. Carter, 'Joseph Agar Beet and the eschatological crisis,' *Proceedings of the Wesley Historical Society* (1998) 51:6, 197–216.
32. Joseph Agar Beet, *The last things* (1897; fifth edition, London: Hodder and Stoughton, 1905), 83–100.
33. Beet, *The last things*, v.
34. Beet, *The last things*, viii, xi.
35. Beet, *The last things*, xiv.
36. See, for example, *The companion Bible*, ed. E.W. Bullinger (1909–22; rpr. London: Lamp Press, n.d.), 162–3.
37. A. E. Knoch, *The unveiling of Jesus Christ* (Los Angeles: Concordant Publishing Concern, 1935).
38. T.K. McCrossan, *The Bible: Its hell and its ages* (Seattle, WA: privately published, 1941).
39. Philip Mauro, *The gospel of the kingdom: An examination of modern dispensationalism* (Swengel, PA: Bible Truth Depot, 1927), 5.
40. Mauro, *The gospel of the kingdom*, 10.
41. C.A. Chader, *God's plan through the ages* (London: Marshall, Morgan & Scott, 1938), viii, dust cover.
42. G.H. Pember, *The great prophecies of the centuries concerning Israel, the Gentiles, and the Church of God* (London: Oliphants, 1941), vii.
43. William J. Rowlands, *Our Lord cometh* (London: Privately published, 1930); Alexander Reese, *The approaching advent of Christ: An examination of the teaching of J.N. Darby and his followers* (London: Marshall, Morgan & Scott, 1937), xi.
44. Reese, *The approaching advent of Christ*, xv.
45. C.F. Hogg and W.E. Vine, *The church and the tribulation: A review of the book entitled 'The Approaching advent of Christ'* (London: Pickering and Inglis, 1938), 9.
46. Hogg and Vine, *The church and the tribulation*, 6.

47. W. Graham Scroggie, *The Lord's return* (London: Pickering and Inglis, n.d.).
48. William Edward Biederwolf, *The millennium Bible* (privately published, 1924), 5.
49. Warfield outlined his reading of Revelation 20:1–10 in 'The millennium and the apocalypse,' in *The Works of Benjamin B. Warfield*, 10 vols (New York: Oxford University Press, 1932), 2: 643–4.
50. Mark Sweetnam, 'Tensions in dispensational eschatology,' in Kenneth G.C. Newport and Crawford Gribben (eds), *Expecting the end: Millennialism in social and historical context* (Baylor, TX: Baylor University Press, 2006), 173–92.
51. Shirley Jackson Case, *The millennial hope: A phase of war-time thinking* (Chicago: University of Chicago Press, 1918), 208.
52. R.H. Charles, *A critical and exegetical commentary on the Revelation of St. John*, International Critical Commentary, 2 volumes (Edinburgh: T & T Clark, 1920), 1: ix, 2: 437.
53. Charles G. Trumball, *The life story of C.I. Scofield* (New York: Oxford University Press, 1920); Joseph M. Canfield, *The incredible Scofield and his book* (Vallecito, California: Ross House Books, 1988); Sweetnam and Mangum, *The Scofield Bible*.
54. 'The Scofield Study Bible: Scofield's use of the critical text and the AV,' *Quarterly Record: The Magazine of the Trinitarian Bible Society* 566 (2004), 21–7; Sweetnam and Mangum, *The Scofield Bible*.
55. The term was sufficiently popularized for Harry Emerson Fosdick to use it in the title of his famous sermon, 'Shall the fundamentalists win?' (1922), in *The Riverside Preachers*, ed. Paul H. Sherry (New York: Pilgrim Press, 1978), 27–38.
56. *The fundamentals: A testimony to the truth*, ed. 'Two Christian Laymen' (Chicago: Testimony Publishing Company, 1910–1915), 1: Foreword.
57. *The fundamentals*, 4: Foreword.
58. *The fundamentals*, 5: 4.
59. *The fundamentals*, 10: Foreword, 128.
60. *The fundamentals*, 11: 100–12, 113–26.
61. 'A statement by the two laymen,' in *The fundamentals*, 12: 4.
62. William G. Moorehead, 'Millennial dawn: A counterfeit of Christianity,' in *The fundamentals: A testimony to the truth*, ed. 'Two Christian Laymen,' 7: 106–27.
63. 'Tributes to Christ and the Bible by brainy men not known as active Christians,' in *The fundamentals: A testimony to the truth*, ed. 'Two Christian Laymen,' 2: 120–6.
64. Wilkinson, *For Zion's sake*, 226; Wilson, *Armageddon now!*, passim.
65. Nick Railton, 'Gog and Magog: The history of a symbol,' *Evangelical Quarterly* 75:1 (2003), 23–43.
66. For accounts of the history of Christian Zionism, see Wilkinson, *For Zion's sake*, and Donald M. Lewis, *The origins of Christian Zionism: Lord Shaftesbury and Evangelical support for a Jewish homeland* (Cambridge: Cambridge University Press, 2009).
67. Leonard Sale-Harrison, *The remarkable Jew: God's great timepiece* (Harrisburg, PA: Evangelical Press; Glasgow: Pickering & Inglis, 1934), 5.
68. Sale-Harrison, *The remarkable Jew*, 5.
69. Sale-Harrison, *The remarkable Jew*, 10.

70. Stephen Spector, *Evangelicals and Israel: The story of American Christian Zionism* (Oxford: Oxford University Press, 2008).

71. Lewis Sperry Chafer, *Systematic theology*, 8 vols (1948; reprinted Dallas: Dallas Theological Seminary, 1975); Jeffery John Richards, 'The eschatology of Lewis Sperry Chafer: His contribution to a systematization of dispensational premillennialism' (unpublished PhD thesis, Drew University, 1985).

72. Ed Hindson, *End times, the middle east, and the New World Order* (Wheaton, IL: Victor Books, 1991), 28.

73. See, for a general discussion of the crisis in the mainstream denominations, Bradley J. Longfield, *The Presbyterian controversy: Fundamentalists, Modernists, and moderates* (Oxford: Oxford University Press, 1991).

74. Daniel W. Draney, *When streams diverge: John Murdock MacInnis and the origins of protestant Fundamentalism in Los Angeles*, Studies in Evangelical History and Thought (Milton Keynes, UK: Paternoster, 2008), 189.

75. Draney, *When streams diverge*, 198.

76. R. Todd Mangum, *The dispensational-covenantal rift: The fissuring of American evangelical theology from 1936 to 1944*, Studies in Evangelical History and Thought (Milton Keynes: Paternoster, 2007).

77. W.J. Grier, *The momentous event: A discussion of Scripture teaching on the second advent* (1945; reprinted Edinburgh: Banner of Truth, 1970).

78. Oswald T. Allis, *Prophecy and the church* (1945; Phillipsburg, NJ: P&R, 1974).

79. Archibald Hughes, *A new heaven and a new earth* (Marshall, Morgan & Scott, 1958); Herman Ridderbos, *The coming of the kingdom* (Philadelphia, PA: P&R, 1962).

80. Iain H. Murray, *D. Martyn Lloyd-Jones: The fight of faith, 1939–1981* (Edinburgh: Banner of Truth, 1990); John Brencher, *Martyn Lloyd-Jones (1899–1981) and twentieth-century evangelicalism*, Studies in Evangelical History and Thought (Milton Keynes: Paternoster, 2002).

81. Paul Boyer, *By the bomb's early light: American thought and culture at the dawn of the Atomic Age* (New York: Pantheon Books, 1985); A.G. Mojtabai, *Blessed assurance: At home with the bomb in Amarillo, Texas* (Albuquerque, NM: University of New Mexico Press, 1986).

82. Billy Graham, *World aflame* (Tadworth, Surrey: The World's Work, 1965), 13.

83. John F. Walvoord, *The return of the Lord* (1955; rpr. Grand Rapids: Zondervan, 1980), 9.

84. Walvoord, *The return of the Lord*, 5.

85. Arthur W. Kac, *The rebirth of the State of Israel – Is it of God or of men?* (Edinburgh: Marshall, Morgan and Scott, 1958), 8.

86. Kac, *The rebirth of the State of Israel*, 301.

87. Walvoord, *The return of the Lord*, 14.

88. Walvoord, *The return of the Lord*, 136.

89. Walvoord, *The return of the Lord*, 15.

90. Walvoord, *The return of the Lord*, 16.

91. Walvoord, *The return of the Lord*, 35.

92. Walvoord, *The return of the Lord*, 11.

93. J. Dwight Pentecost, *Prophecy for today: The middle east crisis and the future of the world* (Grand Rapids, MI: Zondervan, 1961), 16.

94. On Tatford, see Crawford Gribben, 'Novel doctrines, doctrinal novels: F.A. Tatford and Brethren prophecy fiction,' in Neil Dickson (ed.), *Brethren and culture* (forthcoming).
95. Frederick A. Tatford, *Five minutes to midnight* (London: Victory Press, 1970; idem, *It's never been so late before* (Belfast: Ambassador, 1986).
96. George M. Marsden, *Reforming Fundamentalism: Fuller Seminary and the new Evangelicalism* (Grand Rapids, MI: Eerdmans, 1987).
97. On Ladd, see D'Elia, *A place at the table*, passim.
98. D'Elia, *A place at the table*, xiii.
99. Walvoord, *The return of the Lord*, 45–6.
100. Walvoord, *The return of the Lord*, 16.
101. Carpenter, *Revive us again*.

6   The Dominance of Evangelical Millennialism, 1970–2000

1. Hart, *Deconstructing Evangelicalism*, 24.
2. Hart, *Deconstructing Evangelicalism*, 13–14, 17.
3. See, for a general discussion, Paul C. Merkley, *American presidents, religion and Israel: The heirs of Cyrus* (Westport, CT: Praeger, 2004). Clinton grew up in a dispensational church in Arkansas and strongly supported Israel on theological terms; O. Palmer Robertson, *The Israel of God: Yesterday, today, and tomorrow* (Phillipsburg, NJ: P&R, 2000), 1. For a discussion of Bush's eschatological interests, see Spector, *Evangelicals and Israel*, 205–10. On the role of evangelical confession of sin in American public life, see Susan Wise Bauer, *The art of the public grovel: Sexual sin and public confession in America* (Princeton, NJ: Princeton University Press, 2008).
4. Hart, *Deconstructing Evangelicalism*, 17.
5. Stephen Sizer, *Christian Zionism: Road-map to Armageddon?* (Leicester: IVP, 2004), 23. On Falwell, see Merrill Simon, *Jerry Falwell and the Jews* (Middle Village, NY: Jonathan David Publishers, 1984), and Susan Friend Harding, *The book of Jerry Falwell: Fundamentalist language and politics* (Princeton: Princeton University Press, 2000). On Robertson, see Robert Walters, 'Robertson's Holy Crusade,' *The Frederick Post*, Frederick, Maryland, 28 July 1986; David Edwin Harrell, Jr., *Pat Robertson: A personal, religious, and political portrait* (San Francisco, CA: Harper & Row, 1987); Wayne King, 'The record of Pat Robertson on religion and government,' *New York Times*, national edition, 27 December 1987, 20; John W. Robbins, *Pat Robertson: A warning to America* (Jefferson, MD: The Trinity Foundation, 1988); Stephen D. O'Leary and Michael McFarland, 'The political use of mythic discourse: Prophetic interpretation in Pat Robertson's presidential campaign,' *Quarterly Journal of Speech* 75 (1989), 433–52; Ephraim Radner, 'New world order, old world anti-Semitism: Pat Robertson of the Christian coalition,' *Christian Century*, 13 September 1995; Toulouse, 'Pat Robertson: Apocalyptic theology and American foreign policy,' 73–99; Gribben, *Writing the rapture*, 118–27.
6. Sizer, *Christian Zionism: Road-map to Armageddon?* 105.
7. Callum Brown, *The death of Christian Britain* (London: Routledge, 2001).
8. Hart, *Deconstructing Evangelicalism*, 150.
9. Hart, *Deconstructing Evangelicalism*, 15.

10. Hart, *Deconstructing Evangelicalism*, 16.
11. See Gribben, *Writing the rapture*, 129–44.
12. Gribben, *Writing the rapture*, 145–65.
13. Robert William Fogel, *The fourth Great Awakening & the future of egalitarianism* (Chicago: University of Chicago Press, 2000).
14. On the history and sociology of the Jesus People, see Frederick Norman Wagner, 'A theological and historical assessment of the Jesus people phenomenon' (unpublished PhD thesis, Fuller Theological Seminary, 1971); Sally Dobson Bookman, 'Jesus People: A religious movement in a mid-western city' (unpublished PhD thesis, University of California, Berkeley, 1974); Preston David Shires, 'Hippies of the religious right: The counterculture and American evangelicalism in the 1960s and 1970s' (unpublished PhD thesis, University of Nebraska, Lincoln, 2002); and Kevin John Smith, 'The origins, nature, and significance of the Jesus Movement as a revitalization movement' (unpublished DMiss thesis, Asbury Theological Seminary, 2003).
15. I owe this information to Thomas Ice.
16. 'Billy Graham: Man with a Mission,' *Cincinnati Post*. 27 June 2002.
17. The dispensational scheme is set out in Graham, *World aflame*, 194.
18. Simon, *Jerry Falwell and the Jews*, 9.
19. Sizer, *Christian Zionism*, 155.
20. Lindsey, *The late great planet Earth*, 43.
21. *Los Angeles Times*, 23 February 1991, p. F16.
22. Lindsey, *The late great planet Earth*, 43.
23. Lindsey, *The late great planet Earth*, 54.
24. Boyer, *When time shall be no more*, 141, 142; Marsden, 'Fundamentalism as an American Phenomenon,' 319; James Mills, 'The serious implications of a 1971 conversation with Ronald Reagan: A footnote to current history,' *San Diego Magazine* (August 1985), 141; Sizer, *Christian Zionism*, 86–9.
25. Gribben, *Writing the rapture*, 19.
26. James Montgomery Boice, *The last and future world* (Grand Rapids, MI: Zondervan, 1974), ix, 5.
27. Boice, *The last and future world*, 23.
28. Boice, *The last and future world*, 62.
29. Sizer, *Christian Zionism*, 86, quoting a speech by President Jimmy Carter on 1 May 1978, *Department of State Bulletin*, vol. 78 no. 2015 (1978), 4.
30. Wilson, *Armageddon Now!* 12.
31. Sizer, *Christian Zionism*, 214; James Castelli, 'The environmental gospel according to James Watt,' *Chicago Tribune*, 25 October 1981, B2.
32. Ronald Reagan, 'Address to the National Association of Evangelicals, March 8, 1983,' in Paul Boyer (ed.), *Reagan as President: Contemporary views of the man, his politics, and his policies* (Chicago: Ivan R. Dee, 1990), 165–9.
33. 'Hal Lindsey, from *The late great planet Earth*,' in *The Norton Anthology of English Literature*, http://www.wwnorton.com/nto/20century/topic_3/crystal. htm, accessed 6 August 2007.
34. George Eldon Ladd, *A commentary on the Revelation of John* (Grand Rapids, MI: Zondervan, 1972); Robert H. Mounce, *The Book of Revelation*, New International Commentaries on the New Testament (Grand Rapids, MI: Eerdmans, 1977); Robert H. Gundry, *The church and the tribulation* (Grand Rapids, MI: Zondervan, 1973).

35. Bob Stokes, *Conflict, conquest and the second coming* (Rushden, UK: Stanley L. Hunt, 1975), 89.
36. Barry Hankins, *Francis Schaeffer and the shaping of evangelical America* (Grand Rapids, MI: Eerdmans, 2008).
37. Wim Rietkerk, *The future great planet Earth* (Mussoorie, U.P., India: Nivedit Good Books, 1989), 29.
38. Rietkerk, *The future great planet Earth*, 3.
39. Blaising and Bock, *Progressive dispensationalism*.
40. Hindson, *End times, the middle east, and the New World Order*, 13.
41. H. Wayne House and Thomas D. Ice, *Dominion theology: Blessing or curse?* (Portland, OR: Multnomah, 1988), 210.
42. A biography of Bavinck by Ron Gleason is forthcoming from P&R.
43. Bavinck, *The last things*, 91.
44. Bavinck, *The last things*, 110.
45. Bavinck, *The last things*, 121.
46. William Hendricksen, *More than conquerors: An interpretation of the book of Revelation* (1939; Grand Rapids, MI: Baker, 1982), 18–19.
47. G.C. Berkouwer, *The return of Christ*, Studies in dogmatics (Grand Rapids, MI: Eerdmans, 1972), 294.
48. Grier, *The momentous event*; J. Marcellus Kik, *Matthew twenty-four* (Philadelphia, PA: P&R, 1948); idem, *Revelation twenty* (Philadelphia, PA: P&R, 1955); James Hamilton, *Light on the 'last days': An historical review of 'days' long past* (Glasgow: K & R Davidson, 1962).
49. Zens, *Dispensationalism*, 42.
50. John H. Gerstner, *Wrongly dividing the worth of truth: A critique of dispensationalism* (1991; second edition, Morgan, PA: Soli Deo Gloria, 2000), vi.
51. Michael Wilcock, *I saw heaven opened: The message of Revelation*, The Bible Speaks Today (Leicester: IVP, 1975), 181–2.
52. Bruce A. Milne, *I want to know what the Bible says about the end of the world* (1979), republished as *The end of the world* (Eastbourne: Kingsway, 1983), 7.
53. Milne, *The end of the world*, 29, 47.
54. Milne, *The end of the world*, 32.
55. See Crawford Gribben, 'Protestant millennialism, political violence and the Ulster conflict,' *Irish Studies Review* 15:1 (2007), 51–63.
56. Gary DeMar, *Something greater is here: Christian Reconstruction in biblical perspective* (Fort Worth, TX: Dominion Press, 1988), 39.
57. David Chilton, *Paradise restored: A biblical theology of dominion* (Fort Worth, TX: Dominion Press, 1985); DeMar, *Something greater is here*; Kenneth L. Gentry, *The beast of Revelation* (Tyler, TX: Institute for Christian Economics, 1989).
58. Robertson, *The Israel of God*.
59. Robertson, *The Israel of God*, 25.
60. Robertson, *The Israel of God*, 31.
61. Kim Riddlebarger, *A case for amillennialism: Understanding the end times* (Grand Rapids, MI: Baker, 2003), 13.
62. Riddlebarger, *A case for amillennialism*, 229–230.
63. Riddlebarger, *A case for amillennialism*, 11.
64. Lance Lambert, *The uniqueness of Israel* (Eastbourne, UK: Kingsway, 1980), 8.

65. Francis Fukuyama, 'The End of History?' in *The National Interest* (Summer 1989), 4. Fukuyama repeated this claim in *The end of history and the last man* (New York: Free Press, 1992).

66. Brown, *The death of Christian Britain*.

67. The popularity of the Left Behind novels, the series in question, has led Melani McAlister to wonder whether the worldview they represent may in fact now be the American mainstream; 'Prophecy, politics and the popular: the *Left Behind* series and Christian fundamentalism's New World Order,' *South Atlantic Quarterly* 102:4 (2003), 773–98.

68. Amy Johnson Frykholm, *Rapture culture:* Left Behind *in evangelical America* (New York: Oxford University Press, 2004); Bruce David Forbes and Jeanne Halgren Kilde (eds), *Rapture, Revelation, and the End Times: Exploring the Left Behind series* (New York: Palgrave Macmillan, 2004); Peter Althouse, 'Left Behind – fact or fiction: Ecumenical dilemmas of the fundamentalist millenarian tensions within Pentecostalism,' *Journal of Pentecostal Theology* 13 (2005), 187–207; Sherryll Mleynek, 'The rhetoric of the 'Jewish problem' in the *Left Behind* novels,' *Literature and Theology* 19:4 (2005), 367–83; Glenn W. Shuck, *Marks of the beast: The Left Behind novels and the struggle for evangelical identity* (New York: New York University Press, 2005); Malcolm Gold, 'The *Left Behind* series as sacred text,' in Elizabeth Arweck and Peter Collins (eds), *Reading religion in text and context* (Aldershot: Ashgate, 2006), 34–49; Gribben, *Writing the rapture*; Jennie Chapman, 'Selling faith without selling out: Reading the Left Behind novels in the context of popular culture,' in John Wallis and Kenneth G. C. Newport (eds), *Apocalyptic texts and popular culture* (London: Equinox, 2008), 148–72.

69. Mark Lilla, 'Church meets state,' *The New York Times Book Review*, 15 May 2005, 39.

70. Hindson, *End times, the middle east, and the New World Order*, 7.

71. Hindson, *End times, the middle east, and the New World Order*, 8.

72. Jorstad, *The politics of doomsday*; Lippy, 'Waiting for the end: The social context of American apocalyptic religion,' 37–63; Robert Clouse, 'The New Christian Right, America, and the Kingdom of God,' 3–16; Ostling, 'Armageddon and the end times: Prophecies of the last days surface as a campaign issue,' 73; Mills, 'The serious implications of a 1971 conversation with Ronald Reagan: A footnote to current history,' 141; Halsell, *Prophecy and politics*; Weigert, 'Christian eschatological identities and the nuclear context,' 175–91; Ritter, 'Reagan's 1964 TV speech for Goldwater: Millennial themes in American political rhetoric,' 58–72; Wagner, *Anxious for Armageddon*; Wojcik, 'Embracing doomsday: Faith, fatalism, and apocalyptic beliefs in the nuclear age,' 297–330; Haija, 'The Armageddon lobby: Dispensationalist Christian Zionism and the shaping of US policy towards Israel-Palestine,' 75–95; Milich, 'Fundamentalism hot and cold: George W. Bush and the "Return of the Sacred,"' 92–125; Phillips, *American theocracy*.

73. Samuel Huntingdon, *The clash of civilizations* (New York: Simon & Schuster, 1996).

74. Paul S. Boyer, 'When U.S. foreign policy meets Biblical prophecy,' *AlterNet*, 20 February 2003, http://www.alternet.org/story/15221, accessed 8 August 2006.

75. Hart, *Deconstructing Evangelicalism*, 176.

Conclusion

1. Gribben, *Writing the rapture*, 167–70.
2. W.Y. Fullerton, *No ordinary man: The remarkable life of F.B. Meyer* (1929; rpr. Belfast: Ambassador, 1993).
3. Gregory MacDonald, *The evangelical universalist* (2006; rpr. London: SPCK, 2008). Parry revealed his identity as Gregory MacDonald at http://theologicalscribbles.blogspot.com/2009/08/i-am-evangelical-universalist.html, accessed 4 January 2010.
4. In David L. Edwards and John Stott, *Evangelical essentials: A liberal–evangelical dialogue* (Leicester: IVP, 1989); see also Billy Graham, 'Teacher of the faith: John Stott,' *TIME* (18 April 2005), 80.
5. Evangelical Alliance, *The nature of hell* (Carlisle: Paternoster, 2000).
6. Gribben, *The puritan millennium*, 37–8.
7. R.C. Sproul gave Russell's arguments a controversial new lease of life in *The last days according to Jesus: When did Jesus say he would return?* (Grand Rapids: Baker, 1998).
8. See the relevant essays in Gribben and Stunt (eds), *Prisoners of Hope?*, and Gribben and Holmes (eds), *Protestant millennialism, evangelicalism and Irish society, 1790–2005*.
9. Gary North coined the expression 'dispen-sensationalism.'
10. Lindsey, *The late great planet Earth*, 54.
11. This is most evidence in George E. Ladd, *A Theology of the New Testament* (London: Lutterworth, 1975) and Gundry, *The church and the tribulation*.
12. Wilkinson, *For Zion's sake*; Lewis, *The origins of Christian Zionism*.
13. Muhammad Abu-Nimer, *Peace-building by, between and beyond Muslims and evangelical Christians* (London: Lexington Books, 2009).
14. The earliest printing of Tim LaHaye and Jerry B. Jenkins, *Left Behind* (Wheaton, IL: Tyndale House, 1995) included Mother Theresa among those taken by the rapture, but the idea was so controversial that it was omitted from subsequent editions of the same text. I owe this information to Thomas Ice, personal conversation, 14 July 2006.

Bibliography

Manuscripts

Christian Brethren Archive, John Rylands University Library, Manchester, 7181 (7).
Trinity College Dublin MS 2940.

Printed sources

Aberle, David F., 'A note on relative deprivation theory as applied to millenarian and other cult movements,' in Sylvia Thrupp (ed.), *Millennial dreams in action: Studies in revolutionary religious movements* (New York: Schocken Books, 1970), 209–14.

Abu-Nimer, Muhammad, *Peace-building by, between and beyond Muslims and evangelical Christians* (London: Lexington Books, 2009).

Ahearn, Edward J., *Visionary fictions: Apocalyptic writing from Blake to the modern age* (New Haven: Yale University Press, 1996).

Allan, Gordon, 'Southcottian sects from 1790 to the present day,' in Kenneth G.C. Newport and Crawford Gribben (eds), *Expecting the end: Millennialism in social and historical context* (Baylor, TX: Baylor University Press, 2006), 213–36.

Allan, Graham, 'A theory of millennialism: The Irvingite movement as an illustration,' *British Journal of Sociology* 25 (1974), 296–311.

Allis, Oswald T., *Prophecy and the church* (1945; Phillipsburg, NJ: P&R, 1974).

Almond, Gabriel Abraham, et al., *Strong religion: The rise of fundamentalisms around the world* (Chicago: University of Chicago Press, 2003).

Almond, Philip, 'John Napier and the mathematics of the middle future apocalypse,' *Scottish Journal of Theology* 63:1 (2010), 54–69.

Althouse, Peter, 'Left Behind – fact or fiction: Ecumenical dilemmas of the fundamentalist millenarian tensions within Pentecostalism,' *Journal of Pentecostal Theology* 13 (2005), 187–207.

Amanat, Abbas, and Magnus Bernhardsson (eds), *Imagining the end: Visions of apocalypse from the Ancient Middle East to modern America* (London: I.B. Taurus, 2002).

Ammerman, Nancy, *Bible believers: Fundamentalists in the modern world* (New Brunswick, NJ: Rutgers University Press, 1987).

Anderson, Robert Mapes, *Visions of the disinherited: The making of American Pentecostalism* (Oxford: Oxford University Press, 1979).

Archer, John, *The Personall Reigne of Christ upon Earth* (London, 1643).

Ariel, Yaakov, 'Doomsday in Jerusalem? Christian messianic groups and the rebuilding of the Temple,' *Terrorism and Political Violence* 13:1 (2001), 1–14.

Ariel, Yaakov, 'How are Jews and Israel portrayed in the Left Behind series?' in Bruce David Forbes and Jeanne Halgren Kilde (eds), *Rapture, revelation, and the End Times: Exploring the Left Behind series* (New York: Palgrave Macmillan, 2004), 131–66.

Armitage, David and Michael J. Braddick (eds), *The British Atlantic world, 1500–1800*, second edition (Basingstoke: Palgrave Macmillan, 2009).

The art of self-deniall: or, A Christian's first lesson: By that famous Prophett of these times: Tho: Brightman (1646).

Ascol, Thomas, 'The doctrine of grace: A critical analysis of federalism in the theologies of John Gill and Andrew Fuller' (unpublished PhD thesis, Southwestern Baptist Theological Seminary, 1989).

Augustine, *Concerning the City of God against the pagans*, trans. Henry Bettenson (London: Penguin, 1984).

Austin, Kenneth, *From Judaism to Calvinism: The life and writings of Immanuel Tremellius (c. 1510–1580)*, St Andrews Studies in Reformation History (Aldershot: Ashgate, 2007).

Backus, Irena, *Reformation readings of the apocalypse: Geneva, Zurich and Wittenberg* (Oxford: Oxford University Press, 2000).

Backus, Irena, 'The Church Fathers and the canonicity of the Apocalypse in the sixteenth century: Erasmus, Frans Titelmans, and Theodore Beza,' *Sixteenth Century Journal* 29 (1998), 651–65.

Bale, John, *The image of both Churches* (1547); rpt. in *Select works of John Bale*, ed. Henry Christmas (Cambridge: University Press, 1849).

Ball, B.W., *A great expectation: Eschatological thought in English Protestantism to 1660* (Leiden: Brill, 1975).

Balleine, G.R., *Past finding out: The tragic story of Joanna Southcott and her successors* (London: SPCK, 1956).

Balmer, Randall, *Mine eyes have seen the glory: A journey into the evangelical subculture in America* (1989; fourth edition, Oxford: Oxford University Press, 2006).

Balmer, Randall, *Thy kingdom come: How the religious right distorts the faith and threatens America: An evangelical's lament* (New York: Basic Books, 2006).

Balmer, Randall, *Encyclopedia of evangelicalism* (Louisville: Westminster John Knox Press, 2002).

Balmer, Randall, 'Apocalypticism in America: The argot of premillennialism in popular culture,' *Prospects* 13 (1988), 417–33.

Balmer, Randall, 'Divided apocalypse: Thinking about the end in contemporary America,' *Soundings* 66 (1983), 257–80.

Barkun, Michael, *A culture of conspiracy: Apocalyptic visions in contemporary America* (Berkeley: University of California Press, 2003).

Barkun, Michael, *Crucible of the millennium: The Burned-Over District of New York in the 1840s* (Syracuse: Syracuse University Press, 1986).

Barkun, Michael (ed.), *Millennialism and violence* (London: Routledge, 1996).

Barnes, R.B., *Prophecy and gnosis: Apocalypticism in the wake of the Lutheran reformation* (Stanford, CA: Stanford University Press, 1988).

Barron, Bruce, *Heaven on earth? The social and political agendas of Dominion Theology* (Grand Rapids, MI: Zondervan, 1992).

Bauckham, Richard, *Tudor Apocalypse: Sixteenth century apocalypticism, millenarianism and the English Reformation: from John Bale to John Foxe and Thomas Brightman* (Appleford: Sutton Courtenay Press, 1978).

Bauer, Susan Wise, *The art of the public grovel: Sexual sin and public confession in America* (Princeton, NJ: Princeton University Press, 2008).

Baumgartner, Frederic, *Longing for the end: A history of millennialism in Western civilization* (New York: Palgrave, 1999).

Bavinck, Herman, *The last things: Hope for this world and the next*, ed. John Bolt, trans. John Vriend (Grand Rapids, MI: Baker, 1996).

Baxter, Richard, *The glorious kingdom of Christ, described and clearly vindicated* (1691).

Bebbington, David W., 'Response,' in Michael A.G. Haykin and Kenneth J. Stewart (eds), *The emergence of Evangelicalism: Exploring historical continuities* (Nottingham: Apollos, 2008), 417–32.

Bebbington, David W., *The dominance of evangelicalism: The age of Spurgeon and Moody*, A History of Evangelicalism (Leicester: IVP, 2005).

Bebbington, David W., 'Evangelical theology in the English-speaking world during the nineteenth century,' *Scottish Bulletin of Evangelical Theology* 22:2 (2004), 133–50.

Bebbington, David W., *Evangelicalism in Modern Britain: A History from the 1730s to the 1980s* (London: Routledge, 1989).

Bebbington, David W., 'The Advent hope in British Evangelicalism since 1800,' *Scottish Journal of Religious Studies* 9 (1988), 103–10.

Beechick, Allen, *The pre-tribulation rapture* (Denver, CO: Accent, 1980).

Beet, Joseph Agar, *The last things* (1897; fifth edition, London: Hodder and Stoughton, 1905).

Bendle, Mervyn F., 'The apocalyptic imagination and popular culture,' *Journal of Religion and Popular Culture* 11 (2005), available online at http://www.usask.ca/relst/jrpc/index.html.

Berger, James, *After the end: Representations of post-apocalypse* (Minneapolis: University of Minnesota, 1999).

Berkouwer, G.C., *The return of Christ*, Studies in dogmatics (Grand Rapids, MI: Eerdmans, 1972).

Bickersteth, Edward, *Practical guide to the prophecies* (fourth edition, London: R.B. Seeley and W. Burnside, 1835).

Biederwolf, William Edward, *The millennium Bible* (privately published, 1924).

'Billy Graham: Man with a Mission,' *Cincinnati Post*. 27 June 2002.

Biss, C.Y., *Things which must be: Being the substance of a course of lectures* (Aylesbury: Hunt, Barnard & Co., 1880).

Bjork, Rebecca S., 'Reagan and the nuclear freeze: 'Star Wars' as a rhetorical strategy,' *Journal of the American Forensic Association* 24 (1988), 181–92.

Blackstone, W.E., *Jesus is coming* (Chicago: Moody Press, 1898).

Blackwell Dictionary of Evangelical Biography, 1730–1860, ed. Donald M. Lewis (Oxford: Blackwell, 1995).

Blaising, Craig A. and Darrell L. Bock, *Progressive dispensationalism* (Wheaton, IL: Victor, 1993).

Bloch, Ruth, *Visionary republic: Millennial themes in American thought, 1756–1800* (Cambridge: Cambridge University Press, 1985).

Blum, Edward J., *Reforging the white republic: Race, religion, and American nationalism, 1865–1898* (Baton Rouge, LA: Louisiana State University Press, 2005).

Blumenthal, Sidney, 'The Religious Right and Republicans,' in Richard John Neuhaus and Michael Cromartie (eds), *Piety and politics: Evangelicals and Fundamentalists confront the world* (Washington, DC: Ethics and Public Policy Center, 1987).

Boice, James Montgomery, *The last and future world* (Grand Rapids, MI: Zondervan, 1974).

Bonar, Andrew, *The development of Antichrist* (1853; rpr. Chelmsford: Sovereign Grace Advent Testimony, n.d.).

Bonar, Andrew A., *Memoirs and remains of Robert Murray McCheyne* (1844; second edition, 1892; rpr. Edinburgh: Banner of Truth, 1966).
Bonar, Andrew A. and Robert Murray McCheyne, *Narrative of a mission of inquiry to the Jews from the Church of Scotland* (Edinburgh, 1842).
Bonar, Marjory (ed.), *Andrew A. Bonar: Diary and life* (1893; rpr. Edinburgh: Banner of Truth, 1960).
Bookman, Sally Dobson, 'Jesus People: A religious movement in a mid-western city' (unpublished PhD thesis, University of California, Berkeley, 1974).
Boran, Elizabethanne, 'The libraries of Luke Challoner and James Ussher, 1595–1608,' in Helga Robinson-Hammerstein (ed.), *European universities in the age of reformation and counter-reformation* (Dublin: Four Courts, 1998), 98–102.
Borgert, Michael G., 'Harry Bultema and the *Maranatha* controversy in the Christian Reformed Church,' *Calvin Theological Journal* 42:1 (2007), 90–109.
Boyce, James Petigru, *Abstract of systematic theology* (1887; Cape Coral, FL: Founder Press, 2006).
Boyer, Paul, 'The Middle East in modern American prophetic belief,' in Abbas Amanat and Magnus Bernhardsson, *Imagining the end: Visions of apocalypse from the ancient Middle East to modern America* (London: I.B. Tauris Publishers, 2002), 312–35.
Boyer, Paul, *When time shall be no more: Prophecy belief in modern American culture* (Cambridge, MA: Belknap Press of Harvard University Press, 1992).
Boyer, Paul, *By the bomb's early light: American thought and culture at the dawn of the Atomic Age* (New York: Pantheon Books, 1985).
Boyer, Paul (ed.), *Reagan as President: Contemporary views of the man, his politics, and his policies* (Chicago: Ivan R. Dee, 1990).
Bozeman, John, 'Technological millenarianism in the United States,' in Thomas Robbins and Susan Palmer (eds), *Millennium, messiahs and mayhem* (New York: Routledge, 1997), 139–58.
Brady, David, *The contribution of British writers between 1560 and 1830 to the Interpretation of Revelation 13.16–18* (Tübingen: J.C.B. Mohr, 1983).
Brady, David, 'The number of the beast in seventeenth- and eighteenth-century England,' *Evangelical Quarterly* 45 (1973), 219–40.
Brasher, Brenda E. and Lee Quinby, *Gender and apocalyptic desire*, Millennialism and society (London: Equinox, 2006).
Bray, Gerald, *Documents of the English reformation* (Cambridge: James Clarke, 1995).
Bremer, Francis J., and Tom Webster (eds), *Puritans and Puritanism in Europe and America: A comprehensive encyclopedia* (Oxford: ABC-CLIO, 2006).
Brencher, John, *Martyn Lloyd-Jones (1899–1981) and twentieth-century evangelicalism*, Studies in Evangelical History and Thought (Milton Keynes: Paternoster, 2002).
Brereton, Virginia Lieson, *Training God's army: The American Bible School, 1880–1940* (Bloomington, IN: Indiana University Press, 1990).
Brightman, Thomas, *A Most Comfortable Exposition of … Daniel* (1635).
Bromley, David G., 'Violence and New Religious Movements,' in James R. Lewis (ed.), *The Oxford handbook of New Religious Movements* (Oxford: Oxford University Press, 2004), 143–62.
Brothers, Richard, *A revealed knowledge of the prophecies and times*, parts I and II (London, 1794, 1795).

Brouwer, Steve, et al., *Exporting the American Gospel: Global Christian Fundamentalism* (New York: Routledge, 1996).

Brown, Callum, *The death of Christian Britain* (London: Routledge, 2001).

Brown, David, *The restoration of the Jews: The history, principles and bearing of the question* (1861) in Steve Schlissel (ed.), *Hal Lindsey and the restoration of the Jews* (Edmonton, Alberta: Still Waters Revival Books, 1990).

Brown, David, *Christ's second coming: Will it be premillennial?* (1846; 1882 ed., rpt. Edmonton, 1990).

Brown, Ralph, 'Victorian Anglican Evangelicalism: The radical legacy of Edward Irving,' *Journal of Ecclesiastical History* 58:4 (2007), 675–704.

Bruce, Steve, *The rise and fall of the New Christian Right: Conservative Protestant politics in American, 1978–1988* (Oxford: Clarendon Press, 1988).

Bruce, Steve, et al. (eds), *The rapture of politics: The Christian Right as the United States approaches the year 2000* (London: Transaction Publishers, 1995).

Brummett, Barry, 'Premillennial apocalypse as a rhetorical genre,' *Central States Speech Journal* 35 (1984), 84–93.

Bull, Malcolm (ed.), *Apocalypse theory and the ends of the world* (Oxford: Blackwell, 1995).

Bunyan, John, *Works*, ed. George Offor, 3 vols (Glasgow: Blackie and Son, 1860).

Burdon, Christopher, *The Apocalypse in England: Revelation unravelling, 1700–1834* (London: Palgrave Macmillan, 1997).

Burnham, Jonathan D., *A story of conflict: The controversial relationship between Benjamin Wills Newton and John Nelson Darby*, Studies in Evangelical History and Thought (Milton Keynes: Paternoster, 2005).

de Burgh, William, *An exposition of the book of Revelation*, fifth edition (Dublin: Hodges, Smith, & Co., 1857).

Bussard, Dave, *Who will be Left Behind and when?* (Lancaster, PA: Strong Tower Publishing, 2002).

Butler, Jonathan M., *Softly and tenderly Jesus is calling: Heaven and hell in American revivalism, 1870–1920* (Brooklyn: Carlson, 1991).

Calhoun, David B., *Princeton Seminary: The majestic testimony, 1869–1929* (Edinburgh: Banner of Truth, 1996).

Calvin, John, *Institutes of the Christian religion*, eds J.T. McNeill and F.L. Battles (1559; rpt. London: SCM, 1960).

Calvin, John, *The Epistles of Paul the Apostle to the Romans and to the Thessalonians*, trans. Ross Mackenzie (Grand Rapids, MI: Eerdmans, 1972).

Campbell, Iain, review of *The Emergence of Evangelicalism*, at http://www.reformation21.org/shelf-life/the-emergence-of-evangelicalism.php, accessed 8 May 2009.

Canfield, Joseph M., *The incredible Scofield and his book* (Vallecito, California: Ross House Books, 1988).

Capern, Amanda L., 'The Caroline Church: James Ussher and the Irish Dimension,' *Historical Journal* 39 (1996), 57–85.

Capp, Bernard, *The Fifth Monarchy Men: A study in seventeenth-century millenarianism* (London: Faber and Faber, 1972).

Capp, Bernard, '*Godly Rule* and English millenarianism,' *Past and Present* 52 (1971), 106–117.

Carpenter, Joel A., *Revive us again: The reawakening of American Fundamentalism* (Oxford: Oxford University Press, 1997).

Carpenter, M.W., and George Landow, 'Ambiguous revelations: The Apocalypse and Victorian literature,' in C.A. Patrides and J.A. Wittreich (eds), *The Apocalypse in English Renaissance thought and literature* (Manchester: Manchester University Press, 1984), 299–322.

Carter, D., 'Joseph Agar Beet and the eschatological crisis,' *Proceedings of the Wesley Historical Society* (1998) 51:6, 197–216.

Carwardine, Richard, *Transatlantic revivalism: Popular Evangelicalism in Britain and America* (Westport, CT: Greenwood Press, 1978).

Case, Shirley Jackson, *The millennial hope: A phase of war-time thinking* (Chicago, Illinois: University of Chicago Press, 1918).

Castelli, James, 'The environmental gospel according to James Watt,' *Chicago Tribune*, 25 October 1981, B2.

Chader, C.A., *God's plan through the ages* (London: Marshall, Morgan & Scott, 1938).

Chafer, Lewis Sperry, *Systematic theology*, 8 vols (1948; reprinted Dallas: Dallas Theological Seminary, 1975).

Chambers, Don, 'Prelude to the last things: The Church of Scotland's mission to the Jews,' *Records of the Scottish Church History Society* 19:1 (1975), 43–58.

Chandler, Ralph Clark, 'The wicked shall not bear rule: The fundamentalist heritage of the New Christian Right,' in David G. Bromley and Anson Shupe (eds), *New Christian politics* (Macon, GA: Mercer University Press, 1984), 41–58.

Chapman, Jennie, 'Paradoxes of power: Apocalyptic agency in the Left Behind series' (unpublished PhD thesis, University of Manchester, 2010).

Chapman, Jennie, 'Selling faith without selling out: Reading the Left Behind novels in the context of popular culture,' in John Wallis and Kenneth G.C. Newport (eds), *Apocalyptic texts and popular culture* (London: Equinox, 2008), 148–72.

Charles, R.H., *A critical and exegetical commentary on the Revelation of St. John*, International Critical Commentary, 2 volumes (Edinburgh: T & T Clark, 1920).

Chatham, Doug, *The rapture book: Exciting teaching about the next event on the prophetic calendar* (New Kensington, PA: Whitaker House, 1974).

Chi, Joseph, "'Forget not the wombe that bare you, and the brest that gave you sucke': John Cotton's Sermons on Canticles and Revelation and his apocalyptic vision for England' (unpublished PhD thesis, New College, Edinburgh, 2008).

Chilton, David, *The great tribulation* (Fort Worth, Texas: Dominion Press, 1987).

Chilton, David, *Paradise restored: A biblical theology of dominion* (Fort Worth, TX: Dominion Press, 1985).

Christianson, Paul, *Reformers and Babylon: English apocalyptic visions from the Reformation to the eve of the Civil War* (Toronto: University of Toronto Press, 1978).

Clouse, Robert, 'The New Christian Right, America, and the Kingdom of God,' *Christian Scholars Review* 12 (1983), 3–16.

Clouse, Robert, 'The rebirth of millenarianism,' in Peter Toon (ed.), *Puritans, the millennium and the future of Israel: Puritan eschatology 1600 to 1660* (Cambridge: James Clarke, 1970), 42–65.

Clouse, Robert, et al., *The new millennium manual: A once and future guide* (Grand Rapids, MI: Baker, 1999).

Coad, F. Roy, *A history of the Brethren movement* (Exeter: Paternoster, 1968).

Coffey, John, *Politics, religion and the British revolutions: The mind of Samuel Rutherford* (Cambridge: Cambridge University Press, 1997).

Cogley, Richard, 'The fall of the Ottoman Empire and the restoration of Israel in the 'Judeo-centric' strand of Puritan millenarianism,' *Church History* 72 (2003), 303–32.

Cohn, Norman, *Cosmos, chaos and the world to come: The ancient roots of apocalyptic faith* (London: Yale University Press, 1993).

Cohn, Norman, *The pursuit of the millennium* (1957; rpt. London: Mercury Books, 1962).

The companion Bible, ed. E.W. Bullinger (1909–22; rpr. London: Lamp Press, n.d.).

Collins, John J., Bernard McGinn, Stephen J. Stein, 'General introduction,' in Bernard McGinn (ed.), *Encyclopedia of apocalypticism*, 3 vols (New York: Continuum, 1998), 1: vii–xi.

Connors, Richard and Andrew Colin Gow (eds), *Anglo-American millennialism, from Milton to the Millerites* (Leiden: Brill, 2004).

Cotton, John, *The churches resurrection* (London, 1642).

Cox, Harvey, *Fire from heaven: The rise of Pentecostal spirituality and the re-shaping of religion in the twenty-first century* (Reading: Addison-Wesley, 1995).

Crome, Andrew, 'The Jews and the literal sense: Hermeneutical approaches in the apocalyptic commentaries of Thomas Brightman (1562–1607)' (unpublished PhD thesis, University of Manchester, 2009).

Crutchfield, Larry V., *The origins of dispensationalism: The Darby factor* (London: University Press of America, 1992).

Cumming, John, *Prophetic studies; or, Lectures on the book of Daniel* (London: Arthur Hall, 1853).

Cumming, John, *Sabbath evening readings on St Matthew* (London: Arthur Hall, 1853).

Currie, David B., *Rapture: The end-times error that leaves the Bible behind* (Manchester, NH: Sophia Institute Press, 2003).

Daniel, Curt, 'Hyper-Calvinism and John Gill' (unpublished PhD thesis, University of Edinburgh, 1983).

Daley, Brian E., *The hope of the early church: Eschatology in the patristic age* (Cambridge: Cambridge University Press, 1991).

Dallimore, Arnold, *The life of Edward Irving: Forerunner of the Charismatic movement* (Edinburgh: Banner of Truth, 1983).

Dallison, A.R., 'Contemporary criticism of millenarianism,' in Peter Toon (ed.), *Puritans, the millennium and the future of Israel: Puritan eschatology, 1600 to 1660* (Cambridge: James Clarke, 1970), 104–14.

Darby, J.N., *Letters of J.N.D.*, ed. William Kelly (London: Stow Hill Bible and Tract Depot, n.d.).

Das ander Thäil Des Newen Testaments I Darinnen ... Die Episteln ... und die Offenbarung S. Johannis, trans. and annotated by Johannes Piscator (Herborn, 1604).

Davidson, James West, *The logic of millennial thought: Eighteenth-century New England* (New Haven, CT: Yale University Press, 1977).

Dayton, Donald W., 'Some doubts about the usefulness of the category 'Evangelical',' in Donald W. Dayton and Robert K. Johnston (eds), *The variety of American Evangelicalism* (Downers Grove, IL: InterVarsity Press, 1991), 245–51.

Donald W. Dayton and Robert K. Johnston (eds), ''The search for the historical evangelicalism': George Marsden's history of Fuller Seminary as a case study,' *Christian Scholar's Review* 33 (1993), 12–33.

Dayton, Donald W. and Robert K. Johnston (eds), *The variety of American Evangelicalism* (Downers Grove, IL: InterVarsity Press, 1991).

D'Elia, John A., *A place at the table: George Eldon Ladd and the rehabilitation of evangelical scholarship in America* (Oxford: Oxford University Press, 2008).

DeMar, Gary, 'The fiction behind Left Behind,' *Biblical Worldview* 3 (July 2004), 12–17.

DeMar, Gary, *End times fiction: A Biblical consideration of the Left Behind theology* (Nashville, TN: Thomas Nelson, 2001).

DeMar, Gary, *Something greater is here: Christian Reconstruction in biblical perspective* (Fort Worth, TX: Dominion Press, 1988).

Dennett, Edward, *The blessed hope* (1879; rpr Bromley, Kent: Wilson Foundation, 1969).

de Jong, James A., *As the waters cover the sea: Millennial expectations in the rise of Anglo-American missions, 1640–1810* (Kampen: J.H. Kok, 1970).

de Patmos, John, *The Great Disappointment of 1844* (Brookline, MA: Miskatonic University Press, 2001).

Derrida, Jacques, 'Of an apocalyptic tone recently adopted in philosophy,' *Semeia* 23 (1982), 63–97.

Ditchfield, G.M., *The evangelical revival* (London: UCL Press, 1998).

Doan, Ruth Alden, *The Miller heresy, millennialism, and American culture* (Philadelphia, PA: Temple University Press, 1987).

Dobson, Ed, and Ed Hindson, 'Apocalypse now? What fundamentalists believe about the end of the world,' *Policy Review* 38 (1986), 16–23.

Dolan, David, *The end of days* (1995; rpr. Springfield, MO: 2003).

Downes, James Cyril, 'Eschatological doctrines in the writings of John and Charles Wesley' (unpublished PhD thesis, University of Edinburgh, 1960).

Draney, Daniel W., *When streams diverge: John Murdock MacInnis and the origins of protestant Fundamentalism in Los Angeles*, Studies in Evangelical History and Thought (Milton Keynes, UK: Paternoster, 2008).

Drummond, A.L., *Edward Irving and his circle* (London: J. Clarke, 1937).

Drummond, Lewis A., *Spurgeon: Prince of preachers* (Grand Rapids, Michigan: Kregel, 1992).

Durham, Martin, *The Christian Right, the far right and the boundaries of American conservatism* (Manchester: Manchester University Press, 2000).

Eagleton, Terry, *Holy terror* (Oxford: Oxford University Press, 2005).

Edwards, David L. and John Stott, *Evangelical essentials: A liberal-evangelical dialogue* (Leicester: IVP, 1989).

Edwards, Jonathan, *The miscellanies*, ed. Amy Plantinga Pauw, The Works of Jonathan Edwards (New Haven, CT: Yale University Press, 2002).

Edwards, Jonathan, *Apocalyptic writings*, ed. Stephen J. Stein, The Works of Jonathan Edwards (New Haven, CT: Yale University Press, 1977).

Edwards, Jonathan, *The Great Awakening*, ed. C.C. Goen, The Works of Jonathan Edwards (New Haven: Yale University Press, 1972).

Ella, George, *John Gill and justification from eternity: A tercentenary appreciation* (Eggleston: Go Publications, 1998).

Ella, George, *John Gill and the cause of God and truth* (Eggleston: Go Publications, 1995).

'End times,' *TIME* 23 June 2002, available at http://www.time.com/time/covers/1101020701/story3.html, accessed 8 January 2008.

Erwin, John Stuart, 'Like a thief in the night: Cotton Mather's millennialism' (unpublished PhD thesis, Indiana University, 1987).

Evangelical Alliance, *The nature of hell* (Carlisle: Paternoster, 2000).

Fairbairn, Patrick, *The interpretation of prophecy* (1865; Edinburgh: Banner of Truth, 1964).

Faubion, James D., *The shadows and lights of Waco: Millennialism today* (Princeton: Princeton University Press, 2001).

Featherstone, Guy, '"Holy city": The Brethren community at Kyneton, 1900–1911,' *Brethren Historical Review* 5:1 (2008), 2–24.

Fenn, Richard K., *Dreams of glory: The sources of apocalyptic terror* (Aldershot: Ashgate, 2005).

Festinger, Leon, et al., *When prophecy fails* (Minneapolis: University of Minneapolis Press, 1956).

Fiddes, Paul S., *The promised end: Eschatology in theology and literature* (Oxford: Blackwell, 2000).

Fiddes, Paul S., 'Facing the end: The apocalyptic experience in some modern novels,' in John Colwell (ed.), *Called to one hope: Perspectives on the life to come* (Carlisle: Paternoster, 2000), 191–209.

Firth, Katherine, *The apocalyptic tradition in reformation Britain, 1530–1645* (Oxford: Oxford University Press, 1979).

Flake, Carol, *Redemptorama: Culture, politics, and the new Evangelicalism* (Garden City, NY: Anchor Press, 1984).

Flanagan, Thomas, 'The politics of the millennium,' *Terrorism and Political Violence* 7:3 (1995), 164–75.

Flegg, Columba Graham, *Gathered under apostles: A study of the Catholic Apostolic Church* (Oxford: Clarendon Press, 1992).

Flesher, LeAnn Snow, *Left Behind? The facts behind the fiction* (Valley Forge, PA: Judson Press, 2006).

Fogel, Robert William, *The fourth Great Awakening & the future of egalitarianism* (Chicago: University of Chicago Press, 2000).

Forbes, Bruce David, 'How popular are the Left Behind books … and why? A discussion of popular culture,' in Bruce David Forbes and Jeanne Halgren Kilde (eds), *Rapture, Revelation and the End Times: Exploring the Left Behind series* (New York: Palgrave Macmillan, 2004), 5–32.

Forbes, Bruce David and Jeanne Halgren Kilde (eds), *Rapture, Revelation, and the End Times: Exploring the Left Behind series* (New York: Palgrave Macmillan, 2004).

Forbes, Bruce David and Jeffrey H. Mahan (eds), *Religion and popular culture in America* (Berkeley: University of California Press, 2000).

Force, James E. and Richard H. Popkin (eds), *The millenarian turn: Millenarian contexts of science, politics, and everyday Anglo-American life in the seventeenth and eighteenth centuries* (Dordrecht: Kluwer Academic Pubishers, 2001).

Fosdick, Harry Emerson, 'Shall the fundamentalists win?' (1922), in *The Riverside Preachers*, ed. Paul H. Sherry (New York: Pilgrim Press, 1978), 27–38.

Foucault, Michel, *The Order of Things* (1966; London: Routledge, 1989).

Fowler, Robert Booth, *A new engagement: Evangelical political thought, 1966–1976* (Grand Rapids, MI: Eerdmans, 1982).

Fowler, Stanley K., 'John Gill's doctrine of believer baptism,' in Michael A.G. Haykin (ed.), *The life and thought of John Gill: A tercentennial appreciation* (Leiden: E.J. Brill, 1997), 69–91.

Fox, Richard Wrightman, 'The culture of liberal Protestant progressivism, 1875–1925,' *Journal of Interdisciplinary History* 23 (1993), 639–60.

Frank, Douglas W., *Less than conquerors: How evangelicals entered the twentieth century* (Grand Rapids, MI: William B. Eerdmans, 1986).

Frankl, Razelle, *Televangelism: The marketing of popular religion* (Carbondale, IL: Southern Illinois University Press, 1987).

Frere, B.S., *A record of the family of Frere of Suffolk and Norfolk* (privately published, 1982).

Fromow, George H., *Teachers of the faith and the future: B.W. Newton and Dr S. P. Tregelles* (second edition, London: Sovereign Grace Advent Testimony, 1969).

Froom, L.E., *The prophetic faith of our fathers: The historical development of prophetic interpretation*, 4 vols (Washington: Review and Herald, 1948).

Fruchtman, Jack, *The apocalyptic politics of Richard Price and Joseph Priestly: A study in late eighteenth-century English republican millennialism* (Philadelphia, PA: American Philosophical Society, 1983).

Frykholm, Amy Johnson, *Rapture culture:* Left Behind *in evangelical America* (New York: Oxford University Press, 2004).

Frykholm, Amy Johnson, 'What social messages appear in the *Left Behind* books? A literary discussion of millenarian fiction,' in Bruce David Forbes and Jeanne Halgren Kilde (eds), *Rapture, Revelation, and the End Times: Exploring the Left Behind series* (New York: Palgrave Macmillan, 2004), 167–95.

Fuller, Robert, *Naming the Antichrist: The history of an American obsession* (New York: Oxford University Press, 1995).

Fullerton, W.Y., *No ordinary man: The remarkable life of F.B. Meyer* (1929; rpr. Belfast: Ambassador, 1993).

Fulop, Timothy E., ''The future golden day of the race': Millennialism and black Americans in the Nadir, 1877–1901,' *Harvard Theological Review* 84:1 (1991), 75–99.

The fundamentals: A testimony to the truth, ed. 'Two Christian Laymen,' 12 vols (Chicago: Testimony Publishing Company, 1910–1915).

Furniss, Tom, 'Reading the Geneva Bible: Notes Toward An English Revolution?' *Prose Studies* 31:1 (2009), 1–21.

Fukuyama, Francis, *The end of history and the last man* (New York: Free Press, 1992).

Garrett, Clarke, *Respectable folly: Millenarians and the French Revolution in France and England* (Baltimore, MD: Johns Hopkins University Press, 1975).

Gates, David, 'Religion: The pop prophets,' *Newsweek* (May 24, 2004).

Gaustad, Edwin Scott (ed.), *The rise of Adventism: A commentary on the social and religious ferment of mid-nineteenth century America* (New York: Harper and Row, 1974).

Geneva Bible: The annotated New Testament, 1602 edition, ed. Gerald T. Sheppard (New York: Pilgrim Press, 1989).

Gentry, Kenneth L., *The Beast of Revelation* (Tyler, TX: Institute for Christian Economics, 1989).

George, Timothy, 'John Gill,' in Timothy George and David S. Dockery (eds), *Baptist theologians* (Nashville: Broadman Press, 1990), 89–94.

Gibbs, Nancy, 'The Bible and the apocalypse,' *TIME* (July 1, 2002), reprinted in the UK edition of *TIME* (19 August 2002), 46–53.

Gill, John, *A body of divinity* (1769–70; rpt. Grand Rapids: Sovereign Grace Publishers, 1971).

Gillespie, George, *A treatise of miscellany questions* (1649); rpt. in *The Presbyterian's armoury*, ed. W.M. Hetherington (Edinburgh: Robert Ogle, and Oliver & Boyd, 1846).

Ginger, Ray, *Six days or forever? Tennessee vs. John Thomas Scopes* (1958; rpr. Oxford: Oxford University Press, 1974).

Gloege, T., 'Gray, James Martin,' in Timothy Larsen (ed.), *Biographical dictionary of evangelicals* (Leicester: IVP, 2003), 266–7.

Goen, C.C., 'Jonathan Edwards: A new departure in eschatology,' *Church History* 28 (1959), 25–40.

Gold, Malcolm, 'The *Left Behind* series as sacred text,' in Elizabeth Arweck and Peter Collins (eds), *Reading religion in text and context* (Aldershot: Ashgate, 2006), 34–49.

Goodnight, G. Thomas, 'Ronald Reagan's re-formulation of the rhetoric of war: Analysis of the 'Zero Option,' 'Evil Empire,' and 'Star Wars' addresses,' *Quarterly Journal of Speech* 72 (1986), 390–414.

Goodwin, Thomas, *Works*, 12 vols (Edinburgh: James Nichol, 1861–66).

Gorenberg, Gershom, *The end of days: Fundamentalism and the struggle for the Temple Mount* (New York: Oxford University Press, 2002).

Gosse, Edmund, *Father and Son: A study of two temperaments* (1907; London: Penguin, 1989).

Graham, Billy, 'Teacher of the faith: John Stott,' *TIME* (18 April 2005), 80.

Graham, Billy, *World aflame* (Tadworth, Surrey: The World's Work, 1965).

Gribben, Crawford, 'Novel doctrines, doctrinal novels: F.A. Tatford and Brethren prophecy fiction,' in Neil Dickson (ed.), *Brethren and Culture* (forthcoming).

Gribben, Crawford, 'Baptists and millennialism in early modern England,' in Anthony R. Cross and Nicholas J. Wood (ed.), *Exploring Baptist Origins* (Oxford: Regent's Park College, 2010), 101–22.

Gribben, Crawford, *Writing the rapture: Prophecy fiction in evangelical America* (Oxford: Oxford University Press, 2009).

Gribben, Crawford, 'The Church of Scotland and the English apocalyptic imagination, 1630–1650,' *Scottish Historical Review* 88:1 (2009), 34–56.

Gribben, Crawford, 'Evangelical eschatology and 'the Puritan hope',' in Michael Haykin and Kenneth Stewart (eds), *The emergence of evangelicalism: Exploring historical continuities* (Leicester: Apollos, 2008), 375–93.

Gribben, Crawford, 'Protestant millennialism, political violence and the Ulster conflict,' *Irish Studies Review* 15:1 (2007), 51–63.

Gribben, Crawford, *Rapture fiction and the evangelical crisis* (Webster, NY: Evangelical Press, 2006).

Gribben, Crawford, 'Introduction: Antichrist in Ireland – Protestant millennialism and Irish studies,' in Crawford Gribben and Andrew R. Holmes (eds), *Protestant millennialism, evangelicalism and Irish society, 1790–2005* (Basingstoke: Palgrave Macmillan, 2006), 1–30.

Gribben, Crawford, 'The future of millennial expectation,' in Kenneth G.C. Newport and Crawford Gribben (eds), *Expecting the end: Millennialism in social and historical context* (Baylor, TX: Baylor University Press, 2006), 237–40.

Gribben, Crawford, 'After *Left Behind*: The paradox of evangelical pessimism,' in Kenneth G.C. Newport and Crawford Gribben (eds), *Expecting the End: Millennialism in social and historical context* (Baylor, TX: Baylor University Press, 2006), 113–30.

Gribben, Crawford, 'Rapture fictions and the changing evangelical condition,' *Literature and Theology* 18:1 (2004), 77–94.

Gribben, Crawford, 'Before Left Behind,' *Books & Culture* (July/August 2003), 11.

Gribben, Crawford, "The worst sect that a Christian man can meet': Opposition to the Plymouth Brethren in Ireland and Scotland, 1859–1900,' *Scottish Studies Review* 3:2 (2002), 34–53.

Gribben, Crawford, 'The eschatology of the puritan confessions,' *Scottish Bulletin of Evangelical Theology* 20:1 (2002), 51–78.

Gribben, Crawford, 'John Gill and puritan eschatology,' *Evangelical Quarterly* 73:4 (2001), 311–26.

Gribben, Crawford, *The puritan millennium: Literature and theology, 1550–1682* (Dublin: Four Courts, 2000).

Gribben, Crawford and Mark Sweetnam, 'J.N. Darby and the Irish origins of dispensationalism,' *Journal of the Evangelical Theological Society* 52:3 (2009), 569–77.

Gribben, Crawford and Andrew R. Holmes (eds), *Protestant millennialism, evangelicalism and Irish society, 1790–2005* (Basingstoke: Palgrave Macmillan, 2006).

Gribben, Crawford and Timothy C.F. Stunt, 'Introduction,' in Crawford Gribben and Timothy C.F. Stunt (eds), *Prisoners of hope? Aspects of evangelical millennialism in Britain and Ireland, 1800–1880*, Studies in Evangelical History and Thought (Milton Keynes: Paternoster, 2004), 1–17.

Grier, W.J., *The momentous event: A discussion of Scripture teaching on the second advent* (1945; reprinted Edinburgh: Banner of Truth, 1970).

Griffiths, C.W.H., 'Spurgeon's eschatology,' *Watching and waiting: A publication of the Sovereign Grace Advent Testimony* 23:15 (1990), 227.

Gundry, Robert H., *The church and the tribulation* (Grand Rapids, MI: Zondervan, 1973).

Gura, Philip F., *A glimpse of Sion's glory: Puritan radicalism in New England, 1620–1660* (Middletown, CT: Wesleyan University Press, 1984).

Gutierrez, Cathy and Hillel Schwartz (eds), *The end that does: Art, science and millennial accomplishment*, Millennialism and society (London: Equinox, 2006).

Guyatt, Nicholas, *Have a nice doomsday: Why millions of Americans are looking forward to the end of the world* (London: Ebury Press, 2007).

Haija, Rammy M., 'The Armageddon lobby: Dispensationalist Christian Zionism and the shaping of US policy towards Israel-Palestine,' *Holy Land Studies* 5:1 (2006), 75–95.

Hall, Joseph H., 'The controversy over Fundamentalism in the Christian Reformed Church, 1915–1966' (unpublished ThD thesis, Concordia Theological Seminary, 1974).

Hall, Peter (ed.), *Harmony of the protestant confessions* (1842; rpt. Edmonton: Still Waters Revival Books, 1992).

Hall, Thomas, *A Confutation of the Millenarian Opinion* (1657).

Halper, Stefan and Jonathan Clarke, *America alone: The Neo-Conservatives and the global order* (Cambridge: Cambridge University Press, 2004).

Halsell, Grace, *Prophecy and politics: Militant evangelists on the road to nuclear war* (Westport, CT: Lawrence Hill, 1986).

Hamilton, James, *Light on the 'last days': An historical review of 'days' long past* (Glasgow: K. & R. Davidson, 1962).

Hankins, Barry, *Francis Schaeffer and the shaping of evangelical America* (Grand Rapids, MI: Eerdmans, 2008).

Harding, Susan Friend, *The book of Jerry Falwell: Fundamentalist language and politics* (Princeton: Princeton University Press, 2000).

Harrell, David Edwin, Jr., *Pat Robertson: A personal, religious, and political portrait* (San Francisco, CA: Harper & Row, 1987).

Harris, Harriet A., *Fundamentalism and evangelicals* (Oxford: Clarendon Press, 1998; 2008).

Harrison, J.F.C., *The second coming: Popular millenarianism, 1780–1850* (New Brunswick, NJ: Rutgers University Press, 1979),

Hart, D.G., *Deconstructing Evangelicalism: Conservative Protestantism in the age of Billy Graham* (Grand Rapids, MI: Baker, 2004).

Hart, Frank, *Revelation and the rapture unveiled! Ancient Hebrew prophecies for the year 2000 and beyond* (Lafayette, LA: Prescott Press, 1999).

Hatch, Nathan O., *The democratisation of American Christianity* (New Haven, CT: Yale University Press, 1989).

Hatch, Nathan O., *The sacred cause of liberty: Republican thought and the millennium in revolutionary New England* (New Haven, CT: Yale University Press, 1977).

Hatch, Nathan O., 'The origins of civil millennialism in America: New England clergymen, war with France, and the Revolution,' *William and Mary Quarterly* 31 (1974), 407–30.

Haykin, Michael A.G., 'Introduction,' in Michael A.G. Haykin (ed.), *The life and thought of John Gill: A tercentennial appreciation* (Leiden: E.J. Brill, 1997), 1–6.

Haykin, Michael A.G. (ed.), *The life and thought of John Gill: A tercentennial appreciation* (Leiden: E.J. Brill, 1997).

Haykin, Michael, and Kenneth Stewart (eds), *The emergence of evangelicalism: Exploring historical continuities* (Leicester: Apollos, 2008).

Hempton, David N., 'Evangelicals and eschatology,' *Journal of Ecclesiastical History* 31 (1980), 179–94.

Hempton, David N., *Evangelical disenchantment: Nine portraits of faith and doubt* (New Haven, CT: Yale University Press, 2009).

Hendershot, Heather, *Shaking the world for Jesus: Media and conservative evangelical culture* (Chicago: University of Chicago Press, 2004).

Hendricksen, William, *More than conquerors: An interpretation of the book of Revelation* (1939; Grand Rapids, MI: Baker, 1982).

Henry, Carl F.H., *The uneasy conscience of modern Fundamentalism* (Grand Rapids, MI: William B. Eerdmans, 1947).

Herman, Didi, 'Globalism's "siren song": The United Nations and international law in Christian Right thought and prophecy,' *Sociological Review* 49:1 (2001), 56–77.

Hertzler, Daniel, 'Assessing the "Left Behind" phenomenon,' in Loren L. Johns (ed.), *Apocalypticism and millennialism: Shaping a believers church eschatology for the twenty-first century* (Kitchener, Ontario: Pandora Press, 2000).

Hill, Charles E., *Regnum Caelorum: Patterns of millennial thought in early Christianity*, second edition (Grand Rapids, MI: Eerdmans, 2001).

Hill, Christopher, *Antichrist in seventeenth-century England* (London: Oxford University Press, 1971).

Hill, Myrtle, 'Watchmen in Zion: Millennial expectancy in late eighteenth-century Ulster,' in Crawford Gribben and Andrew R. Holmes (eds), *Protestant millennialism, evangelicalism, and Irish society, 1790–2005* (Basingstoke: Palgrave Macmillan, 2006), 31–51.

Hindson, Ed, *End times, the middle east, and the New World Order* (Wheaton, IL: Victor Books, 1991).

Hirst, Julie, *Jane Leade: Biography of a seventeenth-century mystic* (Aldershot: Ashgate, 2005).

Hitchcock, Mark and Thomas Ice, *The truth behind Left Behind: A biblical view of the end times* (Sisters, OR: Multnomah, 2004).

Hoekema, Anthony A., *The Bible and the future* (Grand Rapids, MI: Eerdmans, 1979).

Hofstadter, Richard, *The paranoid style in American politics* (Chicago: University of Chicago Press, 1979).

Hogg, C.F., and W.E. Vine, *The church and the tribulation: A review of the book entitled 'The Approaching advent of Christ'* (London: Pickering and Inglis, 1938).

Holmes, Janice, *Religious revivals in Britain and Ireland, 1859–1905* (Dublin: Irish Academic Press, 2000).

Hopkins, Mark, *Nonconformity's Romantic generation: Evangelical and liberal theologies in Victorian England*, Studies in Evangelical History and Thought (Milton Keynes: Paternoster, 2004).

Horatius Bonar, D.D.: A Memorial (London, 1890).

Hotson, Howard, *Johann Heinrich Alsted, 1588–1638* (Oxford: Oxford University Press, 2000).

Hotson, Howard, *Paradise postponed: Johann Heinrich Alsted and the Birth of Calvinist Millenarianism* (Dordrecht: Kluwer Academic Publishers, 2000).

House, H. Wayne, and Thomas D. Ice, *Dominion theology: Blessing or curse?* (Portland, OR: Multnomah, 1988).

Howard, Tal, 'Charisma and history: The case of Münster, Westphalia, 1534–1535,' *Essays in History* 35 (1993), 48–64.

Howson, Barry H., 'The eschatology of the Calvinistic Baptist John Gill (1697–1771) examined and compared,' *Eusebeia* 5 (2005), 33–66.

Hughes, Archibald, *A new heaven and a new earth* (Marshall, Morgan & Scott, 1958).

Hunt, Stephen (ed.), *Christian millennarianism: From the early church to Waco* (Bloomington, IN: Indiana University Press, 2001).

Hunter, James Davison, *Evangelicalism: The coming generation* (Chicago: University of Chicago Press, 1987).

Hunter, James Davison, *American evangelicalism: Conservative Protestantism and the quandary of modernity* (New Brunswick, NJ: Rutgers University Press, 1983).

Huntingdon, Samuel, *The clash of civilizations* (New York: Simon & Schuster, 1996).

Hutton, Sarah, 'The appropriation of Joseph Mede: Millenarianism in the 1640s,' in James E. Force and Richard H. Popkin (eds), *Millenarianism and Messianism in Early Modern European Culture: The Millenarian Turn* (Dordrecht: Kluwer Academic Publishers, 2001), 1–13.

Ice, Thomas, and Randall Price, *Ready to rebuild: The imminent plan to rebuild the last days temple* (Eugene, OR: Harvest House Publishers, 1992).

Ice, Thomas, and Kenneth L. Gentry Jr., *The great tribulation: past or future? Two evangelicals debate the question* (Grand Rapids, MI: Kregel, 1999).

Ironside, H.A., *Wrongly dividing the word of truth* (Neptune, NJ: Loizeaux Borthers, third edition, 1938).

Jeffrey, Kenneth S., *When the Lord walked the land: The 1858–62 revival in the north east of Scotland*, Studies in Evangelical History and Thought (Carlisle, 2002).

Jenkins, Philip, *Mystics and messiahs: Cults and new religions in American history* (Oxford: Oxford University Press, 2000).

Jensen, Michael, '"Simply" reading the Geneva Bible: The Geneva Bible and its readers,' *Literature and Theology* 9 (1995), 30–45.

Johnson, Paul E., *A shopkeeper's millennium: Society and revivals in Rochester, New York, 1815–1837* (New York: Wang and Hill, 1978).

Johnson, Warren, 'The Anglican apocalypse in Restoration England,' *Journal of Ecclesiastical History* 55:33 (2004), 467–501.

Johnson, Warren, 'The patience of the saints, the apocalypse and moderate nonconformity in Restoration England,' *Canadian Journal of History* 38 (2003), 505–16.

Johnson, Warren, 'Apocalypticism in Restoration England' (unpublished PhD thesis, University of Cambridge, 2000).

Jones, Darryl, 'The liberal Antichrist: *Left Behind* in America,' in Kenneth G.C. Newport and Crawford Gribben (eds), *Expecting the end: Millennialism in social and historical context* (Baylor, TX: Baylor University Press, 2006), 97–112.

Jorstad, Erling, *Popular religion in America: The evangelical voice* (Westport, CT: Greenwood Press, 1993).

Jorstad, Erling, *The politics of doomsday: Fundamentalists of the far right* (Nashville, TN: Abingdon Press, 1970).

Jue, Jeffrey K., *Heaven upon earth: Joseph Mede (1586–1638) and the legacy of millenarianism* (Dordrecht: Kluwer Academic Publications, 2006).

Juergensmeyer, Mark, *Terror in the mind of God: The global rise of religious violence* (Berkeley: University of California Press, 2003).

Kac, Arthur W., *The rebirth of the State of Israel – Is it of God or of men?* (Edinburgh: Marshall, Morgan and Scott, 1958).

Katz, David and Richard Popkin, *Messianic revolution: Radical religious politics to the end of the second millennium* (New York: Penguin, 1999).

Kay, William K., 'Pre-millennial tensions: What pentecostal ministers look forward to,' in Martyn Percy (ed.), *Calling time: Religion and change at the turn of the millennium* (Sheffield: Sheffield Academic Press, 2000), 93–113.

Keeble, N.H., *The literary culture of nonconformity in later seventeenth-century England* (Leicester: Leicester University Press, 1987).

Keith, Alexander, *Evidence of the truth of the Christian religion, derived from the literal fulfilment of prophecy* (1828; Edinburgh: Waugh and Innes, 1832).

Kellog, S.H., 'Christ's coming: Will it be premillennial?' in Nathaniel West (ed.), *Premillennial essays of the Prophetic Conference held in the Church of the Holy Trinity, New York City* (Chicago, IL: Fleming H. Revell, 1879), 47–77.

Kennedy, Douglas, 'Selling rapture,' *Guardian*, 9 July 2005.

Kik, J. Marcellus, *Revelation twenty* (Philadelphia, PA: P&R, 1955).

Kik, J. Marcellus, *Matthew twenty-four* (Philadelphia, PA: P&R, 1948).

Kilde, Jeanne Halgren, 'How did Left Behind's particular vision of the end times develop? A historical look at millenarian thought,' in Bruce David Forbes and

Jeanne Halgren Kilde (eds), *Rapture, Revelation, and the End Times: Exploring the Left Behind series* (New York: Palgrave Macmillan, 2004), 33–70.

Kilroy, Phil, 'Sermon and pamphlet literature in the Irish Reformed Church, 1613–34,' *Archivium Hibernicum* 33 (1975), 110–21.

King, Wayne, 'The record of Pat Robertson on religion and government,' *New York Times*, national edition, 27 December 1987, 20.

Kintz, Linda and Julia Lesage (eds), *Media, culture, and the religious right* (Minneapolis, MN: University of Minnesota Press, 1998).

Kirk, Tim, *I want to be 'Left Behind': An examination of the ideas behind the popular series and the end times* (New York: Writers Club Press, 2002).

Kirsch, Jonathan, 'Hal Lindsey,' *Publishers Weekly*, 14 March 1977, 30–2.

Knoch, A.E., *The unveiling of Jesus Christ* (Los Angeles: Concordant Publishing Concern, 1935).

Knox, Ronald, *Enthusiasm* (Oxford: Clarendon Press, 1950).

Krapohl, Robert Henry, 'A search for purity: The controversial life of John Nelson Darby' (unpublished PhD thesis, Baylor University, 1988).

Kraus, C. Norman, *Dispensationalism in America: Its rise and development* (Richmond, VA: John Knox Press, 1958).

Ladd, George Eldon, *A commentary on the Revelation of John* (Grand Rapids, MI: Zondervan, 1972).

Ladd, George Eldon, *A theology of the New Testament* (London: Lutterworth, 1975).

LaHaye, Tim, 'Introduction,' in Mark Hitchcock and Thomas Ice, *The truth behind Left Behind: A biblical view of the end times* (Sisters, OR: Multnomah, 2004), 5–9.

LaHaye, Tim, 'Russia on edge' in William T. James (ed.), *Foreshadows of wrath and redemption* (Eugene, OR: Harvest House, 1999), 147–74.

LaHaye, Tim, 'America's perilous times have come,' in William T. James (ed.), *Forewarning: Approaching the final battle between heaven and hell* (Eugene, OR: Harvest House, 1998), 235–69.

LaHaye, Tim, *The battle for the mind: A subtle warfare* (Old Tappan, NJ: Revell, 1980).

LaHaye, Tim and Jerry B. Jenkins, *The Rapture* (Wheaton, IL: Tyndale House, 2007).

LaHaye, Tim and Jerry B. Jenkins, *Kingdom Come* (Wheaton, IL: Tyndale House, 2007).

LaHaye, Tim and Jerry B. Jenkins, *John's Story: The last eyewitness* (Wheaton, IL: Tyndale House, 2006).

LaHaye, Tim and Jerry B. Jenkins, *The Regime* (Wheaton, IL: Tyndale House, 2005).

LaHaye, Tim and Jerry B. Jenkins, *The Rising* (Wheaton, IL: Tyndale House, 2005).

LaHaye, Tim and Jerry B. Jenkins, *The Glorious Appearing* (Wheaton, IL: Tyndale House, 2004).

LaHaye, Tim and Jerry B. Jenkins, *Armageddon* (Wheaton, IL: Tyndale House, 2003).

LaHaye, Tim and Jerry B. Jenkins, *The Remnant* (Wheaton, IL: Tyndale House, 2002).

LaHaye, Tim and Jerry B. Jenkins, *Desecration* (Wheaton, IL: Tyndale House, 2001).

LaHaye, Tim and Jerry B. Jenkins, *Are we living in the end times?* (Wheaton, IL: Tyndale House, 2001).

LaHaye, Tim and Jerry B. Jenkins, *The Indwelling* (Wheaton, IL: Tyndale House, 2000).

LaHaye, Tim and Jerry B. Jenkins, *The Mark* (Wheaton, IL: Tyndale House, 2000).

LaHaye, Tim and Jerry B. Jenkins, *Apollyon* (Wheaton, IL: Tyndale House, 1999).

LaHaye, Tim and Jerry B. Jenkins, *Assassins* (Wheaton, IL: Tyndale House, 1999).

LaHaye, Tim and Jerry B. Jenkins, *Soul Harvest* (Wheaton, IL: Tyndale House, 1998).

LaHaye, Tim and Jerry B. Jenkins, *Nicolae* (Wheaton, IL: Tyndale House, 1997).

LaHaye, Tim and Jerry B. Jenkins, *Tribulation Force* (Wheaton, IL: Tyndale House, 1996).

LaHaye, Tim and Jerry B. Jenkins, *Left Behind* (Wheaton, IL: Tyndale House, 1995).

LaHaye, Tim, et al., *The authorized Left Behind handbook* (Wheaton, IL: Tyndale House, 2005).

LaHaye, Tim, et al., *These will not be left behind* (Wheaton, IL: Tyndale House, 2003).

Lalonde, Peter and Patti, *Left Behind* (Eugene, OR: Harvest House Publishers, n.d.).

Lalonde, Peter and Paul Lalonde, *Tribulation* (Niagra Falls, NY: This Week in Bible Prophecy, 2001).

Lalonde, Peter and Paul Lalonde, *Judgment* (Niagra Falls, NY: This Week in Bible Prophecy, 2001).

Lalonde, Peter and Paul Lalonde, *Revelation* (Niagra Falls, NY: This Week in Bible Prophecy, 1999).

Lalonde, Peter and Paul Lalonde, *Apocalypse* (Niagra Falls, NY: This Week in Bible Prophecy, 1998).

Lambert, Lance, *The uniqueness of Israel* (Eastbourne, UK: Kingsway, 1980).

Lamont, William, *Richard Baxter and the millennium: Protestant imperialism and the English revolution* (London: Croom Helm, 1979).

Lamont, William, *Godly Rule: Politics and religion, 1603–60* (London: Macmillan, 1969).

Landes, Richard, et al. (eds), 'Millennialism,' in James R. Lewis (ed.), *The Oxford handbook of new religious movements* (Oxford: Oxford University Press, 2004), 333–58.

Landes, Richard, et al. (eds), *The apocalyptic year 1000: Religious expectation and social change, 950–1050* (Oxford: Oxford University Press, 2003).

Larkin, Clarence, *The book of Revelation* (Glenside, PA: Clarence Larkin Estate, 1919).

Larkin, Clarence, *Dispensational truth* (Glenside, PA: Clarence Larkin Estate, 1918).

Larsen, Timothy, 'The reception given *Evangelicalism in Modern Britain* since its publication in 1989,' in Michael A.G. Haykin and Kenneth J. Stewart (eds), *The emergence of Evangelicalism: Exploring historical continuities* (Nottingham: Apollos, 2008), 21–36.

Larson, Timothy T. (ed.), *Biographical dictionary of evangelicals* (Leicester: IVP, 2003).

Laursen, John Christian and Richard H. Popkin (eds), *Continental millenarians: Protestants, Catholics, heretics* (Dordrecht: Kluwer Academic Publishers, 2001).

Leeman, Saul, 'Was Bishop Ussher's chronology influenced by a midrash?' *Semeia* 8 (1977), 127

'*Left Behind* fans clamor for *The Remnant*,' www.leftbehind.com, accessed 7 August 2002.

Leighton, C.D.A., 'Antichrist's revolution: Some Anglican apocalypticists in the age of the French wars,' *Journal of Religious History* 24 (2000), 125–42.

Levin, David (ed.), *Jonathan Edwards: A Profile* (New York: Hill & Wang, 1969).

Lewis, Alan E., 'Eschatology,' in Donald M. McKim (ed.), *Encyclopaedia of the Reformed faith* (Edinburgh: St Andrews Press, 1992), 122–4.

Lewis, Donald M., *The origins of Christian Zionism: Lord Shaftesbury and evangelical support for a Jewish homeland* (Cambridge: Cambridge University Press, 2009).

Lienesch, Michael, *Redeeming America: Piety and politics in the new Christian right* (Chapel Hill, NC: University of North Carolina Press, 1993).

Lilla, Mark, 'Church meets state,' *New York Times Book Review*, 15 May 2005, 39.

Lindermayer, Orestis, 'Europe as Antichrist: North American pre-millenarianism,' in Stephen Hunt (ed.), *Christian millenarianism: From the early church to Waco* (Bloomington, IN: Indiana University Press, 2001), 39–49.

Lindsey, Hal, 'Hal Lindsey, from *The late great planet Earth*,' in *The Norton Anthology of English Literature*, http://www.wwnorton.com/nto/20century/topic_3/crystal.htm, accessed 6 August 2007.

Lindsey, Hal, *Blood Moon* (Palos Verdes, CA: Western Front Publishing, 1996).

Lindsey, Hal, *The 1980's: Countdown to armageddon* (New York: Bantam, 1981).

Lindsey, Hal, *The terminal generation* (Old Tappan, NJ: Spire Books, 1976).

Lindsey, Hal, *The late great planet Earth* (1970; rpr. London: Marshall Pickering, 1971).

Lippy, C.H., 'Waiting for the end: The social context of American apocalyptic religion,' in L. Zamora (ed.), *The apocalyptic vision in America: Interdisciplinary essays on myth and culture* (Bowling Green, OH: Bowling Green University Popular Press, 1982), 37–63.

Long, Kathryn Teresa, *The revival of 1857–58: Interpreting an American religious awakening* (Oxford: Oxford University Press, 1998).

Longfield, Bradley J., *The Presbyterian controversy: Fundamentalists, Modernists, and moderates* (Oxford: Oxford University Press, 1991).

Ludwigson, Raymond, *A survey of Bible prophecy* (Grand Rapids, MI: Zondervan, 1973).

Ludwigson, Raymond, 'The apocalyptic interpretation of history of American premillennial groups' (unpublished PhD thesis, University of Iowa, 1944).

MacCulloch, Diarmaid, *Reformation: Europe's house divided* (London: Penguin, 2004).

MacDonald, Gregory, *The evangelical universalist* (2006; rpr. London: SPCK, 2008).

MacInnes, Allan I., *The British revolution, 1629–60* (Basingstoke: Palgrave Macmillan, 2004).

MacLeod, David J., 'Walter Scott, a link in dispensationalism between Darby and Scofield?' *Bibliotheca Sacra* 153:610 (1996), 155–76.

McAlister, Melani, 'Prophecy, politics and the popular: The *Left Behind* series and Christian fundamentalism's New World Order,' *South Atlantic Quarterly* 102:4 (2003), 773–98.

McCosh, James, *The Ulster revival and its physiological accidents: A paper read before the Evangelical Alliance, September 22, 1859* (Belfast, 1859).

McCrossan, T.K. *The Bible: Its hell and its ages* (Seattle, WA: privately published, 1941).

McDannell, Colleen, *Material Christianity: Religion and popular culture in America* (New Haven: Yale University Press, 1995).

McFarlane, Graham W., *Christ and the Spirit: The doctrine of the incarnation according to Edward Irving* (Carlisle: Paternoster, 1996).

McGinn Bernard (ed.), *Encyclopedia of apocalypticism*, 3 vols (New York: Continuum, 1998).

McKeever, James, *The rapture book: Victory in the end times* (Medford, OR: Omega Publications, 1988).

Maddex, Jack, 'Proslavery millennialism: Social eschatology in Antebellum Southern Calvinism,' *American Quarterly* 31:1 (1979), 46–62.

Mangum, R. Todd, *The dispensational–covenantal rift: The fissuring of American evangelical theology from 1936 to 1944*, Studies in Evangelical History and Thought (Milton Keynes: Paternoster, 2007).

Manton, Thomas, *The complete works of Thomas Manton*, ed. Thomas Smith, 22 vols (London: James Nisbet & Co., 1870–75).

Martin, William, *With God on our side: The rise of the religious right in America* (New York: Broadway Books, 1996).

Marsden, George M., *Fundamentalism and American culture: The shaping of twentieth-century evangelicalism, 1870–1925* (Oxford: Oxford University Press, 1980; new edition, 2006).

Marsden, George M., *Jonathan Edwards: A life* (New Haven: Yale University Press, 2003).

Marsden, George M., *Reforming Fundamentalism: Fuller Seminary and the new Evangelicalism* (1987; second edition, Grand Rapids, MI: Eerdmans, 1995).

Marsden, George M., 'Fundamentalism as an American phenomenon,' in D.G. Hart (ed.), *Reckoning with the past: Historical essays on American evangelicalism from the Institute for the Study of American Evangelicals* (Grand Rapids: Baker, 1995), 303–21.

Marsden, George M., *Understanding Fundamentalism and Evangelicalism* (Grand Rapids, MI: Eerdmans, 1991).

Marsden, George M., *Religion and American culture* (New York: Harcourt Brace Jovanovich College Publishers, 1990).

Marsden, George M. (ed.), *Evangelicalism and modern America* (Grand Rapids, MI: Eerdmans, 1984).

Martin, Marty, 'Protestantism and capitalism: Print culture and individualism,' in Leonard I. Sweet (ed.), *Communication and change in American religious history* (Grand Rapids, MI: Eerdmans, 1993), 91–107.

Martin, William, 'Waiting for the end: The growing interest in apocalyptic prophecy,' *Atlantic* (June 1982), 31–7.

Maudlin, Michael G., 'Holy smoke! The darkness is back,' *Christianity Today* 15 (1989), 58–9.

Mauro, Philip, *The gospel of the kingdom: An examination of modern dispensationalism* (Swengel, PA: Bible Truth Depot, 1927).

Mede, Joseph, *The Key of the Revelation* (London, 1643).

Melling, Philip H., *Fundamentalism in America: Millennialism, identity and militant religion* (Edinburgh: Edinburgh University Press, 1999).

Merkley, Paul C., *American presidents, religion and Israel: The heirs of Cyrus* (Westport, CT: Praeger, 2004).

Milich, Klaus J., 'Fundamentalism hot and cold: George W. Bush and the "Return of the Sacred,"' *Cultural Critique* 62 (2006), 92–125.

Mills, James, 'The serious implications of a 1971 conversation with Ronald Reagan: A footnote to current history,' *San Diego Magazine* (August 1985), 141.

Milne, Bruce A., *I want to know what the Bible says about the end of the world* (1979), republished as *The end of the world* (Eastbourne: Kingsway, 1983).

Milne, Garnet Howard, *The Westminster Confession of Faith and the cessation of special revelation: The majority puritan viewpoint on whether extra-biblical prophecy is still possible*, Studies in Christian History and Thought (Milton Keynes: Paternoster, 2007).

Milton, Anthony, *Catholic and Reformed: The Roman and protestant churches in English protestant thought, 1600–1640* (Cambridge: Cambridge University Press, 1995).

Mixon, Harold and Mary Frances Hopkins, 'Apocalypticism in secular public discourse: A proposed theory,' *Central States Speech Journal* 39 (1988), 244–57.

Mleynek, Sherryll, 'The rhetoric of the "Jewish problem" in the *Left Behind* novels,' *Literature and Theology* 19:4 (2005), 367–83.

Mojtabai, A.G., *Blessed assurance: At home with the bomb in Amarillo, Texas* (Albuquerque, NM: University of New Mexico Press, 1986).

Moltmann, Jürgen, *Theology of hope: On the ground and implications of a Christian eschatology* (London: SCM Press, 1967, 2002).

Moltmann, Jürgen, *The coming of God: Christian eschatology* (London: SCM, 1996).

Monseth, Francis Wesley, 'Millennialism in American Lutheranism in light of Augsburg Confession, article xvii' (unpublished PhD thesis, Concordia Theological Seminary, 1986).

Moorehead, William G., 'Millennial dawn: A counterfeit of Christianity,' in *The fundamentals: A testimony to the truth*, ed. 'Two Christian Laymen,' 12 vols (Chicago: Testimony Publishing Company, 1910–1915), 7. 106–27.

Moorhead, James H., *World without end: Mainstream American protestant visions of the last things, 1880–1925* (Bloomington, IN: Indiana University Press, 2000).

Moorhead, James H., 'Apocalypticism in mainstream Protestantism: 1800 to the present,' in Bernard McGinn (ed.), *Encyclopedia of apocalypticism*, 3 vols (New York: Continuum, 1998), 3: 72–107.

Moorhead, James H., 'Between progress and apocalypse: A reassessment of millennialism in American religious thought, 1800–1880,' *Journal of American History* 71:3 (1984), 524–42.

Moorhead, James H., 'The erosion of postmillennialism in American religious thought, 1865–1925,' *Church History* 53:1 (1984), 61–77.

Moorhead, James H., 'Millennialism,' in Samuel S. Hill (ed.) *Encyclopaedia of religion in the South* (Macon, GA: Mercer University Press, 1984), 477–79.

Moorhead, James H., *American apocalypse: Yankee protestants and the Civil War, 1860–1869* (New Haven: Yale University Press, 1978).

Morden, Peter J., *Offering Christ to the world: Andrew Fuller (1754–1815) and the revival of eighteenth century Particular Baptist life* (Milton Keynes: Paternoster, 2003).

Mounce, Robert H., *The Book of Revelation*, New International Commentaries on the New Testament (Grand Rapids, MI: Eerdmans, 1977).

Muirhead, I.A., 'The revival as a dimension of Scottish church history,' *Records of the Scottish Church History Society* 20 (1980), 179–96.

Muller, Richard, *Post-Reformation Reformed dogmatics*, second edition, 4 volumes (Grand Rapids, MI: Baker Academic, 2003).

Muller, Richard, 'John Gill and the Reformed tradition: A study in the reception of Protestant Orthodoxy in the eighteenth century,' in Michael A.G. Haykin (ed.), *The life and thought of John Gill: A tercentennial appreciation* (Leiden: E.J. Brill, 1997), 51–68.

Muller, Richard, *Christ and the decree: Christology and predestination in Reformed theology from Calvin to Perkins* (Durham, NC: Labyrinth, 1986).

Murdoch, Alexander, *Scotland and America, c. 1600–c. 1800* (Basingstoke: Palgrave Macmillan, 2009).

Murdock, Graeme, *Calvinism on the frontier, 1600–1660: International Calvinism and the Reformed Church in Hungary and Transylvania* (Oxford: Clarendon Press, 2000).

Murray, Iain H., *Spurgeon v. hyper-Calvinism: The battle for gospel preaching* (Edinburgh: Banner of Truth, 1995).

Murray, Iain H., *D. Martyn Lloyd-Jones: The fight of faith, 1939–1981* (Edinburgh: Banner of Truth, 1990).

Murray, Iain H., *The puritan hope: Revival and the interpretation of prophecy* (Edinburgh: Banner of Truth, 1971).

Napier, John, *A plaine discovery of the whole revelation* (1593; 2nd ed. 1611).

Nash, Ronald H., *Evangelicals in America: Who they are, what they believe* (Nashville, TN: Abingdon Press, 1987).

Nebeker, Gary L., 'John Nelson Darby and Trinity College, Dublin: A study in eschatological contrasts,' *Fides et Historia* 34 (2002), 87–108.

Nelson, John Wiley, *Your God is alive and well and appearing in popular culture* (Philadelphia: Westminster Press, 1976).

Nelson, Ronald R., 'Apocalyptic speculation and the French revolution,' *Evangelical Quarterly* 53 (1981), 194–206.

Nettles, Thomas J., *James Petigru Boyce: A Southern Baptist Statesman* (Phillipsburg, NJ: P&R, 2009).

Nettles, Thomas J., *By his grace and for his glory: A historical, theological and practical study of the doctrines of grace in Baptist life* (Grand Rapids: Baker Book House, 1986).

Newport, Kenneth G.C., *Apocalypse and millennium: Studies in biblical eisegesis* (Cambridge: Cambridge University Press, 2000).

Newport, Kenneth G.C., 'Benjamin Keach, William of Orange and the book of Revelation: A study in English prophetical exegesis,' *Baptist Quarterly* 36 (1995–96), pp. 43–51.

Newton, B.W., *Thoughts on the Apocalypse* (1843; second edition, London: Partridge and Oakey, 1853).

Noll, Mark A., *The Civil War as a theological crisis* (Chapel Hill, NC: University of North Carolina Press, 2006).

Noll, Mark A., *The rise of Evangelicalism: The age of Edwards, Whitefield, and the Wesleys*, A History of Evangelicalism (Leicester: IVP, 2004).

Noll, Mark A., *The scandal of the evangelical mind* (Leicester: IVP, 1994).

Noll, Mark A., *A history of Christianity in the United States and Canada* (Grand Rapids, MI: Eerdmans, 1992).

North, Gary, 'Publisher's preface,' Dwight Wilson, *Armageddon now! The premillenarian response to Russia and Israel since 1917* (1977; Tyler, TX: Institute for Christian Economics, 1991), ix–xxiv.

North, Gary, *Millennialism and social theory* (Tyler, TX: Institute for Christian Economics, 1990).

North, Gary, *Is the world running down? Crisis in the Christian worldview* (Tyler, TX: Institute for Christian Economics, 1988).

North, Gary, 'Towards the recovery of hope,' *Banner of Truth* 88 (1971), 12–16.

Northcott, Michael, *An angel directs the storm: Apocalyptic religion and American empire* (London: I.B. Taurus, 2004).

Numbers, Ronald L., and Jonathan M. Butler, *The disappointed: Millerism and millenarianism in the nineteenth century* (Bloomington, IN: Indiana University Press, 1987).

O'Leary, Stephen D., *Arguing the apocalypse: A theory of millennial rhetoric* (Oxford: Oxford University Press, 1994).

O'Leary, Stephen D., and Michael McFarland, 'The political use of mythic discourse: Prophetic interpretation in Pat Robertson's presidential campaign,' *Quarterly Journal of Speech* 75 (1989), 433–52.

O'Leary, Stephen D., and Glen S. McGhee (eds), *War in heaven/Heaven on earth: Theories in the apocalyptic*, Millennialism and society (London: Equinox, 2005).

O'Farrell, Patrick, 'Millennialism, messianism and Utopianism in Irish history,' *Anglo-Irish Studies* 2 (1976), 45–68.

Oliver, Robert, 'John Gill: Orthodox dissenter,' *Strict Baptist Historical Society Bulletin* 23 (1996), 3–18.

Oliver, W.H., *Prophets and millennialists: The uses of Biblical prophecy in England from the 1790s to the 1840s* (Auckland, New Zealand: Auckland University Press, 1978).

Olson, Carl E., *Will Catholics be 'Left Behind'? A Catholic critique of the rapture and today's prophecy preachers* (San Francisco: Ignatius Press, 2003).

Olsen, Palle J., 'Was John Foxe a millenarian?' *Journal of Ecclesiastical History* 45:4 (1994), 600–24.

Olson, Theodore, *Millennialism, utopianism, and progress* (Toronto: Toronto University Press, 1982).

Ostling, Richard N., 'Armageddon and the end times: Prophecies of the last days surface as a campaign issue,' *TIME* (November 5, 1984), 73.

Paik, Peter Yoonsuk, 'Smart bombs, serial killing, and the rapture: The vanishing bodies of imperial apocalypticism,' *Postmodern Culture* 14:1 (2003), available at http://muse.jhu.edu/journals/pmc/index.html, accessed 19 January 2008.

Parry, Robin, 'I am the evangelical universalist,' http://theologicalscribbles.blogspot.com/2009/08/i-am-evangelical-universalist.html, accessed 4 January 2010.

Patrides, C.A., and Joseph Wittreich (eds), *The apocalypse in English Renaissance thought and literature: Patterns, antecedents and repercussions* (Manchester: Manchester University Press, 1984).

Pember, G.H., *The great prophecies of the centuries concerning Israel, the Gentiles, and the Church of God* (London: Oliphants, 1941).

Pentecost, J. Dwight, *Prophecy for today: The middle east crisis and the future of the world* (Grand Rapids, MI: Zondervan, 1961).

Pentecost, J. Dwight, *Things to come: A study in biblical eschatology* (Grand Rapids, MI: Zondervan, 1958).

Penton, M. James, *Apocalypse delayed: The story of Jehovah's Witnesses* (1985; second edition, Toronto: University of Toronto Press, 1997).

Percy, Martyn, 'Whose time is it anyway? Evangelicals, the millennium and millenarianism,' in Stephen Hunt (ed.), *Christian millenarianism: From the early church to Waco* (Bloomington, IN: Indiana University Press, 2001), 26–38.

Percy, Martyn (ed.), *Calling time: Religion and change at the turn of the millennium* (Sheffield: Sheffield Academic Press, 2000).

Peretti, Frank, *Piercing the Darkness* (1989; Eastbourne: Minstrel, 1990).

Peretti, Frank, *This Present Darkness* (1986; Eastbourne: Minstrel, 1989).

Perkins, William, *Works* (1612).

Pettegree, Andrew, *Reformation and the culture of persuasion* (Cambridge: Cambridge University Press, 2005).

Peterson, Rodney L., *Preaching in the last days: The theme of 'two witnesses' in the sixteenth and seventeenth centuries* (Oxford: Oxford University Press, 1993).

Pfoertner, George Baxter, 'The profits of doom,' *The Independent on Sunday* magazine supplement (12 November 2000), 10.

Phillips, Kevin, *American theocracy: The peril and politics of radical religion, oil, and borrowed money in the 21st century* (New York: Viking, 2006).

Phillips, Kevin, *The emerging Republican majority* (New York: Arlington House, 1969).

Pibworth, Nigel, 'Benjamin Wills Newton (1807–1899): A theological biography' (unpublished manuscript).

Pope, Alexander, *An essay on man, in four epistles, to which is added the universal prayer* (Hartford, CT: H. Benton, 1825).

Popkin, Richard H. (ed.), *Millenarianism and messianism in English literature and thought, 1650–1800* (Leiden: E.J. Brill, 1988).

Popkin, Richard H., 'The triumphant apocalypse and the catastrophic apocalypse,' in Avner Cohen and Steven Lee (eds), *Nuclear weapons and the future of humanity* (Totowa, NJ: Rowman & Allanheld, 1986), 131–49.

Preston, John, *The breastplate of faith and love* (1630).

Purcell, Joseph, 'Left Behind: Some kind of super Christian' (unpublished MA thesis, University of Manchester, 2007).

Purcell, Joseph, 'Left Behind: Depictions of Europe as an American other in the premillennial imagination' (unpublished BA thesis, University of Manchester, 2006).

Quandt, Jean, 'Religion and social thought: The secularization of postmillennialism,' *American Quarterly* 25 (1973), 390–409.

Quebedeaux, Richard, *The worldly evangelicals* (San Francisco: Harper and Row, 1978).

Quinby, Lee, *Millennial seduction* (Ithaca, NY: Cornell University Press, 1999).

Quistorp, Heinrich, *Calvin's doctrine of the last things* (London: Lutterworth Press, 1955).

Radner, Ephraim, 'New world order, old world anti-Semitism — Pat Robertson of the Christian coalition,' *Christian Century*, 13 September 1995.

Railton, Nick, 'Gog and Magog: The history of a symbol,' *Evangelical Quarterly* 75:1 (2003), 23–43.

Randall, Ian M., *Communities of conviction: Baptist beginnings in Europe* (Schwarzenfeld, Germany: Neufeld Verlag, 2009).

Reagan, Ronald, 'Address to the National Association of Evangelicals, March 8, 1983,' in Paul Boyer (ed.), *Reagan as President: Contemporary views of the man, his politics, and his policies* (Chicago: Ivan R. Dee, 1990), 165–9.

Reagan, Ronald, *A time for choosing: The speeches of Ronald Reagan, 1961–1982*, ed. Alfred Balitzer and Gerald M. Bonetto (Chicago: Regnery Gateway, 1983).

Reasoner, Mark, 'What does the Bible say about the end times? A biblical studies discussion of interpretive methods,' in Bruce David Forbes and Jeanne Halgren Kilde (eds), *Rapture, Revelation and the End Times: Exploring the Left Behind series* (New York: Palgrave Macmillan, 2004), 71–98.

Reese, Alexander, *The approaching advent of Christ: An examination of the teaching of J.N. Darby and his followers* (London: Marshall, Morgan & Scott, 1937).

Reeves, Marjory, *The influence of prophecy in the later Middle Ages* (Oxford: Clarendon Press, 1969).

Reid, William, *Plymouth Brethrenism unveiled and refuted* (Edinburgh, 1875).

Reverend Mr. Brightmans Judgement (1642).

Review of Keith's *Evidence* in *Quarterly Journal of Prophecy* 1:2 (1849), 192.

Revivals and the Millennial Advent Foretold by the Prophets and the Apostles (Belfast, 1859).

Richards, Jeffery John, 'The eschatology of Lewis Sperry Chafer: His contribution to a systematization of dispensational premillennialism' (unpublished PhD thesis, Drew University, 1985).

Ridderbos, Herman, *The coming of the kingdom* (Philadelphia, PA: P&R, 1962).

Riddlebarger, Kim, *A case for amillennialism: Understanding the end times* (Grand Rapids, MI: Baker, 2003).

Rippon, John, *A brief memoir of the life and writings of the late Rev. John Gill, D.D.* (1838; rpt Harrisonburg: Gano Books, 1992).

Ritter, Kurt, 'Reagan's 1964 TV speech for Goldwater: Millennial themes in American political rhetoric,' in Martin J. Medhurst and Thomas W. Benson (eds), *Rhetorical dimensions in media: A critical casebook*, second edition (Dubuque, IA: Kendall / Hunt, 1991), 58–72.

Robbins, Thomas and Susan Palmer (eds), *Millennium, messiahs and mayhem* (New York: Routledge, 1997).

Robbins, John W., *Pat Robertson: A warning to America* (Jefferson, MD: The Trinity Foundation, 1988).

Robert, Dana L., '"The crisis of missions": Premillennial mission theory and the origins of independent evangelical missions,' in Joel A. Carpenter and Wilbert R. Shenk (eds), *Earthen vessels: American evangelicals and foreign missions, 1880–1980* (Grand Rapids, MI: Eerdmans, 1990), 29–46.

Robertson, O. Palmer, *The Israel of God: Yesterday, today, and tomorrow* (Phillipsburg, NJ: P&R, 2000).

Rogers, Richard Lee, 'A testimony to the whole world: Evangelicalism and millennialism in the northeastern United States, 1790–1850' (unpublished PhD thesis, Princeton University, 1996).

Romanowski, William D., *Pop culture wars: Religion and the role of entertainment in American life* (Downers Grove, IL: InterVarsity, 1996).

Rossing, Barbara R., *The rapture exposed: The message of hope in the Book of Revelation* (Boulder, CO: Westview Press, 2004).

Rowe, David L., *Thunder and trumpets: Millerites and dissenting religion in upstate New York, 1800–1850* (Chico, CA: Scholars Press, 1985).

Rowland, Christopher and John Barton (eds), *Apocalyptic in history and tradition* (Sheffield: Sheffield Academic Press, 2002).

Rowland, Christopher, 'Afterword,' *Journal for the Study of the New Testament* 25:2 (2002), 255–62.
Rowlands, William J., *Our Lord cometh* (London: privately published, 1930).
Ryle, J.C., *Coming events and present duties* (1867), reprinted as *Prophecy* (Fearn, Ross-shire, UK: Christian Focus, 1991).
Ryrie, Charles Caldwell, *Dispensationalism today* (Chicago: Moody Press, 1965).
Sale-Harrison, Leonard, *The remarkable Jew: God's great timepiece* (Harrisburg, PA: Evangelical Press; Glasgow: Pickering & Inglis, 1934).
Sandeen, Ernest R., *The roots of fundamentalism: British and American millenarianism* (Chicago: University of Chicago Press, 1970).
Sanders, Mike, *The poetry of Chartism: Aesthetics, politics, history* (Cambridge: Cambridge University Press, 2009).
Schall, James V., 'Apocalypse as a secular enterprise,' *Scottish Journal of Theology* 29 (1976), 357–73.
Shantz, Douglas, 'Millennialism and apocalypticism in recent historical scholarship,' in Crawford Gribben and Timothy C.F. Stunt (eds), *Prisoners of hope? Aspects of evangelical millennialism in Britain and Ireland, 1800–1880*, Studies in Evangelical History and Thought (Milton Keynes: Paternoster, 2004), 18–43.
Shepherd, Norman, 'Postmillennialism,' in *Zondervan pictorial encyclopedia of the Bible*, ed. Merrill C. Tenney (Grand Rapids, MI: Zondervan, 1975), 4. 822–23.
Schlissel, Steve (ed.), *Hal Lindsey and the restoration of the Jews* (Edmonton, Alberta: Still Waters Revival Books, 1990).
'The Scofield Study Bible: Scofield's use of the critical text and the AV,' *Quarterly Record: Magazine of the Trinitarian Bible Society* 566 (2004), 21–7.
Scholz, Susanne, 'The Christian Right's discourse on gender and the Bible,' *Journal of Feminist Studies in Religion* 21 (2005), 81–100.
Schultze, Quentin J., 'Keeping the faith: American evangelicals and the mass media,' in Quentin J. Schultze (ed.), *American evangelicals and the mass media* (Grand Rapids, MI: Academie Books, 1990), 23–45.
Schwartz, Hillel, *The French Prophets: The history of a millenarian group in eighteenth-century England* (Los Angeles: University of California Press, 1980).
Schwartz, Hillel, 'The end of the beginning: Millenarian studies, 1969–1975,' *Religious Studies Review* 2 (1976), 1–15.
Scott, A.J., *The rapture is coming* (Cambridgeshire: Upfront Publishing, 2005).
Scroggie, W. Graham, *The Lord's return* (London: Pickering and Inglis, n.d.).
Shedden, David W., 'Presbyterian premillennialism and the *Presbyterian Review*' (unpublished ThM thesis, Princeton Theological Seminary, 2007).
Shipps, Jan, *Mormonism: The story of a new religious tradition* (Champaign, IL: University of Illinois Press, 1987).
Shires, Preston David, 'Hippies of the religious right: The counterculture and American evangelicalism in the 1960s and 1970s' (unpublished PhD thesis, University of Nebraska, Lincoln, 2002).
Shuck, Glenn W., *Marks of the beast: The Left Behind novels and the struggle for evangelical identity* (New York: New York University Press, 2005).
Sibbes, Richard, *Works*, ed. A.B. Grosart, 6 vols (Edinburgh: James Nichol, 1862–64).
Simon, Merrill, *Jerry Falwell and the Jews* (Middle Village, NY: Jonathan David Publishers, 1984).

Sizer, Stephen R., *Christian Zionism: Road-map to Armageddon?* (Leicester: IVP, 2004).

Smith, David E., 'Millennial scholarship in America,' *American Quarterly* 17 (1965), 535–49.

Smith, G.S., 'West, Nathaniel (1826–1906),' in D.G. Hart (ed.), *Dictionary of the Presbyterian and Reformed tradition in America* (Downers Grove, Illinois: IVP, 1999), 273.

Smith, Kevin John, 'The origins, nature, and significance of the Jesus Movement as a revitalization movement' (unpublished DMiss thesis, Asbury Theological Seminary, 2003).

Smith, Timothy L., 'Righteousness and hope: Christian holiness and the millennial vision in America, 1800–1900,' *American Quarterly* 31 (1979), 21–45.

Smolinksi, Reiner, 'Caveat Emptor: Pre- and postmillennialism in the late reformation period,' in James E. Force and Richard H. Popkin (eds), *Millenarianism and Messianism in early modern European culture: The millenarian turn* (Dordrecht: Kluwer Academic Publishers, 2001), 145–69,

Spector, Stephen, *Evangelicals and Israel: The story of American Christian Zionism* (Oxford: Oxford University Press, 2008).

Spivey, James, 'The millennium,' in Paul Basden (ed.), *Has our theology changed? Southern Baptist thought since 1845* (Nashville: B&H, 1994), 230–62.

Sproul, R.C., *The last days according to Jesus: When did Jesus say he would return?* (Grand Rapids: Baker, 1998).

Spurgeon, Charles H., 'Spurgeon's Confession of Faith,' *The Sword and Trowel* 26 (August 1891), 446–8.

Spurgeon, Charles H., *Commentating and commentaries* (London: Passmore and Alabaster, 1876).

Standaert, Michael, *Skipping towards armageddon: The politics and propaganda of the Left Behind novels and the LaHaye empire* (Brooklyn, NY: Soft Skull Press, 2006).

Stanley, Brian, *The global diffusion of Evangelicalism: The age of Graham and Stott*, A History of Evangelicalism (Leicester: IVP, forthcoming).

'A statement by the two laymen,' in *The fundamentals: A testimony to the truth*, ed. 'Two Christian Laymen,' 12 vols (Chicago: Textimony Publishing Company, 1910–1915), 12: 4.

Stein, Stephen J., 'American millennialism: Towards construction of a new architectonic of American apocalypticism,' in Abbas Amanat and Magnus Bernhardsson (eds), *Imagining the end: Visions of apocalypse from the Ancient Middle East to modern America* (London: I.B. Taurus, 2002), 187–211.

Stein, Stephen J., *The Shaker experience in America: A history of the United Society of Believers* (New Haven, CT: Yale University Press, 1992).

Stein, Stephen J., 'Providence and the apocalypse in the early writings of Jonathan Edwards,' *Early American Literature* 13:3 (1978–1979), 250–67.

Stein, Stephen J., 'Editor's introduction,' in Jonathan Edwards, *Apocalyptic Writings*, ed. Stephen J. Stein, The Works of Jonathan Edwards (New Haven, CT: Yale University Press, 1977), 1–93.

Stine, Milton H., *Studies on the religious problem of our country* (York, PA: Lutheran Printing House, 1888).

Stoker, Bram, *Dracula* (1897; rpr. Oxford: Oxford University Press, 1996).

Stokes, Bob, *Conflict, conquest and the second coming* (Rushden, UK: Stanley L. Hunt, 1975).

Stout, Harry S., *Upon the altar of the nation: A moral history of the Civil War* (New York: Viking, 2006).

Stover, Mark, 'A kinder, gentler teaching of contempt? Jews and Judaism in contemporary protestant evangelical children's fiction,' *Journal of Religion & Society* 7 (2005), available online at http://moses.creighton.edu/JRS/, accessed 19 January 2008.

Stunt, Timothy C.F., 'Influences in the early development of J.N. Darby,' in Crawford Gribben and Timothy C.F. Stunt (eds), *Prisoners of hope? Aspects of evangelical millennialism in Britain and Ireland, 1800–1880*, Studies in Evangelical History and Thought (Milton Keynes: Paternoster, 2004), 44–67.

Stunt, Timothy C.F., *From awakening to secession: Radical evangelicals in Switzerland and Britain, 1815–35* (Edinburgh: T&T Clark, 2000).

Strachan, Gordon, *The Pentecostal theology of Edward Irving* (London: DLT, 1973).

Strandberg, Todd and Terry James, *Are you rapture ready? Signs, prophecies, warnings, threats, and suspicions that the endtime is now* (New York: Dutton, 2003).

Strozier, Charles B., *Apocalypse: On the psychology of fundamentalism in America* (Boston, MA: Beacon Press, 1994).

Sturm, Tristan, 'Prophetic eyes: The theatricality of Mark Hitchcock's premillennial geopolitics,' *Geopolitics* 11 (2006), 231–55.

Svigel, Michael J., 'The phantom heresy: Did the Council of Ephesus (431) condemn chiliasm?' *Trinity Journal* 24 n.s. (2003), 105–12.

Swanson, Dennis M., 'The millennial position of Spurgeon,' *The Master's Seminary Journal* 7:2 (1996), 183–212.

Sweet, Leonard I., *Communication and change in American religious history* (Grand Rapids, MI: Eerdmans, 1993).

Sweet, Leonard I., *The evangelical tradition in America* (Macon, GA: Mercer University Press, 1984).

Sweet, Leonard I., 'Millennialism in America: Recent studies,' *Theological Studies* 40 (1979), 510–31.

Sweetnam, Mark S., 'Defining dispensationalism: A cultural studies perspective,' *Journal of Religious History* 34:2 (2010), 191–212.

Sweetnam, Mark, 'Tensions in dispensational eschatology,' in Kenneth G.C. Newport and Crawford Gribben (eds), *Expecting the end: Millennialism in social and historical context* (Baylor, TX: Baylor University Press, 2006), 173–92.

Sweetnam, Mark and Todd Mangum, *The Scofield Bible: Its history and impact on the evangelical church* (Milton Keynes: Paternoster, 2009).

Tatford, Frederick Albert, *It's never been so late before* (Belfast: Ambassador, 1986).

Tatford, Frederick Albert, *Ten nations: What now? The European Community and its future* (Eastbourne: Upperton Press, 1980).

Tatford, Frederick Albert, *Middle East cauldron* (Eastbourne: Prophetic Witness Publishing House, 1971).

Tatford, Frederick Albert, *Five minutes to midnight* (London: Victory Press, 1971).

Tatford, Frederick Albert, *Going into Europe: The Common Market and prophecy* (Eastbourne: Prophetic Witness Publishing House, 1971).

Tatford, Frederick Albert, *Israel and her future* (Eastbourne: Prophetic Witness Publishing House, 1971).

Tatford, Frederick Albert, *Daniel's seventy weeks* (Eastbourne: Prophetic Witness Publishing House, 1971).

Tatford, Frederick Albert, *The clock strikes* (London: Lakeland, 1970).

Tatford, Frederick Albert, *The Jew and prophecy* (Eastbourne: Bible and Advent Testimony Movement, 1969).

Tatford, Frederick Albert, *Will there be a millennium?* (Eastbourne: Prophetic Witness Publishing House, 1969).

Tatford, Frederick Albert, *China and prophecy* (Eastbourne: Bible and Advent Testimony Movement, 1968).

Tatford, Frederick Albert, *Russia and prophecy* (Eastbourne: Bible and Advent Testimony Movement, 1968).

Tatford, Frederick Albert, *Egypt and prophecy* (Eastbourne: Bible and Advent Testimony Movement, 1968).

Tatford, Frederick Albert, *A one world church and prophecy* (Eastbourne: Bible and Advent Testimony Movement, 1967).

Tatford, Frederick Albert, *God's program of the ages* (Grand Rapids, MI: Kregel Publications, 1967).

Tatford, Frederick Albert, *Climax of the ages: Studies in the prophecy of Daniel* (London: Oliphants, 1964).

Tatford, Frederick Albert, *The Middle East: War theatre of prophecy* (London: Advent Testimony and Preparation Movement, 1959).

Tatford, Frederick Albert, *The rapture and the tribulation* (Blackburn: Durham & Sons, 1957).

Tatford, Frederick Albert, *Prophecy's last word* (London: Pickering & Inglis, 1947).

Thigpen, Paul, *The rapture trap: A Catholic response to 'End Times' fever* (West Chester, PA: Ascension Press, 2001).

Thompson, Damian, *Waiting for Antichrist: Charisma and apocalypse in a Pentecostal church* (Oxford: Oxford University Press, 2004).

Thompson, Damian, *The end of time: Faith and fear in the shadow of the millennium* (revised edition, London: Vintage, 1999).

Thompson, Donald W. (dir.), *Prodigal planet* (1983).

Thompson, Donald W. (dir.), *Image of the beast* (1980).

Thompson, Donald W. (dir.), *A distant thunder* (1978).

Thompson, Donald W. (dir.), *Thief in the night* (1972).

Thrupp, Sylvia (ed.), *Millennial dreams in Action: Studies in revolutionary religious movements* (New York: Schocken Books, 1970).

Tinder, Glenn, 'Eschatology and politics,' *Review of Politics* 27 (1965), 311–33.

Tiryakian, Edward A., 'Modernity as an eschatological setting: A new vista for the study of religions,' *History of Religions* 25:4 (1986), 378–86.

Tollinger, W.V., 'Moorehead, William Gallogly (1836–1914),' in D.G. Hart (ed.), *Dictionary of the Presbyterian and Reformed tradition in America* (Downers Grove, Illinois: IVP, 1999), 164.

Toon, Peter, *The emergence of hyper-Calvinism in English non-conformity* (London: The Olive Tree, 1967).

Toon, Peter (ed.), *Puritans, the millennium and the future of Israel: Puritan eschatology 1600 to 1660* (Cambridge: James Clarke, 1970).

Torrance, T.F., 'The eschatology of the reformation,' *Eschatology: Scottish Journal of Theology Occasional Papers* 2 (1953), 36–62.

Toulouse, Mark G., 'Pat Robertson: Apocalyptic theology and American foreign policy,' *Journal of Church and State* 31:1 (1989), 73–99.

Tregelles, S.P., *The hope of Christ's second coming* (1864; second edition, London: Samuel Bagster and Sons, 1886).

Treloar, Geoff, *The disruption of Evangelicalism: The age of Mott, Machen and McPherson*, A History of Evangelicalism (Leicester: IVP, forthcoming).

'Tributes to Christ and the Bible by brainy men not known as active Christians,' in *The fundamentals: A testimony to the truth*, ed. 'Two Christian Laymen,' 12 vols (Chicago: Testimony Publishing Company, 1910–1915), 2: 120–6.

Trumball, Charles G., *The life story of C.I. Scofield* (New York: Oxford University Press, 1920).

Tuveson, Ernest Lee, *Redeemer nation: The idea of America's millennial role* (Chicago: University of Chicago Press, 1968).

Tuveson, Ernest Lee, *Millennium and utopia: A study in the background of the idea of progress* (Berkeley: University of California Press, 1949).

Urban, Hugh B., 'America, Left Behind: Bush, the neoconservatives, and evangelical Christian fiction,' *Journal of Religion & Society* 8 (2006), 1–15.

Urban, Hugh B., 'Religion and secrecy in the Bush administration: The gentleman, the prince and the simulacrum,' *Esoterica* 7 (2005), 1–36.

Ussher, James, *The whole works of James Ussher*, ed. C.R. Erlington and J.R. Todd, 17 vols (Dublin: Hodges and Smith, 1847–64).

Valenze, Deborah M., 'Prophecy and popular literature in eighteenth-century England,' *Journal of Ecclesiastical History* 29:1 (1978), 78–82.

Van Asselt, W.J., 'Chiliasm and Reformed eschatology in the seventeenth and eighteenth centuries,' in A. van Egmond and D. van Keulen (eds), *Christian hope in Context*, Studies in Reformed Theology 4 (Zoetermeer: Meinema, 2001), 11–29.

Van Asselt, W.J., 'Structural elements in the eschatology of Johannes Cocceius,' *Calvin Theological Journal* 34 (1999), 76–104.

Wagar, W. Warren, *Terminal visions: The literature of last things* (Bloomington, IN: Indiana University Press, 1982).

Wagner, Donald E., *Anxious for Armageddon: A call to partnership for middle eastern and western Christians* (Scottdale, PA: Herald Press, 1995).

Wagner, Frederick Norman, 'A theological and historical assessment of the Jesus people phenomenon' (unpublished PhD thesis, Fuller Theological Seminary, 1971).

Wallis, John, 'Celling the end times: The contours of contemporary rapture films,' *Journal of Religion and Popular Culture* 19 (2008).

Wallis, John, and Kenneth G.C. Newport (eds), *The end all around us: Apocalyptic texts and popular culture* (London: Equinox, 2008).

Walters, Robert, 'Robertson's Holy Crusade,' *Frederick Post*, Frederick, Maryland, July 28, 1986

Walvoord, John F., *Armageddon, oil, and the middle east crisis: What the Bible says about the future of the middle east and the end of western civilization*, revised edition (Grand Rapids: Zondervan, 1991).

Walvoord, John F., *The return of the Lord* (1955; Grand Rapids: Zondervan, 1980).

Ward, W.R., *Early Evangelicalism: A global intellectual history, 1670–1789* (Cambridge: Cambridge University Press, 2006).

Warfield, B.B., 'The millennium and the apocalypse,' in *The Works of Benjamin B. Warfield*, 10 vols (New York: Oxford University Press, 1932), 2: 643–64.

Watt, David Harrington, *Transforming faith: Explorations of twentieth-century American Evangelicalism* (New Brunswick, NJ: Rutgers University Press, 1991).

Watt, David Harrington, 'The private hopes of American fundamentalists and evangelicals, 1925–1975,' *Religion and American Culture* 1:2 (1991), 155–75.

Weber, Eugene, *Apocalypses: Prophecies, cults, and millennial beliefs through the ages* (Cambridge, MA: Harvard University Press, 1999).

Weber, Timothy, *On the road to armageddon: How evangelicals became Israel's best friend* (Grand Rapids, MI: Baker, 2005).

Weber, Timothy, 'Premillennialism and the branches of evangelicalism,' in Donald W. Dayton and Robert K. Johnston (eds), *The variety of American Evangelicalism* (Downers Grove, IL: InterVarsity Press, 1991), 5–21.

Weber, Timothy , *Living in the shadow of the second coming: American premillennialism, 1875–1982* (Grand Rapids, MI: Academie Books, 1983).

Weigert, Andrew J., 'Christian eschatological identities and the nuclear context,' *Journal for the Scientific Study of Religion* 27 (1988), 175–91.

Weir, John, *The Ulster awakening: Its origin, progress, and fruit: With notes of a tour of personal observation and inquiry* (London, 1860).

Wells, David F., *No place for truth, or Whatever happened to evangelical theology?* (Grand Rapids, MI: Eerdmans, 1993).

Werly, John M., 'Premillennialism and the paranoid style,' *American Studies* 18 (1977), 39–55.

Wessinger, Catherine (ed.), *Millennialism, persecution, and violence: Historical cases* (Syracuse: Syracuse University Press, 2000).

Whalen, Robert K., '"Christians love the Jews!" The development of American philo-Semitism, 1790–1860,' *Religion and American Culture* 6:2 (1996), 225–59.

Whalen, Robert K., 'Millenarianism and millennialism in America, 1790–1880' (unpublished PhD thesis, State University of New York, Stony Brook, 1972).

Wilcox, William Clyde, *God's warriors: The Christian right in twentieth-century America* (Baltimore: Johns Hopkins University Press, 1992).

Wilkinson, Paul, *For Zion's sake: Christian Zionism and the role of John Nelson Darby*, Studies in Evangelical History and Thought (Milton Keynes: Paternoster, 2007).

Wilks, Michael (ed.), *Prophecy and eschatology: Studies in church history, Subsidia 10* (Oxford: Blackwell, 1994).

Williams, Ann (ed.), *Prophecy and millenarianism: Essays in honour of Marjorie Reeves* (Harlow: Longman, 1980).

Williams, Stephen, 'Thirty years of hope: A generation of writing on eschatology,' in K.E. Brower and M.W. Elliot (eds), *'The reader must understand': Eschatology in Bible and theology* (Leicester, 1997), 243–62.

Williamson, Arthur H., *Apocalypse then: Prophecy and the making of the modern world* (Santa Barbara, CA: Praeger, 2008).

Wills, Gregory A., *Democratic religion: Freedom, authority, and church discipline in the Baptist South, 1785–1900* (Oxford: Oxford University Press, 1997).

Wilmington, H.L., *The king is coming* (Wheaton, IL: Tyndale House, 1973).

Wilson, Bryan R., *Magic and the millennium: A sociological study of religious movements of protest among tribal and third-world peoples* (London: Harper and Row, 1973).

Wilson, Dwight, *Armageddon now! The premillenarian response to Russia and Israel since 1917* (1977; Tyler, TX: Institute for Christian Economics, 1991).

Wilt, C., 'Erdman, William Jacob (1834–1923),' in D.G. Hart (ed.), *Dictionary of the Presbyterian and Reformed tradition in America* (Downers Grove, Illinois: IVP, 1999), 92.

Withrow, Brandon G., 'A future of hope: Jonathan Edwards and millennial expectations,' *Trinity Journal* 22 (2001), 75–98.

Wojcik, Daniel, 'Embracing doomsday: Faith, fatalism, and apocalyptic beliefs in the nuclear age,' *Western Folklore* 55:4 (1996), 297–330.

Wolffe, John, *The expansion of Evangelicalism: The age of Wilberforce, More, Chalmers and Finney*, A History of Evangelicalism (Leicester: IVP, 2007).

Worthen, Molly, 'The Chalcedon problem: Rousas John Rushdoony and the origins of Christian Reconstructionism,' *Church History* (2008), 399–437.

Zakai, Avihu, *Exile and kingdom: History and apocalypse in the puritan migration to America* (Cambridge: Cambridge University Press, 1992).

Zakai, Avihu, 'Reformation, history and eschatology in English Protestantism,' *History and Theory* 26:3 (1987), 300–18.

Zamora, Lois Parkinsons (ed.), *The apocalyptic vision in America: Interdisciplinary essays on myth and culture* (Bowling Green, OH: Bowling Green University Popular Press, 1982).

Zamora, Lois Parkinsons (ed.), *Writing the apocalypse: Historical vision in contemporary U.S. and Latin American fiction* (Cambridge: Cambridge University Press, 1989).

Zens, Jon, *Dispensationalism: A Reformed inquiry into its leading figures and features* (Phillipsburg, NJ: P&R, 1978).

Index